Football Intelligence

Soccer is the biggest game in the world and has proved to be an unprecedented phenomenon of social impact, inhabiting a prominent place in the daily lives of millions of human beings, a game that has impact even in the most remote places. In an ever-changing world of soccer coaching and tactics, player intelligence has become increasingly important, providing the essential ability to act effectively in a given moment. Therefore, in recent years, the tactical component has been increasingly valued and diffused. Around the world, this dimension of sport performance is being studied and applied by many professionals in the field, from the youth academies all the way through to the professional level.

This book is designed to help those who devote much of their time to improving the quality of the game, by coaching and training highly informed, creative and intelligent players. These coaches devote their time and energy to improve players' and teams' performances. In turn, match analysts, physiotherapists, psychologists, clinicians and the sport science team dedicate themselves to optimize resources that help boost the performance levels of the players, the coaches and the team.

Football Intelligence: Training and Tactics for Soccer Success presents procedures and ideas that, besides assisting in the task of evaluating the tactical performance of soccer players and teams, also allows improving their expression throughout the learning and training phase. This book will be key reading for football coaches and players alike, as well as students and practitioners of sport psychology and performance analysis.

Israel Teoldo holds a PhD in Sport Sciences at the Faculty of Sports of the University of Porto and spent a year as a Postdoctoral Fellow in Sport Sciences at Brunel University London, UK. He is Reader in Soccer at the Department of Physical Education of the Federal University of Viçosa and is in charge of the postgraduate course in Soccer and of the Centre of Research and Studies in Soccer (NUPEF). He is a creator of TacticUP, NUPEF and UFV Soccer Academy. He is a FIFA Coach Educator and consultant at CBF and CONMEBOL.

José Guilherme holds a PhD in Sport Sciences and is a lecturer at the Faculty of Sports of the University of Porto, Portugal. He is a member of the Centre of Research, Education, Innovation and Intervention in Sport and of the Centre for Team Sports Studies. Professor Guilherme has worked as coach and as assistant coach of the Portuguese National Team.

Júlio Garganta holds a PhD in Sport Sciences and is a lecturer at the Faculty of Sports of the University of Porto, Portugal. He is in charge of FADEUP's Football Office in the last two decades and is a member of the Centre of Research, Education, Innovation and Intervention in Sport. He is a collaborator of several Portuguese and foreign universities, in undergraduate and postgraduate courses.

"This book was written by three genuine superstars of research, theory and practice in top-level soccer. This is a book that refreshes our knowledge with respect to cutting-edge technical and tactical aspects, among others, through the perspective of complexity. No one who is aware of the evolution and development of soccer can fail to read this book written by professors Israel Teoldo, José Guilherme and Júlio Garganta."

João Paulo Medina, *Sports Executive*

"A compendium of genuine concepts that brings to the light of our discernment a logical and simple comprehension about the game and the training, despite all its complexity. Therefore, it is a book that rebuilds and organizes our way of thinking about the game and the training."

Ricardo Drubscky, *Coach*

"All the tactical complexity of soccer condensed into an intelligent book, which leads us to an understanding of important concepts, therefore opening new paths for a better preparation and assessment of a soccer team."

Ney Franco, *Coach*

Football Intelligence
Training and Tactics for Soccer Success

Israel Teoldo, José Guilherme and Júlio Garganta

NEW YORK AND LONDON

Cover image: © RapidEye / Getty Images

First published 2022
by Routledge
605 Third Avenue, New York, NY 10158

and by Routledge
2 Park Square, Milton Park, Abingdon, Oxon, OX14 4RN

Routledge is an imprint of the Taylor & Francis Group, an informa business

© 2022 Israel Teoldo, José Guilherme and Júlio Garganta

The right of Israel Teoldo, José Guilherme and Júlio Garganta to be identified as authors of this work has been asserted by them in accordance with sections 77 and 78 of the Copyright, Designs and Patents Act 1988.

All rights reserved. No part of this book may be reprinted or reproduced or utilised in any form or by any electronic, mechanical, or other means, now known or hereafter invented, including photocopying and recording, or in any information storage or retrieval system, without permission in writing from the publishers.

Trademark notice: Product or corporate names may be trademarks or registered trademarks, and are used only for identification and explanation without intent to infringe.

British Library Cataloguing-in-Publication Data
A catalogue record for this book is available from the British Library

Library of Congress Cataloging-in-Publication Data
Names: Teoldo, Israel, author. | Guilherme, José, author. | Garganta, Júlio, author.
Title: Football intelligence : training and tactics for soccer success / Israel Teoldo, José Guilherme, and Júlio Garganta.
Description: New York, N.Y. : Routledge, 2022. | Includes bibliographical references and index. |
Identifiers: LCCN 2021045880 (print) | LCCN 2021045881 (ebook) | ISBN 9781032121604 (hardback) | ISBN 9781032121505 (paperback) | ISBN 9781003223375 (ebook)
Subjects: LCSH: Soccer—Training. | Soccer—Psychological aspects. | Soccer players—Psychology.
Classification: LCC GV943.9.T7 T46 2022 (print) | LCC GV943.9.T7 (ebook) | DDC 796.33407/7—dc23/eng/20211022
LC record available at https://lccn.loc.gov/2021045880
LC ebook record available at https://lccn.loc.gov/2021045881

ISBN: 978-1-032-12160-4 (hbk)
ISBN: 978-1-032-12150-5 (pbk)
ISBN: 978-1-003-22337-5 (ebk)

DOI: 10.4324/9781003223375

Typeset in Baskerville
by Apex CoVantage, LLC

This book is dedicated to all those who have devoted much of their time to soccer and to the people involved in it, who help colouring the world and making it a better place to live and get along.

Contents

List of Figures   viii
List of Charts   xi
Forewords   xii
Introduction   xviii

SECTION I
Understanding the Soccer Game and Its Dynamics   1

1   **Soccer: A Game of Tactical Knowledge**   3

2   **Tactics in Soccer**   17

3   **Tactical Modelling in Soccer**   74

SECTION II
Improving Quality Play: Training and Assessment as Key Elements for Intelligence and Creativity   87

4   **Periodization of Tactical Training**   89

5   **Instruments for Assessment of Tactical Behaviour**   135

6   **Contributions for the Observation and Interpretation of the Soccer Game**   190

References   209
Index   220

Figures

1.1	Representation of the arrangement of the players on the field	7
1.2	Representation of the different arrangements of the players on the field	7
1.3	Representation of the "Classical System" or "Pyramid"	8
1.4	Representation of Herbert Chapman's "WM System"	9
1.5	Representation of Vittorio Pozzo's "WW System"	10
1.6	Representation of Hugo Meisl's "System"	11
1.7	Representation of Gustav Sebes' "System", with the positioning of the players when defending and attacking	12
1.8	Representation of the 1-4-2-4 and 1-4-3-3 "Systems" used by the Brazilian Team in the 1958 and 1962 World Cups, respectively	12
1.9	X Diagonal of the "WM" and asymmetric "WM" systems, respectively	13
2.1	Elements that comprise tactics and are related to the organization in the field and decision-making	19
2.2	Phases, objectives and offensive and defensive aspects within the phases of play of the soccer game	21
2.3	Examples of tactical schemes (communication channels) within a team	23
2.4	Spatial references used in the conception of the core tactical principles	26
2.5	Illustration of the trajectories of the ball for a 15-metre pass, when the opponent is 5.5 and 9.15 metres away from the player in possession of the ball	28
2.6	Phases of play, objectives and the general, operational and core tactical principles of the soccer game	30
2.7	Management of space according to the core tactical principles of the offensive phase	32
2.8	Management of space in the principle of penetration	34
2.9	Management of space for the principle of offensive coverage	36
2.10	Management of space for the principle of depth mobility	39
2.11	Management of space for the principle of width and length	42

2.12	Management of space for the principle of offensive unity	45
2.13	Management of space according to the core tactical principles of the defensive phase	46
2.14	Management of space for the principle of delay	49
2.15	Representation of the idea of risk to goal	50
2.16	Management of space for the principle of defensive coverage	53
2.17	Management of space for the principle of balance	56
2.18	Management of space for the principle of concentration	58
2.19	Reduction of the effective play-space through the use of the offside rule	59
2.20	Management of space for the principle of defensive unity	63
2.21	The layout of the players in three geometric configurations: diamond, box (square) and triangle	65
3.1	Inseparability of conception, principles, organization, systems implemented and respective game plan	82
3.2	The model of play as meta level of tactical behaviours, both in competition and training	83
4.1	(Gk+ 6) versus (6+Gk) drill with man-to-man marking	101
4.2	(Gk+ 6) versus (6+Gk) drill with zone defence organization	102
4.3	(Gk+ 4) versus (2+Gk) drill + 2 floaters	103
4.4	Diagonal positioning in a 1-4-3-3 structure	103
4.5	Lines in depth in a 1-4-3-3 structure	104
4.6	Lines in width in a 1-4-3-3 structure	105
4.7	(Gk+4) versus (4+Gk) drill + 2 side floaters in a diamond shape	105
4.8	(Gk+4) versus (4+Gk) drill + 2 side floaters in a square shape	106
4.9	Example proposed to demonstrate the importance of coach's intervention in the drill	107
5.1	Nomogram for assessing performance in team sports	144
5.2	Example of assessment of a player's action zones	145
5.3	Nomogram with two performance scores	146
5.4	Structure and organization of the KORA:O.O test	148
5.5	Structure and organization of the KORA:R.E test	149
5.6	Structural organization of FUT-SAT's variables	151
5.7	Representation of the physical structure of FUT-SAT's field test	167
5.8	Graphical information generated by FUT-SAT through software *Soccer View®*	168
5.9	Representative image of the moment when the participant has to make the decision for the sequence of play, according to TacticUP®	170
5.10	Graphic information scheme	171
5.11	Result of the individual response time	173
5.12	Results from different defensive midfielders	175
5.13	Athletes' performance and response time for the principles of offensive and defensive coverage	176

5.14	Assessment of two players in three different moments over the year	178
5.15	Comparison between assessments performed by TacticUP® and by the coach	179
5.16	Representative picture of the moment the player in possession of the ball should make the decision for the sequence of the play	182
5.17	Representative picture of the options of solution for the play	182
5.18	Representative picture of the life-size video of the declarative knowledge test for tactical actions in the defensive phase	183
5.19	Representative picture of a participant's answer, according to the protocol of the decision-making test	184
5.20	Representative picture of a participant's answer, according to the protocol of the situational probability test	185
5.21	Hardware of Vienna Test System (VTS)	187
6.1	Reciprocity between training and competition	191
6.2	Means and methods used in the observation, analysis and interpretation of the soccer game	194
6.3	Evolution of the processes of analysis and interpretation of the soccer game, during the transition from the quantitative to qualitative records	195
6.4	The soccer game as a consequence of the way(s) through which the organization of the different phases and moments is managed, with respect to the tactical concepts and principles	200
6.5	The soccer game as a phenomenon resulting from various polarities	201
6.6	Macrocategories that frame the tactical observation of the soccer game	202
6.7	Summarized example of sectorial characteristics of a team	205
6.8	Example of basic positional arrangement and movement tendencies	206
6.9	Example 1 of description of offensive routines	206
6.10	Example 2 of description of offensive routines	207

Charts

2.1	Characteristics of the principle of penetration	33
2.2	Characteristics of the principle of offensive coverage	35
2.3	Characteristics of the principle of depth mobility	38
2.4	Characteristics of the principle of width and length	40
2.5	Characteristics of the principle of offensive unity	43
2.6	Characteristics of the principle of delay	47
2.7	Characteristics of the principle of defensive coverage	52
2.8	Characteristics of the principle of balance	54
2.9	Characteristics of the principle of concentration	57
2.10	Characteristics of the principle of defensive unity	60
2.11	Proposal for spatial organization and adaptations for the game	66
5.1	Categories, sub-categories, variables and definitions of FUT-SAT's Observation Instrument	152
5.2	Spatial references, tactical actions and performance indicators of the core tactical principles assessed through FUT-SAT	154
5.3	References of values for the arrangements of FUT-SAT's field test	165
6.1	Comparison between the elementary and complex perspectives used in the context of performance analysis	196

Foreword

To preface a book by acknowledged experts and researchers in soccer such as Israel Teoldo, Júlio Garganta and José Guilherme is not an easy task.

As Júlio Garganta often says, soccer is played with ideas; well-played soccer is played with good ideas and poor-played soccer, with bad or sometimes no ideas at all. This insight by itself provides us with a taste of the rich content developed by the authors throughout this book.

The passion that distinguishes almost everything that is involved with soccer is something fantastic. However, when the central topic is the game, the subject deserves to be considered with the perception of how complex playing is. That is precisely what the authors do. To the extent that the book offers an immersion into the complexity of the tactical dimension, the more attractive the subject becomes. That reminds me of Constantin Brancusi, when stating that "simplicity is complexity resolved".

Thus, the great deal is to produce ideas that enable the development of an atmosphere that facilitates the generation of solutions for playing simple, but also with quality and effectiveness. Also, everything is developed within logic—the internal logic of the game, the logic of comprehension. Logic that does not intend to be different, and therefore it is. And it is different because, even in an extremely competitive environment, there is still plenty of space and importance to reflect upon and preserve throughout the entire process, the social, anthropological and philosophical aspects, which are so important when it comes to dealing with people.

The logic is also different because, when coming up with "the game/training back to the players", implicitly, does not neglect the importance of soccer games practiced in public areas, such as streets, vacant lots, beaches, etc. In this aspect, one of the core ideas refers to the typical freedom of this recreational practices, in which participants are allowed to play the role of the "real owners of the game", not only by emulating their idols, in an attempt to reproduce their body and gestural expressions, but also to do so in a scenario of endless creativity.

Within this environment, children and teenagers used to learn how to play the game through playing, as they picked up its spirit and played every possible role, thus developing their motor and coordinative skills, as well as their cognitive, perceptual, attentional and decision-making aspects. All this is translated into a "game-specific knowledge", and is expressed in a natural, spontaneous, ludic and creative manner, becoming captivating and resulting in the vaunted passion for the "ball game".

This is how, in an up-to-date context, with great sensibility and within the big picture in which the game is incorporated, the authors manage to convey in this work a deep knowledge regarding the development of the skills necessary to its practice.

Based upon systemic thinking, they show that a team is something different from its players, who cease to be isolated parts to become a unit along with the others and thus acquire a new expression.

By potentializing training and the different forms of assessment, Israel Teoldo, Júlio Garganta and José Guilherme propose a new way to effectively prepare players and specially the team, raison d'être of the game itself.

Through the interactions, permeated by intentions (behaviours), players and teams are capable of materializing the ideas originally proposed. Thus, they become capable through the broad repertoire, which is systematically acquired and applied in training sessions. Besides, they are encouraged to reflect upon what to do in the different moments or phases of play, thus being allowed, within certain contexts, to make more appropriate decisions to the different demands and as effectively as possible. Therefore, we understand that "training makes the game, which justifies or validates training" (Júlio Garganta).

These are some of the ingredients that the beloved reader will find in this seminal work about the pedagogy of soccer, written by three of the greatest exponents in this area, and that will certainly make you reflect critically about several aspects of teaching soccer, by confronting traditional and present methods.

Enjoy your reading!

Paulo Autuori
International Brazilian Soccer Coach

Foreword

To preface a book with so many tested theoretical contents about soccer is for me something rather rewarding and odd at the same time. This is because after 40 years of work in Brazil and abroad, I am still regarded, pejoratively, as a theoretical coach. All because I value the game in which the player does not only play but also reads it, thinks it and generates ideas.

I have always believed that our (Brazilian) way of observing and understanding the game was rather subjective. It was enough to observe and analyse the plays of each player, and we had all the indicators we needed to understand the team's performance.

We have got used to think of a team as the sum of individual performances and of areas that are drawn together as a whole. We have managed to get where we are now by developing the technique of our players who, by their exuberance and brilliance, have made us five-time world champions.

Nevertheless, nowadays we begin to understand that the path that will lead us back to victories and world titles goes through a quite accurate adjustment to what this book so cleverly presents us.

The new soccer, in contrast with soccer played three decades ago, shows us that we can no longer "play" without any of the 11 team players, in the different moments of the game: attack, defence and offensive and defensive transitions. And that does not refer to having a player sent-off, but rather a player who is on the field and does not perform collective actions to achieve the goal.

In this context, the authors, PhDs in their activities, show us that it is not enough to play the game, everyone does that, that it is not enough to know what to do during the game, many do that, but, above all, it is necessary to know the reason for every detail of this complex system, which possesses several games within a game (playing at home or away, early or closing moments of the match, early or final stages of a competition, scoring or conceding first, among others).

Therefore, this book allows us to step into the world of objectivity of soccer, providing us with tools that facilitate our work with our smart goal in an accurate way, without, forcibly, neglecting the beauty of the game.

The didactic and evaluative tools presented here enable the anticipation of scenarios and, in view of the content presented, make this a bedside book for the coaches who want to become winners in a profession not only so cruel and difficult but also honourable and beautiful.

Enjoy your reading!

Renê Simões
International Brazilian Soccer Coach

Foreword

My thoughts on soccer and the concepts I apply bring ideas to a game that prioritizes the synchrony, from all the tactical aspects to the players' technical excellence. The concepts that I usually develop with my players range from the clear definition of their positions according to the game and involve, among other aspects, qualified possession of the ball, in-depth triangulations, aggressive marking and speed in actions of transitional play.

I believe that in order to develop these concepts and maximize the athletic quality of a team we should be prepared for intelligently managing to obtain the full potential of our players in the different game (physical, technical, tactical and emotional) components.

In search of this purpose, this book comes at the right time and with an important mission: to support coaches and soccer practitioners in general, to accumulate knowledge so as to fundamentally enable us to display increasingly more efforts that qualify our game.

The authors of this book alert to the interrelation between the concepts of tactics and strategy, the development of tactics through the model and the principles of play, the creation and occupation of spaces, positioning and movement of players, which I consider key concepts for when we are preparing to play a match. By performing this preparation, we generate a strategy, anticipate potential situations, seek to provide athletes and the team with options of offensive movements and defensive positioning that will allow us to achieve our goals. A well-done and grounded preparation enables us, during the game, to endorse or, if necessary, to rethink the initial strategy, as the game speaks and shows us other routes, which implies that, all of a sudden, we should choose for plan B, tactical alternatives that were also practiced during pre-match.

In one of the chapters within this book, the authors highlight the tactical modelling, which is the expression of what we plan and intend for the game and how we interpret its essence. In order for soccer to be played with ideas, modelling of training and play should provide athletes with conditions to think, to propose the game. Through this organization, we are able to qualify their decision-making and thus have players who are more active than reactive to the game. I say this because, for me, it is more pleasing to watch athletes and teams that do not display a systematically reactive play.

As a means to examine whether the players understand the concepts I show them, I have been systematically searching for tools to assess, operationalize and guide training according to how I think soccer and how I prefer my teams to behave on the field. I am an apologist for teams that possess creative players, with good technical level (good reception, good passing, etc.) that read the game well, are intense, fast, dynamic, competitive and supportive. Obviously, I am aware that all these qualities are hard to find within the same team, however, the more qualities my team possesses, the closer to excellence in performance and, consequently, of victories we will be.

Particularly, 2014 was a year of professional qualification. I dedicated in my personal and professional life some time to watch, on site, Bayern Munich, Barcelona, Real Madrid, Arsenal, Manchester City, Atletico Madrid matches, among other teams, and to follow decisive matches such as the Champions League and Copa Libertadores finals. In these opportunities I managed to interact with top-level professionals such as Carlos Bianchi and Carlo Ancelotti and to have several interesting conversations, in which I could review and confirm my concepts on soccer. I also used this time to read and study about the (General, Operational, Core and Specific) tactical principles and how to apply them to the training method I adopt, so as to allow my team to play as a proponent of the game. Through the knowledge gained I could think of new and motivating training sessions, which could, among other things, support players' positioning on the field in several situations such as defensive and offensive coverages, development of set pieces in offensive dead ball situations, defenders' positioning and movement in set pieces, team's intra- and inter-lines' organization, and "aggressive" and "fast" transitions of play, such as "lose-and-press" and counter-attacking, among others.

Therefore, in face of the growing importance of the tactical component for quality play—and we could intimately observe this importance during the World Cup matches in Brazil—this excellent book by the trio of professors Israel Teoldo, Guilherme Oliveira and Júlio Garganta comes to convey ideas that allow to enlighten soccer and, as direct promoters of this spectacle, I believe that all of us should enjoy this effect. Thus, I hope you, reader, might enjoy this reading. My technical staff colleagues and I are already doing so!

Enjoy your reading.

Adenor Leonardo Bachi (Tite—Coach of Brazilian National Team)
Adenor Leonardo Bachi (Tite)

Introduction

Soccer has proved to be an unprecedented phenomenon of social impact, inhabiting a prominent place in the daily lives of millions of human beings, a phenomenon that may be witnessed even in the most remote places of the planet.

On the match stage and behind the scenes of practice and training, the demands of specialization are increasingly greater and more refined, which justifies an increased responsibility and a more accurate competence by all those involved.

The players play the game. The coaches devote their time and energy to improve players and teams' performances. In turn, match analysts, physiotherapists, psychologists, clinicians and the remaining staff dedicate themselves to optimize resources that help boosting the performance levels of players, teams, coaches and others.

In this context, practice in youth academies and top-level professional teams has posed continuously different and challenging problems, with respect to the relevance of the training to play according to ideas and playing styles that allow the materialization of these ideas. Therefore, modern training methodologies are incessantly urged to include practices related to representativeness and specificity of the models and conceptions of play, in order to ensure a significant transfer of sport performance, from training to competition, and to make preparation increasingly consistent.

It is clear, therefore, that the progress of soccer depends, more and more, on the need to create and systematize a body of knowledge that supports the evolution of practices. Hence, it seems relevant to study soccer, in its various fields, in order to help understand the constraints that favour or hinder the progress of players, teams and of the game itself. At the same time, it is necessary to spread knowledge, so as to benefit from it.

The authors of this book have devoted a significant part of their academic, professional and personal time to this enthralling team sport and, over the years, have come to realize that there is not only one single "geography of knowledge" in soccer, just as there is no single answer to the questions: How to train? How to play?

Effectively, the richness of soccer seems to lie, largely, in the fact that it can be played, practiced and thought of in plural. Hence we are in favour of neither the globalization of training methods nor the standardization of playing styles. On the contrary, we acknowledge that the different perspectives, training and forms of expression of teams and players, comprise an important asset, so that this sport never ceases to be an art and, as such, remains very much alive and keeps stirring emotions.

This work is a result of the study, practice and reflection of its authors, always taking soccer playing and training in soccer as mottos, and was conceived with the purpose of spreading and sharing a way of prospecting and evaluating the game of soccer, according to logics and principles. From a conceptual organization, several drills are presented and evaluation procedures are suggested, and may be applied to gather information regarding the tactical performance of players and teams.

It should be said, however, that the systematization of conceptions and knowledge presented here should not be outlined as a prescription. On the contrary, they are intended to also constitute a contribution that challenges other ways to see and understand soccer.

We wish to dedicate this book to all those who admit that the act of training with quality is the most influential condition in the improvement of players, teams and in the positive transformation of soccer.

Section I
Understanding the Soccer Game and Its Dynamics

1 Soccer

A Game of Tactical Knowledge

1.1 Tactics as a Complex Dimension

Throughout the years, soccer has been analysed through different perspectives that have emerged due to the use of paradigms that were created by part of the scientific community, which began to apply them to understand the reality of the phenomena (Capra, 1996; Morin, 1991).

Over the last centuries, the evolution of knowledge and expertise was based on paradigms that separated the phenomena or the objects of study so as to understand them in a more simplified manner (Morin, 1991). These approaches not only facilitated countless discoveries and promoted exponential growth in science but also made it clear that the complexity of certain phenomena and fields could not be studied from such angle. That is, they could not be simplified and had to be studied inside the limits of their inherent complexity; otherwise they would cease to exist. Trying to solve this issue, new fields of study, theories and investigation methodologies emerged in the Sixties in a more consistent manner, attempting to understand the phenomena in their complex nature (Benkirane, 2002; Capra, 1996; Morin, 1991; Stacey, 1995).

The attempt to comprehend and understand soccer games is also going through this dichotomy of paradigms. On the one hand the game is split into four dimensions (tactical, technical, physical and psychological), but on the other hand new approaches appear, describing the game as a full and complex creation, in which any attempt of breaking it apart is regarded as a mutilator of its essence. While in the first approach these different dimensions are broken down to the smallest detail, in the second approach, the study of the whole, the dimension or the detail are inseparable from the complexity intrinsic to it.

Given these different approaches, elaborated with the purpose of understanding and acting effectively and efficiently within the game and, consequently, within the training that generates it, we understand that the concept of tactics in soccer should also be considered in light of its own complexity.

In this context, if the definitions of tactics from different authors (Garganta & Oliveira, 1996; Gréhaigne, 1992; Mahlo, 1974; Teodorescu, 1984) point towards the behaviours that the player and/or team assume to deal in a correct way with the problems systematically presented by the game regarding the occupation of

DOI: 10.4324/9781003223375-2

the field, it is reasonable to say that the concept of tactics may be considered as the management (positioning and displacement/movement) of the playing space by players and teams.

This concept is related to what may be observed of the behaviour of players and the team in the field. Thus, we emphasize that this is a simple way to conceive tactics, given that underlying each positioning and displacement/movement there is a complex process that involves multiple aspects of players' cognition—(central and peripheral) perception and memory, information processing, attention/concentration and the (procedural and declarative) knowledge among them—which subsidize a more creative and/or intelligent decision-making from the players and the team, leading to the solution of the problems posed by the game.

Such comprehension of tactics takes this dimension to an emergent process (Frade, 1990; Laughlin, 2008), resulting in the interaction between a combination of factors, ideas and specific knowledge (Guilherme, 2004; Mahlo, 1974) among the different actors of a team: players, coach and the surrounding context (Guilherme, 2004). Therefore, the tactical dimension of a soccer team should be understood as a unique structure distinguished by its non-linear and spiralling complexity and dynamics. In summary, it is about a specific cultural context generated by the interaction of its different actors, which enables the emergence of a collective identity over time.

This idea of the tactical dimension as a unique structure, in which each team uncovers their own measure in a *sui generis* manner, contrasts with the abstract idea through which it is often presented. Thus, when we talk about a team's tactical dimension we do not mean a general concept, but rather a specific one, which contextualizes and gives meaning and consistency to all other dimensions.

In this case, as defined by Gibson (1979), the specificity refers to a qualifying concept of a relation of interaction between variables. These variables represent the specific information of a given context (Laughlin, 2008). As such, the variables are only considered specific if the informational links between them maintain a relation of dependence (Beek, Jacobs, Daffertshofer, & Huys, 2003). Therefore, the tactical dimension assumes in each team a different organism, with its own identity and particularities, which emerge from the relation of complicity with other dimensions. These, however, also exhibit particular characteristics influenced by the specific informational context generated by the respective interactions.

As a consequence of such properties, the technical, physical or psychological dimensions are meaningless without the tactical one to contextualize them, in the same way that the tactical dimension cannot express itself if any of the others is not present. With this statement we do not intend to convey the idea that the tactical dimension is more important than the others, but rather to highlight that it plays the role of generator, catalyst and specific informational coordinator of each team.

This understanding of tactics refers to the interaction of distinct variables: the ideas and specific knowledge of the different actors.

The ideas are related to the direction we give to the way of solving problems. Usually, coaches know the style of play they intend to implement in their teams. They know what they want in the different moments of play, they know what they intend when the team is in offensive or defensive organization or in the respective transitions (defence-attack and attack-defence). These are the ideas conveyed to the players through training, the process of incorporating the play (Maciel, 2011), which drives the paths to be followed by the teams and their respective players. The coaches' ideas function as a guiding light. Therefore, the play that is created is closely related to the ideas transmitted by the coach.

The players' specific knowledge is related to the interaction between their particular tactical understanding and expertise related to distinguishing motor skills applied to the context (Guilherme, 2004). The specific tactical knowledge leads us to the knowledge the player possesses that allows him/her to play, selecting the options that seem appropriate when facing different situations. This one is related to the declarative and procedural knowledge. With respect to both concepts, procedural knowledge is related to the motor skills which ensures the feasibility of the action intended to operationalize the decision (Guilherme, 2004).

When there is an interaction between the player's specific knowledge, and the coach's ideas of play, the outcome is a collective project of dynamic play, simultaneously and paradoxically, predictable and unpredictable.

The predictability emerges from the ideas of play the coach conveys and is structured on a macro level. On the other hand, the unpredictability rises from the interpretation and interaction structured on a micro level that the different players make from those ideas, with their own knowledge, perception and particularities.

Let us make an analogy to better understand and evoke the idea. Say the ideas of play the coach intends to convey are represented by the colour blue. When the idea of this colour is transmitted, it will be interpreted by the players and each one will recognize this blue in a peculiar way, according to their experiences, characteristics, skills, limitations, preferences and emotions. When these different blues expressed by the players interact, the resulting shade of blue that emerges is unpredictable.

Through this analogy we have just presented, we intend to demonstrate that the predictability is the understanding that the interaction between the coach's ideas and the players' specific knowledge will be represented by the colour blue, and not by red, green or yellow. However, the shade of blue that will rise from every interaction is unknown to us. This is the unpredictability, the shade of blue, on the macro level, and the different players' shades, on the micro level.

The combination of the coaches' ideas, the respective interpretation by the players and the resulting rebuilding of these ideas through the training process is what enables the players to continuously find new individual and collective paths.

At this point, we intend to highlight that tactic is a complex dimension related to the team's identity and also to the operational process of building this identity. Next we will seek to understand the tactical evolution that game and the player had over time.

1.2 The Paths Taken by Tactics

From its origins to the present day, soccer has been through different phases, characterized by equally distinct demonstrations of play (Guilherme, 2004). These phases grant understanding of the evolution of the game, the player and, at the same time, of the concept of tactics.

As mentioned earlier, the current definition of tactics refers to the behaviours the player and/or the team performs to solve the problems that arise from the game. We also verified that the patterns of these behaviours come from the interaction between various levels, specifically the coaches' ideas and the players' specific knowledge. Thus, we understand tactics as a concept from which emerges a particular and specific informational context that is gradually built and recreated in a spiralling way, as its actors interact in training and matches.

Therefore, we are aware that the onset of tactics in the soccer game is in the origin of the game itself, regardless of the completely different nuances currently observed.

1.3 The Game Begins, Tactics Emerge

The emancipation of soccer as a game happened at the occasion of its institutionalization through The Football Association, in 1863, in England. However, its practice as a recognized sport started in the early years of this century.

The first known rules were proposed in 1815 by the Eton College. However, it was only in 1848 in Cambridge, in a meeting between the most prestigious Universities at the time, that the first standardized rules were created, strongly influenced by rugby (Sebastián, 1996). The particularities highlighted, such as the prohibition of passing the ball to a more advanced teammate, which would be considered offside, constrained the progression of the team and the players in the field, thus determining the characteristics of the game and player at that time (Castelo, 1996). The solution found to overcome this issue was the progression through individual actions. The player in possession of the ball would move forward trying to dribble all opponents that appeared and, if successful, would shoot at goal. However, if any of the opponents took away the ball, he/she would be the one to perform the same actions of progression and dribble. The teammates of the player leading the progression were concerned about supporting him/her and, if he/she lost possession of the ball, they would try to recover it and start a new action of dribbling penetration. The players of the opposite team would try to prevent this advancement, and when they gained the ball, they would try to advance themselves through dribble. Because of these characteristics, this period of soccer was mentioned to as the dribbler's period (Castelo, 1996). The arrangement of the players on the field employed at the time consisted of one goalkeeper, one defender and nine forwards (1–1–9) (Figure 1.1). This solution turned the game into a set of individualized actions with little collective meaning.

After the foundation of The Football Association in 1863 there was an attempt to permanently emancipate soccer from rugby. This effort enabled the introduction

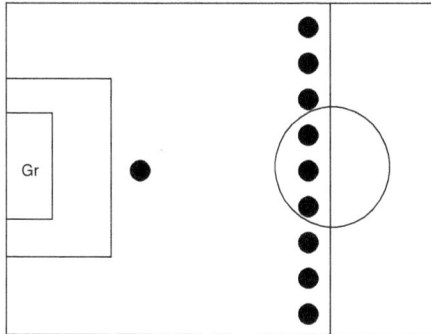

Figure 1.1 Representation of the arrangement of the players on the field: (1-1-9) one goalkeeper, one defender and nine forwards
Source: Guilherme (2004)

of changes to the rules in 1866, which was decisive for the evolution and the path that the game started to follow.

The most relevant adjustment, among many, was the modification in the offside rule. A player would then be considered offside only if he/she received the ball without having at least three opponents between himself/herself and the opposite goal line. This alteration made forward passes possible, thus progressively turning soccer from a game of essentially individual features into a game of collective ones (Gréhaigne, 1992).

With the purpose of creating new solutions to the possibilities and characteristics the game began to present, the arrangements of the players started to change. There was a decrease in the number of forwards and an increase in the number of players with defensive and organizational tasks, that is the concern gradually shifted to lessen the imbalance between the number of players in defence and attack (Figure 1.2) (Castelo, 1996).

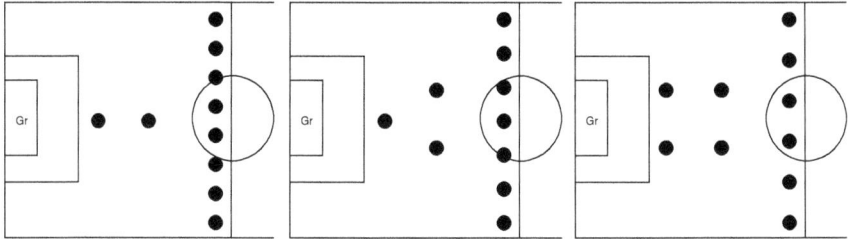

Figure 1.2 Representation of the different arrangements of the players on the field: (1-1-1-8) one goalkeeper, one defender, one midfielder and eight forwards; (1-1-2-7) one goalkeeper, one defender, two midfielders and seven forwards; (1-2-2-6) one goalkeeper, two defenders, two midfielders and six forwards*Source*: Guilherme (2004)

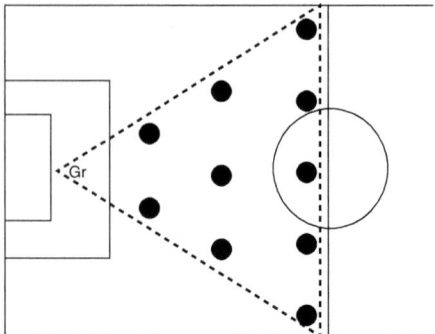

Figure 1.3 Representation of the "Classical System" or "Pyramid": (1-2-3-5) one goalkeeper, two defenders, three midfielders and five forwards
Source: Guilherme (2004)

These changes were progressive for around 20 years, until 1884, when as a consequence of the evolution that had been observed there came which was considered the first soccer system, the "Classical System" or "Pyramid" (Figure 1.3). This system was organized with players arranged in: one goalkeeper, two defenders, three midfielders and five forwards (1-2-3-5). It was considered the first soccer system because, for the first time, the three sectors of the team were took into account: defence, midfield and attack, allowing a certain balance between offensive and defensive actions (Castelo, 1996; Mendes, 1979).

In comparison with the game played in previous decades, the meaning of the game had definitively changed. Due to the generalized possibility of passing, the game was no longer a set of individual actions of dribbling progression, but rather a more collective one.

This stage of adaptation and evolution (in)to a game with different, more collective characteristics, lasted around 50 years. Another change in the offside rule, proposed in 1925, reduced for two the number of opponents the attacker were allowed to have between himself/herself and the opposite goal line when he/she received the ball, led the game to a considerable evolution. From that point forwards, the doors to the development of tactics were also opened, since the ideas for solving problems of the game started to diversify. As an example of the alterations observed then, the centre-backs who previously played in projection (one in front and the other behind) started to play in line to benefit from the offside rule. Those players positioned up the field, by the side corridors, known as wingers, progressed to play close to the line of the centre-backs, thus shaping the "W" of notorious systems, which have been very successful since the 1930s.

Because of the emergence of three new coaches, from three different countries, who revolutionized the characteristics of soccer and influenced the following generations, that decade was considered, in turn, quite rich. Herbert Chapman

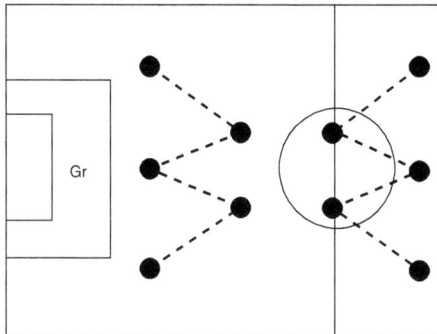

Figure 1.4 Representation of Herbert Chapman's "WM System"
Source: Guilherme (2004)

appeared in England, while Italy and Austria saw the rise of Vittorio Pozzo and Hugo Meisl, respectively. In 1932, Herbert Chapman, Arsenal's coach, developed a new playing "system" called "WM" (Figure 1.4). This "system" became revolutionary because it provided, for the first time, a numerical balance between defenders and forwards and, as a result, individual defence appears as a collective concern (Sebastián, 1996). If we project the letters that make the acronym for this system among teams, we will notice that the "W" (attack) projected on the "M" (defence) provides the exact fit of the marking for each player: the centre-back marking the centre forward, the full-backs marking the two midfielders and the defensive midfielder marking the attacking midfielder. In addition, this system enabled a balanced occupation, for that time, of all playing spaces: defence, midfield and attack. These positional characteristics brought out a more collective game compared to the one practiced up to that point, and it was from that time on that the tactical dimension started being acknowledged in the characteristics and qualities the game exhibited (Guilherme, 2004).

The "WM system", also known as "magic square" due to the square-shaped positioning of the four midfield players, was of paramount importance for the evolution of the characteristics of the game and the players. The game began to show a more collective meaning (Castelo, 1996), while the player became an integral part of a group with previously established tasks and objectives, in which the final result was not the sum of all players' roles, but rather of the relations they took on. For the first time, there was an idea of an organized team, both collectively and individually (Guilherme, 2004).

Vittorio Pozzo, coach of the Italian National Team crowned World Champions in 1934 and 1938, and gold medallist at the Olympic Games in Berlin, in 1936, was also a very important coach at that time, due to the titles won and his ideas of play. Pozzo's ideas of play were based on off-ball play and on the preparation he demanded from the team. He wanted the team to display a very rigorous and

10 *Understanding the Soccer Game*

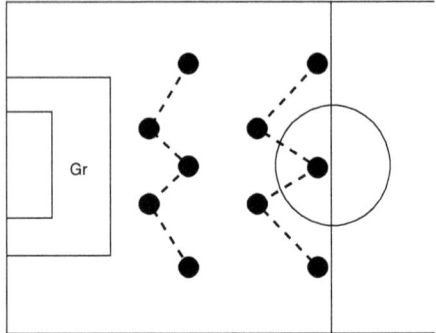

Figure 1.5 Representation of Vittorio Pozzo's "WW System"
Source: Guilherme (2004)

safe defensive organization, with the purpose of regaining possession and counter attack, through a fast and in-depth play. He was the precursor of counter attacking and positional shifts between forwards. The playing "system" displayed was the so-called WW (Figure 1.5), an adaptation of the "classical system": five defenders, two midfielders and three forwards. With respect to team conditioning, due to the influence of the military dictatorship that ruled the country at the time, he imposed a quite demanding and rigorous physical and psychological preparation, as he understood this was the path to success (Sebastián, 1996).

Hugo Meisl, coach of the Austrian National Team and creator of the so-called *Wunderteam*, dazzled the entire Europe between 1931 and 1935 with the quality of his game. Meisl gathered the renowned technique of the Austrian players and his new ideas of play that were revolutionary at the time and that inspired the following generations. In defensive terms they were the first team to collectively constrain their opponents. It was not only the players with defensive tasks who performed it but also those in the offensive, thus giving rise to the ideas of collective defensive organization and pressing. In offensive terms, he demanded great mobility from all players, required players to constantly shift positions in order to create additional problems to the opponents, and also expected the players with defensive tasks to be involved in the offensive ones (Sebastián, 1996).

These ideas, which then were completely revolutionary and performed by players with great technique, allowed for the soccer game to be played as never seen before. The structure employed by Meisl was an adaptation of the "classical system" with some alterations that had the purpose of creating balance between all three sectors and a rational occupation of the playing space (Figure 1.6).

The *Wunderteam* was considered back then the ultimate expression of attacking soccer (Márcio et al., 1992; Sebastián, 1996). Its continuity was not possible due to the death of its creator in 1937, and because its players were involved in the war during several years. For these reasons Meisl's ideas were neglected at the time,

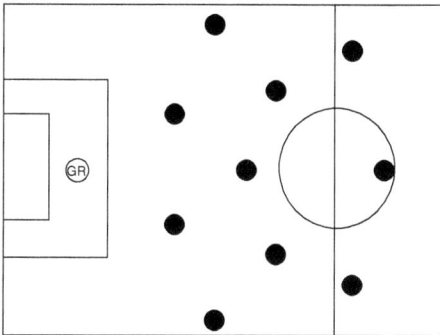

Figure 1.6 Representation of Hugo Meisl's "System"
Source: Guilherme (2004)

maybe because they were far too evolved. Nevertheless, they later inspired several coaches who were also very important for the evolution of the game.

The importance of all three coaches mentioned was decisive due to the ideas introduced, the paths that they opened and, consequently, the ideological versatility that soccer began to exhibit, that is for the first time ever, the relevance of the tactical dimension started taking shape.

The predominance of the "WM" system lasted until the early 1950s, more precisely November, 1953, when England was beaten at home by Hungary 6–3 and again, after a few months, in 1954, in Hungary, 7–1. During the 20 years within this period, some variations of the "WM" emerged, always with the purpose of improving it. However, the true changes only occurred in the 1950s, with the Hungarian and Brazilian National Teams (Sebastián, 1996).

The Hungarian team, coached by Gustav Sebes, featured a group of players of great technical quality, but it was the tactical characteristics that made it different and were responsible for their achievements (Mendes, 1979). The key aspect of the Hungarian team was the dynamics the players and, as a result, the team were able to impose to their offensive game. However, another element displayed was the distinctive positional organization of the players when defending and attacking (Figure 1.7). This change brought several problems to their opponents, due to the static positional approach that existed at the time.

From this point forward, the dynamics, that is the players' and team's mobility with and without the ball proved to be key aspects of the game. It was the return of a more incisive and definitive version of Hugo Meisl's ideas.

The Brazilian team was also decisive within this period due to the new systems it displayed. At first, the "1-4-2-4", (one goalkeeper, four defenders, two midfielders and four forwards), in 1958 and, later, in 1962 the "1-4-3-3" (one goalkeeper, four defenders, three midfielders and three forwards), the latter because it adapted to the players' skills and characteristics (Figure 1.8).

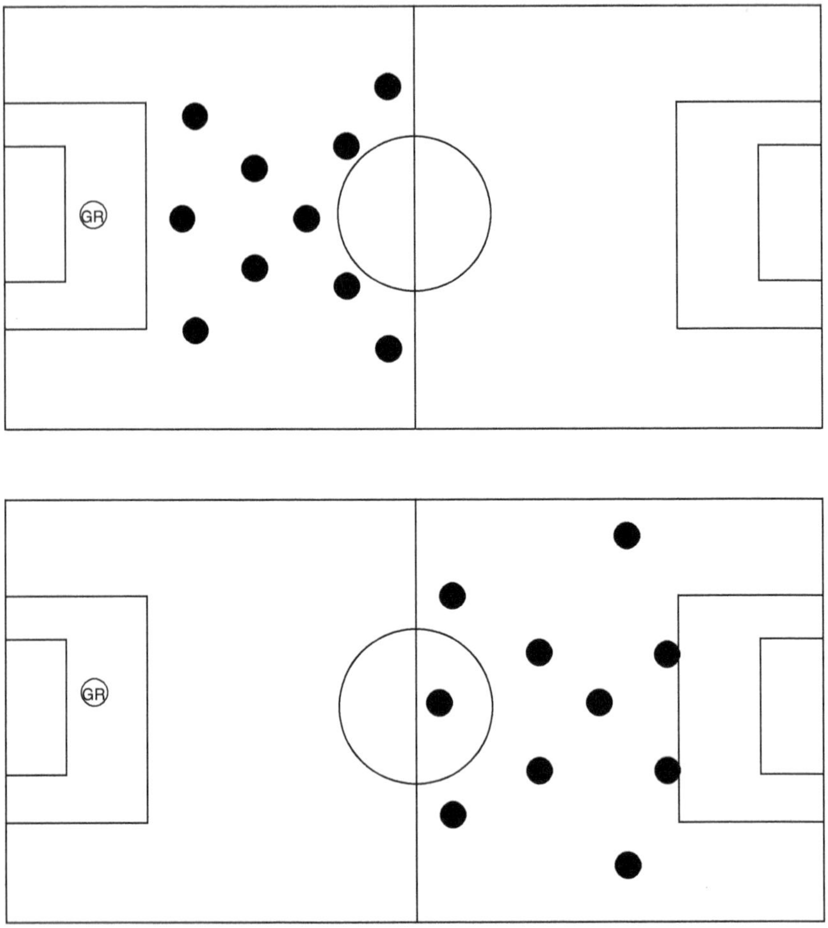

Figure 1.7 Representation of Gustav Sebes' "System", with the positioning of the players when defending and attacking

Source: Guilherme (2004)

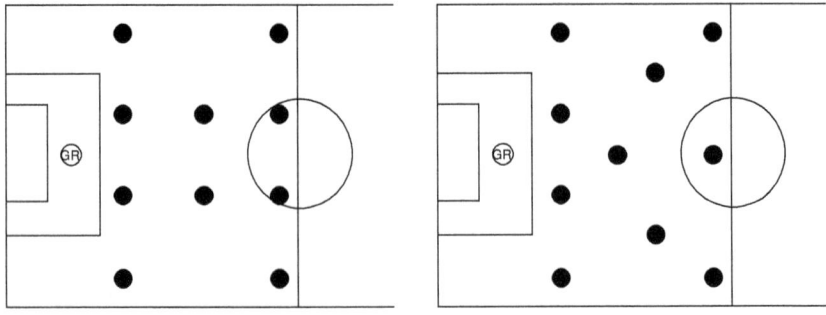

Figure 1.8 Representation of the 1-4-2-4 and 1-4-3-3 "Systems" used by the Brazilian Team in the 1958 and 1962 World Cups, respectively

Source: Guilherme (2004)

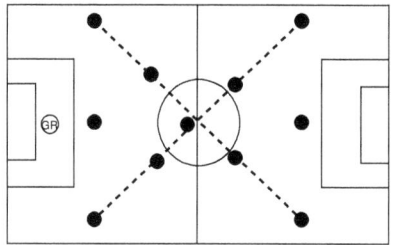 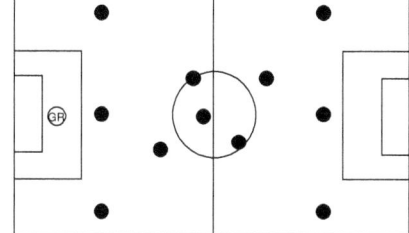

Figure 1.9 X Diagonal of the "WM" and asymmetric "WM" systems, respectively
Source: Guilherme (2004)

The former (1-4-2-4) system was the consequence of the evolution of some years of experiences and adaptations of South American soccer. After the application of the "WM" and "WW" systems in Brazil, mainly in the Flamengo and Fluminense teams during the 1930s and 1940s, alternatives for the expression of the game appeared, slowly displaying the essence of Brazilian soccer (Parreira, 2005).

The first change ever recorded was from the X diagonal of the "WM" System to the asymmetric "WM" (see Figure 1.9), causing one of the midfielders to be pushed forward and the other to be pulled back. Thus, two new functions emerged in soccer: attacking midfielder and centre-forward.

Because the centre-forward often penetrated the penalty box unmarked, forcing the centre-back to divide his attention between him/her and the target man, the fourth defender emerged to mark him/her. Besides, the freedom granted to the full-backs to progress to the offensive half made the defensive coverage of the space vacated by them essential to preserve defensive balance. As a result came the 1-4-2-4, a winning system used by the Brazilian Team during the 1958 World Cup, in Sweden.

Conversely, the 1-4-3-3 system was an evolution of the former caused by some organizational and functional adjustments to the players' characteristics and skills. This innovative system also allowed Brazil to win the 1962 World Cup, in Chile.

The essential characteristics of these systems were: the balance between the defensive and offensive play, which allowed for an easy and rapid turn from a strong defence into a strong attack and vice versa; a dynamics of team and players which allowed them to generate defensive and offensive edge within the area where the ball was being played; and, lastly, the acknowledgement of the physical dimension as core aspect of this playing style. Both systems were successful at that time, because at first they encouraged by the proposed dynamics that did not exist until then, and also because its demands required of the midfielders who often took part in the defensive and offensive actions of the team (Castelo, 1996; Mendes, 1979; Sebastián, 1996).

Thereafter, the physical dimension started being permanently recognized as decisive for the evolution of the game (Castelo, 1996; Mendes, 1979; Sebastián, 1996).

In spite of the importance of this recognition, it has not always been interpreted with the intention of protecting the essence of the game and, as a consequence, its qualitative evolution. Since the different dimensions of the game were not acknowledged by most of the sports people in its complex uniqueness, there was the interpretation of the possibility of splitting them. If in some cases, as we will refer to later, this fact was not evidenced as a limitation for the evolution of the game and the player, in others, it was found that the direction through which it went led the game to winding paths, in which the quality of the play and the players was even up.

One of the most crucial examples of this line of reasoning was the 1966 World Cup, held in England. The champion and runner-up, England and Germany, respectively, were distinguished as the greatest exponents of what was known at the time as the "physical style". This style of play was distinguished by the supremacy of the physical dimension above all others. The players would run a lot and often went to the challenges with great vigour. Many of the technical and puny players were replaced by the strong, tall and robust ones. The game was described as ugly and violent due to the excessive number of dangerous fouls, lacking technical quality and artless, driven by the absence of skills and creativity displayed by the players (Mendes, 1979).

This style of play, adopted by many European countries and, consequently, important teams after the 1960s, was the answer to the recognition of the need of increased playing dynamics. This challenge was introduced by Gustav Sebes, in the 1950s, and by the Brazilian National teams in 1958 and 1962, though with completely distinct nuances, since, as we mentioned, the dynamics of the teams emerged from the creative and innovative ideas of play presented and from the technical skills of the different players.

Yet, the continuity and evolution of the ideas patented by the Brazilian team in South America and the resurgence in Europe of innovative ideas of play, proposed by the Dutch National team and by Ajax, through the coaches Rinus Michels and Stephan Kovacs, were crucial for generating alternatives to the physical style that had been established in the Old Continent.

Rinus Michels, Ajax's and future Netherlands' coach, created an idea of play that would be called "Total Football". The characteristics that supported this idea elected the technical skills and players' freedom and intelligence as the most important values of expression (Cruyff, 2002). Passing, constant mobility of the forwards without the ball, continuous support to the player in possession of the ball, versatility of tasks, control of the pace of play, with accelerations, decelerations or breaks generating adaptation problems for the opponents, and the superior technical skills of the different players, supported by the physical dimension, were regarded as basic fundamentals for the offensive play. The reduction of the playing space, thus approximating the areas both in width and length and packing the team, the permanent search for recovering possession in every zone of the field and pressing the player in possession of the ball also supported by good physical strength were the characteristics of the defensive play (Cruyff, 2002; Mendes, 1979; Olivares, 1978; Sebastián, 1996).

According to what we have just mentioned, the late 1960s and the 1970s saw the rise of distinct ideas about the game. These ideas came from the same concern: the need for greater dynamics of play. However, taking into account the main concerns of each to solve the problem, the game began evidencing distinct forms of expression, which, in a simplified manner, may be named "technical-tactical" and "tactical-physical" (Guilherme, 2004).

The "technical-tactical" form, mainly displayed by the Dutch, Brazilian and Argentinian national teams, as well as some domestic teams of these countries, was characterized by a playing style essentially based on the tactical and technical dimensions. The physical dimension also played an important role, but only as a support to the others rather than as a generator of the process. This style of play was expressed in different ways, but focused on the qualitative relation between the offensive and defensive processes and, above all, on their connection with the players' technical skills. Technique does not appear constrained, but it is rather a conditioning factor. It interacts with the tactical dimension to generate a more qualitative play, which, in consequence, compels the player to create new paths to respond to the ever-growing demands the game begins to exhibit. There is an evolutionary process of spiralling interaction between the game and the player (Guilherme, 2004).

The "tactical-physical" form, exhibited by the English, German, Italian and Spanish national teams, among others, was characterized by a playing style based on the tactical and physical dimensions. Technique emerges from the need of solving problems in the game, but with a secondary importance in relation to and constrained by the other dimensions. For these reasons, in many teams over the years players were selected not according to technical superiority, but to tactical characteristics based on discipline, organizational capabilities and superior physical skills. This style of play can also manifest in different ways: more offensive or more defensive, but always strongly linked to the tactical and physical dimensions.

From the late 1960s up to present days, there has been an ongoing battle between these two styles of play. In some periods, a more "tactical-physical" style has dominated. Some of the highlights of this style were the 1966 World Cup, won by England, the 1982 World Cup, won by Italy and the 1990 World Cup, won by Germany.

In other periods, it was the more "technical-tactical" style that prevailed, particularly when supported by technically evolved players, and when those skills work in favour of the team. Some examples of this style are the Brazilian teams of 1958 and 1962, the Netherlands in 1974, Brazil in 1982, Argentina in 1986 and the current Spanish team. At club level, some European teams were also noteworthy: Rinus Michels' and Stephan Kovacs' Ajax of the early 1970s, Arrigo Sacchi's Milan of the late 1980s, Johan Cruyff's Barcelona of the early 1990s and, more recently, Pep Guardiola's Barcelona, Bayern München and Manchester City are some clear examples.

Despite this evident dichotomy in understanding soccer, it was what, over the years, provided moments of clear evolution of the game and the player: The game because of the new ideas that coaches proposed when facing the problems that arose, especially regarding gradual decrease of playing time and space. The player because he/she not only interpreted the new ideas presented but also reinvented them, at both tactical and physical dimensions, propelling the game to ever more elaborate levels.

According to what we have just observed, the evolution that the game has undergone over the years has different aspects, though it always aimed at solving tactical problems that emerged.

The first period was defined by the emancipation and identification of soccer as a sport with its own characteristics: the creation and restructuring of rules allowed the change from a game with mainly individual expressions into a collective one.

The second was defined by the implementation and evolution of the "playing systems" and by the appearance of players with great technical skills who responded to tactical evolutions, promoting and propelling them to even more advanced levels. The logic that underpinned the effort to solve the evidenced tactical problems was the continuous attempt to balance the power between attack and defence. Some did so by favouring offensive characteristics, while others the defensive ones. Both ways succeeded, but the most exciting were those who focused on the offensive characteristics, supported by the superior technical skills of their players.

The third period came from the acknowledgement of the need to increase the dynamics of the game. The paths to the achievement of these goals diverged. On one side were the advocates of a more "tactical-physical" style, while the ones who preferred a more "technical-tactical" one stood on the opposite side, with mixed expressions in between. The consequence of this significant and permanent increase of "dynamics" reflected in the constant reduction of space and time, thus constraining the teams' and players' defensive and offensive play.

Currently, the teams wield their collective and individual competencies through their ideas and respective qualities. While defending, they try to constrain space and time more and better. When attacking, they try to create space and time to better decide and act, sometimes in high intensity, other times with a rhythmic variability with the purpose of limiting the opponents' adaptations. Thus, the styles of play are distinct. We are being increasingly exposed to peculiar ideas of play; however, those characterized by the triumphs and aesthetics are the ones based on a game played in collective way, in which the technical excellence and diversity and the intelligence and creativity are acclaimed (Cruyff, 2002; Valdano, 2002).

So that these styles of play can be expressed, we propose the analysis of soccer as a complex game and, therefore, the understanding of the concept of tactics through this perspective. Instead of understanding it as an abstract dimension, appreciate it as a specifying one that promotes the interaction and identification of all other dimensions and, consequently, of the team.

2 Tactics in Soccer

We start this chapter by recalling one of the papers published by Prof. Júlio Garganta (2006a), in which he reflects on the absence in the Olympic motto *Citius, Altius, Fortius* of a major component of team sports, particularly soccer: *Intelligentia*. Since the main action of players and teams is developed based on the type of opposition between opponents, the type of cooperation involving teammates, on the degrees of freedom and variability and the characteristics of technical skills to respond to the specific demands of the game, how could we conceive soccer without considering the intelligence of its elements?

In soccer, as stressed by Gréhaigne (1991), the performance of its elements (players and teams) is closely related to the tactical and strategic aspects of the game, since they deal at every moment with the space, time, organization and information available in the match. The essentiality of these aspects becomes more evident if we consider that: (i) most of the actions in a match occur without the players being in direct contact with the ball; (ii) players with limited mastery of technical skills are able to play a soccer match with minimal organization if they possess a reasonable level of tactical comprehension (Oslin, Mitchell, & Griffin, 1998) and (iii) the lack of tactical knowledge may compromise the efficient and/or effective execution of technical skills (Mesquita, Farias, Oliveira, & Pereira, 2009).

This tactical/strategic essentiality becomes even more evident when we verify that the movements (walking, jogging, running) and positions that players assume at every moment in the field are closely related with the game configuration and with the goal that was set. Given the convenience that every action has a tactical purpose, the analysis of indicators such as the distance covered during a match, the "heat maps" of displacements in the field, or players' heart rate may be of greater relevance when related to the tactical and strategic applications of the game, particularly with respect to the playing style, to the offensive and defensive methods adopted by the team, and to the positional and functional roles of the players (Garganta, 1997, 2001, 2009).

In this respect, we intend to present here concepts that seem relevant for both the teaching/training process and the match, such as tactics and strategy, phases and moments of play, system and scheme of play and tactical principles.

DOI: 10.4324/9781003223375-3

1.1 Tactics and Strategy: Two Sides of the Same Coin

In the context of soccer, the concepts of tactics and strategy are, not rarely, mistaken and put into similarity. Indeed, these concepts are somehow strongly interrelated, and to separate one from the other is not an easy task when they are not well clarified and/or defined.

In order to facilitate understanding, it is possible to verify that the origin of the word strategy derives from the Latin *stratègós*, that in military expeditions is intimately linked to the art of planning war operations. Thus, we can assume that strategy in soccer is the way a team plans for a particular match or situation (tournament, championship, game period, etc.). This concept is volatile by nature, and may be completely changed from one match to the next, or even within the same match, depending on the events that occur. The change in strategy may also occur during a season with respect to the preparation of the players and the team, depending on the results achieved in previously played matches, and what is expected from the following ones. Therefore, when a strategy is set up for the team to perform, outlines are built and short-, medium- or long-term objectives are established. All this is represented by a strategic plan that aims to anticipate events and/or situations through previous knowledge one has of them, in order to increase the probability of success of future behaviours to be adopted in the field by the players and the team.

In turn, these behaviours will be performed based on the tactics developed through the model of play and the game principles. As mentioned in Chapter 1, tactics (from the Greek *taktikê*—which in military context means the art of disposing and using the troops through the combat ground), to our knowledge, is the way players manage/occupy the playing spaces, through their positioning and movements.

In this respect, we advocate that the player's action necessarily leads to the interaction of the other elements of the game and the team operates as a unity whose relations outweigh the individual values (Garganta, 2005). This means that understanding and assimilating the game without ball possession is as important as the perfect mastery of technical skills, because it will enable the actions performed by the players who are distant from the centre of play to have implications for the players who are positioned closer to the ball. This means that the game without ball possession has two goals: (i) intervention of the highest possible number of players in the game and (ii) the possibility of, through movements in the field, drawing the attention of opponents and force them to move to zones of lesser intervention, mainly in the centre of play, so as to make room for other teammates and support the actions of the player in possession of the ball (Castelo, 1996). Thus, as we highlighted in Chapter 1, in order to have good space management within the game, the player must be aware and well (in)formed about the multiplicities of spaces that exist in a game, namely, in three important scales of interaction, in which the macro represents the fixed and dynamic spaces that encompass all the collective plan (collective tactics); the meso represents the first line of opposition and the first line of support on a group level (group tactics), especially in the game centre; and the micro represents the spaces between the player and the ball (i), between the player with the ball and the defender (ii), behind the defender (iii), behind the player with the ball (iv) (individual tactics)

Through the development of this idea, it is possible to state that tactics are related to organizational and decision-making factors, which are present among the inter- and intra-team relations, and may be examined under the individual or collective point of view. Expressed on the functional structure of the game that results from the actions of players and teams around the ball, tactics are presented as a product of the interaction between the individual aspects related to decision-making and the external aspects that come from the organization in the field (Figure 2.1) (Lamas & Seabra, 2006; Pinto & Garganta, 1996).

Considering this information, the *strategic-tactical knowledge* takes on a key role, since it arises not only from the understanding of the competition rules and management and organization of the game, but also from the awareness of the conditions of situational regulation (Barth, 1994; Garganta, 2006b). From the assumption that each team will behave as a dynamic system that exists from its organization in space and time, the efficacy of the individual and collective behaviours will depend on the commitment between its identity and integrity. Thus, what makes the game is the transformation of causality in chance, in other words, to seize the moment; and strategy and tactics are the elements that teach how to do that (Garganta, 2006b).

To this extent, what is required from the players is a permanent strategic-tactical disposition whose quality depends on the players' knowledge about the game and his/her ability to perceive and interpret the available information. At this level, the materialization of the strategic planning will occur through the tactical behaviours

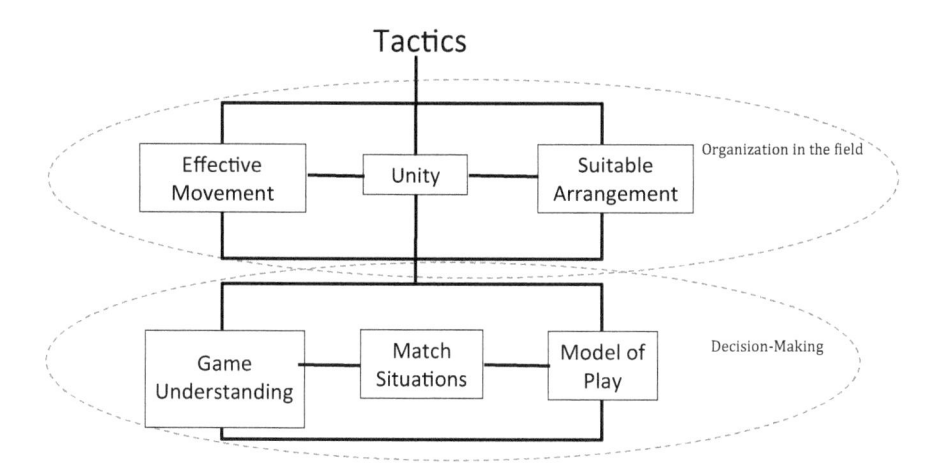

Figure 2.1 Elements that comprise tactics and are related to the organization in the field and decision-making

Source: The authors

performed according to the specific situational game conditions to gain maximum benefit from advantages that arise from the dynamic interactions between the players, namely with regards to the (i) numerical, (ii) positional, (iii) dynamic movement, (iv) qualitative and (v) relationship/integration.

1.2 The Internal Logic and the Phases of Play in the Soccer Game

Soccer is distinguished by the simultaneous existence of cooperation and opposition, which at every moment leads to a collective relational dynamic that compels players to make continuous judgements and decisions, being the players' actions, reactions and interactions that built the singularity and diversity of the chain of events that culminates in the scoring in the opponent's goal and the prevention of such in their own goal (Castelo, 1996; Júlio & Araújo, 2005).

In addition to these factors, it is important to emphasize the probability of the association between the performance elements (energetic functional, anthropometric, psychological, social, technical and tactical), aspects related to chance[1] (Eigen & Winkler, 1989; Garganta & Cunha e Silva, 2000) and the chaotic variables[2] (Werner, 1995) contributes to the structure and outcome of the game (Garganta & Cunha e Silva, 2000; Werner, 1995).

Although it is not possible to standardize the sequence of actions, the possibilities of combination being countless, soccer might be considered a macrosystem that comprises subsystems or team organizational levels of collective and individual opposition. In this system, players' actions are incorporated into a structure that follows a particular model, according to certain principles and rules that develop in two opposite phases, attack and defence (Gréhaigne, 2001; Teodorescu, 1984).

In the defensive phase, players continuously attempt to neutralize attackers' actions to achieve a stable position in order to regain possession of the ball; whereas in the offensive phase, they intend to generate, in a self-organized way, disorder in the opposite defence with the aim of upsetting the balance and scoring a goal (Garganta, 1996).

From this structure, it can be said that the game interactions translate into the rationalization and objectification of the set of basic and specific tactical tasks and missions that guide the behaviours of all players in the field (Castelo, 1996), given that in each of the phases of play there are related objectives concerning the defensive and offensive aspects of the actions (as shown in Figure 2.2).

The logic of the game present in these two phases is expressed by the intent of players' cooperation and organization with the purpose of beating the opponents, either attacking (keeping the defensive balance in mind) or defending (being ready to attack). Accordingly, all players' attitudes and behaviours are focused on the game objectives: avoid conceding goals in their own net and score goals in the opposite net. Furthermore, players who are not directly involved in the defensive process should mentally prepare the attack by searching for empty spaces that may be used for the development of offensive actions, whereas those who are not

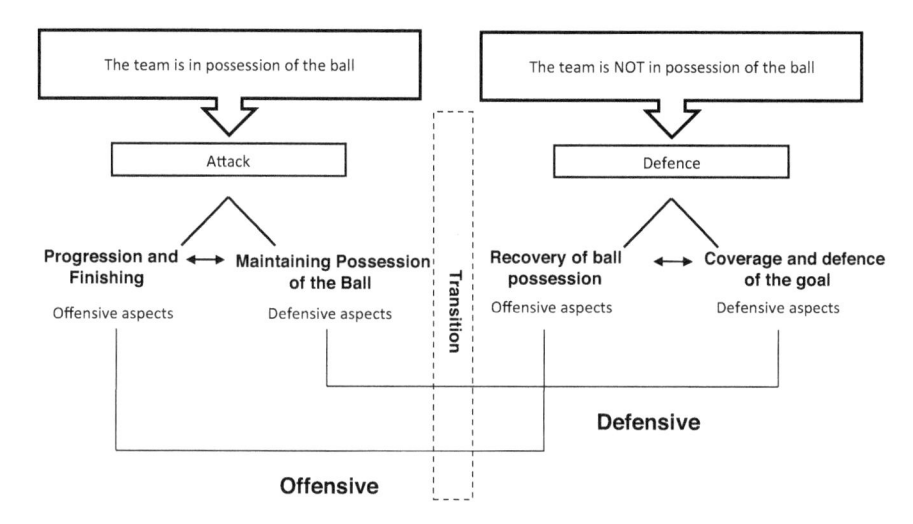

Figure 2.2 Phases, objectives and offensive and defensive aspects within the phases of play of the soccer game (modified from Gréhaigne et al., 1997)
Source: The authors

actively participating in these actions are required to think the game defensively (Castelo, 1996; Gréhaigne, Godbout, & Bouthier, 1997).

From this idea, one assumes a conception of balance that enables attacking without compromising defensive security when in possession, and by analogy, defending without losing the capacity to score goals (Silva, 2004). Based on this logic, the player should be capable of attacking, but should also be positioned, oriented and ready to act efficiently in case of loss of possession, adapting their behaviours to the defensive objectives of the situation. In a non-possession situation, it is appropriate to consider the opposite, that is, the player should defend, but, in a situation of recovery of possession he/she should also be prepared for efficiently developing behaviours consistent with the attacking objectives (Cervera & Malavés, 2001).

In view of these characteristics from the game operational complicity, we also highlight the transitions between these phases of play (attack-defence and defence-attack) that gain more importance each and every day. The argument for this is based on the frequent changes of possession, which impose to the players high ability to adapt to the various moments of the game, in which the collective organization becomes more difficult and vulnerable (Barreira & Garganta, 2007; Garganta, 2006a).

Since they are responsible for most of the situations that unbalance the outcome of the game, attack-defence and defence-attack transitions can be described as moments of the game that, combined with the dynamics of the interrelations that are established within the field, are associated with the player's and team's thinking skills and tactical adaptability in the first moments following the loss or recovery of possession. On this subject, Guilherme (2004) states that these seconds are extremely important, since the teams are disorganized for the new functions, and that the objective is to take advantage of the opposition's disorganization.

Because it possesses this attribute and importance, it is believed that the faster the ability of the player and the team to switch between the phases of play is, therefore appropriating the mentality, the principles and the specific behaviours within each of these transitions, the more and better conditions will be achieved in order to beat the opponent and accomplish the objective of the game.

1.3 Scheme and System of Play

Once the unitary and collective mentality of the game is thoroughly paced, it becomes essential to understand the existing relationships in all actions performed by the players, since each of them must necessarily interact with the other game elements. Therefore, comprehending the existing connections between players' actions and the variables correlated with team performance is a key step to grasp the elements that provide balance to the offensive, defensive and transitional (attack-defence and defence-attack) actions.

At this point, the concepts of system of play and scheme of play support the understanding of the dynamics displayed in the field and the arrangements adopted by the players. Scheme (from the Latin "*schema*") of play refers to the relations established between players, that is their communication channels. In this sense, it is not only the actual form of the figure represented between these channels, but rather how these relations are manifested, and how their potentials and limitations underpin the establishment of functions that assist the development of such links.

As an example of the concept described earlier, we can see in Figure 2.3 the communication channels (lines linking the players) within this team. Through the links represented we can see how relations are established, based on the thickness of the line that symbolizes the connection. Among the numerous information displayed in this figure, it is possible to verify that the team represented there prefers to start their attacks along the sides of the field, particularly the left side. In addition, the relations drawn between players of different areas may also be observed. In this respect, we see that the midfield area (attacking and defensive midfielders, ns. 10, 8 and 6) connects with the offensive area by means of central play and through passes. Similarly, the connection of the defensive area with the offensive one, especially on the right side, occurs indirectly; but on the left side there is a direct link between the centre-back (n. 4) and the forward (n. 7), although in lesser intensity when compared to the connection that this same centre-back has with other players (ns. 6, 8, 11 and 5) from adjacent areas.

Hence, it is from the schemes, that is the communication channels established between the players, that the team's system of play emerges. The system would then be the representation of the whole, which in soccer is usually classified as the union of defence, midfield and attack. Thus, it would be represented by the

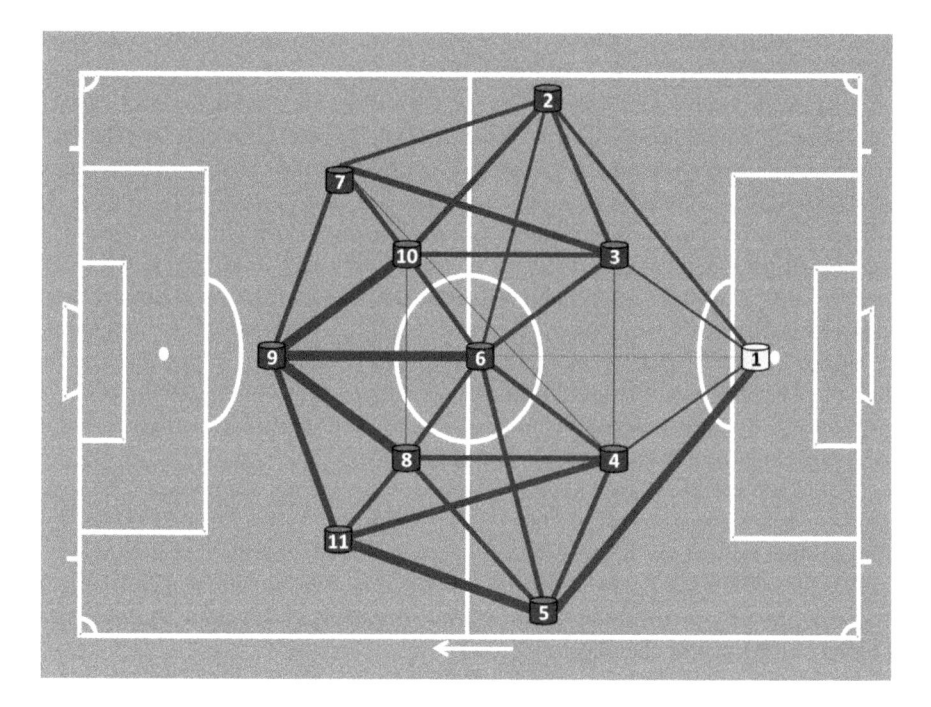

Figure 2.3 Examples of tactical schemes (communication channels) within a team.
Source: The authors

famous numbers (1-4-4-2, 1-3-5-2, 1-4-2-3-1, among others) that give an idea about the arrangement of the players in the field.

In this context, the concept of System of Play (from the Latin *"systema"*) is closely linked to the idea of combining parts that together make up a unique identity that competes for a result. This means that even if we have the same parts in equally represented systems, they are unlikely to behave in the same way. There may be similarities, but there will hardly be equality. That is, if we have two teams playing in 1-4-4-2 (therefore, in equally represented systems), they will not behave in the same way. Obviously, there may be similarities in some actions, but each one will articulate their game through the actions performed by the players, as means to express their identity and achieve the expected result.

To further elucidate the concept presented here, especially with regards to the unique identity of the systems, we will call for a metaphor with some of the systems that are present in our day-to-day lives: nervous system, digestive system, cardiovascular system and ecosystem, among others. Let us take the digestive system as a random example. The digestive system consists of the following parts: mouth, pharynx, oesophagus, stomach, small intestine, large intestine and anus. If we compare two or more people who have no issues in this system, we will verify that they possess all of the parts mentioned, correct? However, we will also verify that their digestive systems work differently. One of them may have the need to go to the restroom more often during the day or at night, while another one may be more sensible to lactose or to a chemical reagent. Still, generally speaking, they all possess complete digestive system (with all parts) that works satisfactorily according to its purpose, which is to digest food, absorb the necessary nutrients to sustain life and eject what is not used. From this example it is possible to verify that, although systems may be similar, each one has its own way of functioning, its identity according to the specificities that are developed throughout life. This also occurs with the tactical systems in soccer. They are often made up of the same parts (1-4-4-2, 1-3-5-2, 1-4-3-3), but their functioning will depend on the relations that were built over time by their players, through training sessions and matches.

Likewise, if we also draw an analogy between the exchange of players in a system of play of a soccer team, and the exchange of organs in one of the systems mentioned, we will understand how its identity may be modified and that the adaption process may take more or less time.

Within a team, if we exchange a player for another, the adaptation time may be more or less extended, depending on the modifications that this new player will foster in the system, causing more or less changes in its identity. If this new piece within the system still needs to develop its relations with, or tune its behaviour to those of the others, this adaptation will take more time and may also promote changes in the rest of the players.

Again, metaphorically, if we make changes in any of our systems, transplanting, for example, a heart in the cardiovascular system, the adaptation of the parts will depend on this new piece. This means that, although the same parts remain (blood, heart and blood vessels), the new heart will now give this system a different identity. The operation will now be different from what it was before. The reactions of this "new" cardiovascular system when facing everyday situations that lead to emotion, stress or anxiety, for example, will undergo an adaptation period, in which there will be similarities and differences with the previous system. In soccer, preserving due proportions, this adaptation occurs in a similar way. Exchanging players requires an adaptation period in training sessions and games, in order to ensure that the proposed modification in the system of play will generate behaviour and performance alterations in the team.

1.4 Tactical Principles of the Game

As previously mentioned, tactics in soccer may be comprehended as how players manage the playing space through their spatial organizations within the field, under the circumstances of the match regarding the movements of the ball and the action alternatives of their teammates and opponents (Duprat, 2007). This way of understanding tactics gives special emphasis to the movements and positioning, highlighting the player's skills for occupying and/or creating free spaces following the most suitable tactical principles for that given moment.

The tactical principles are referred to as a set of norms that provides players the possibility of rapidly achieving calculated solutions for problems that arise from the situations they face (Garganta & Pinto, 1994). Because of this nature, they need to be understood as well as observed in players' behaviour, since they are intended to facilitate the achievement of the objectives that lead to score or to avoid taking goals. Collectively, their execution helps the team to better control the game, both in the offensive and defensive phases. With respect to the attack, applying the tactical principles may help maintain ball possession, performing variations in its circulation, changing the pace of the game, and materializing tactical actions aiming to break up opponents' balance and, consequently, to score a goal more easily (Aboutoihi, 2006; Zerhouni, 1980). Regarding the defence, tactical principles assist the rapid and synchronized collective movements so as to restrict the opponent's play to zones of easier recovery of possession and/or risk to goal. Therefore, the more appropriate and qualified the execution of the tactical principles is, the better will be the team's or player's performances.

2.4.1 Characterization of the Tactical Principles

The tactical principles arise from the theoretical construction regarding the logic of the game, and are operationalized in players' tactical-technical behaviours. Therefore, players need to be aware of such principles in order to simplify the transmission and operationalization of concepts, supporting the selection and execution of the necessary action. The principles show a certain degree of generalization of movements and are closely related to players' actions and motor mechanisms, as well as tactical awareness and knowledge (Castelo, 1994).

Soccer specialized literature has been using different designations to mention and describe tactical principles (Aboutoihi, 2006; Bauer & Ueberle, 1988; Bayer, 1994; Castelo, 1996; Garganta & Pinto, 1994; Mombaerts, 1991; Pereni & Di Cesare, 1998; Teodorescu, 1984; Wrzos, 1984; Zerhouni, 1980). Amongst the variety of concepts presented by different authors, it is possible to notice a certain agreement of ideas on four theoretical constructs that relate to players' tactical organization in the field of play. These constructs are identified as general, operational, core and specific principles.

General principles are so named because they are transversal in relation to other invasion team sports, to the different phases of play and to the other categories of principles, based on three concepts that come from spatial and numerical relations between teammates and opponents within the zones of challenge for the ball: (i) do not allow numerical inferiority, (ii) avoid numerical equality and (iii) seek for numerical superiority (Garganta & Pinto, 1994; Queiroz, 1983).

Operational principles are related to the necessary actions for achieving the goal of the game (Bayer, 1994). Therefore, they are related to attitudinal concepts for both phases of play. The principles of the defensive phase include actions to: (i) neutralize shooting situations, (ii) regain possession of the ball, (iii) prevent opponents' progression, (iv) protect the goal and (v) decrease effective play-space, whereas the offensive phase includes the following principles: (i) maintain ball possession, (ii) build up offensive actions, (iii) progress through the opponent's half, (iv) create shooting opportunities and (v) shoot on goal.

26 Understanding the Soccer Game

Core principles represent a set of ground rules that guide players' and team's actions in both phases of play (defence and attack), with the main purpose of facilitating the management of space by the players. Their execution grants the creation of imbalances in the opponent's organization, the stabilization of the arrangement of the team itself and an adequate intervention in and out the "centre of play".

The core principles described in here take into account the propositions of various authors (Zerhouni, 1980; Teodorescu, 1984; Wrzos, 1984; Bauer & Ueberle, 1988; Mombaerts, 1991; Bayer, 1994; Garganta & Pinto, 1994; Castelo, 1996; Pereni & Di Cesare, 1998; Aboutoihi, 2006), but with a concept based on the static spatial references existing in the laws of the game, and on some dynamic spatial references. This concept was developed with the purpose of eliminating the conceptual superposition present in some definitions and providing to each of the core principles an ecological and unique character.

The static and dynamic spatial references used in the conception of the core principles are shown in the observational grid (see Figure 2.4). This grid highlights the official line markings on the field (penalty area, goal area, centre circle, etc.) with its offensive and defensive halves. From these markings it is also possible to see the corridors (left, central and right), the areas (defensive, pre-defensive, pre-offensive and offensive) and the zones of play (LD-left defensive, CD-central defensive, RD-right defensive, LPD-left pre-defensive, CPD-central pre-defensive, RPD-right pre-defensive, LPO-left pre-offensive, CPO-central pre-offensive, RPO-right pre-offensive, LO-left offensive, CO-central offensive and RO-right offensive).

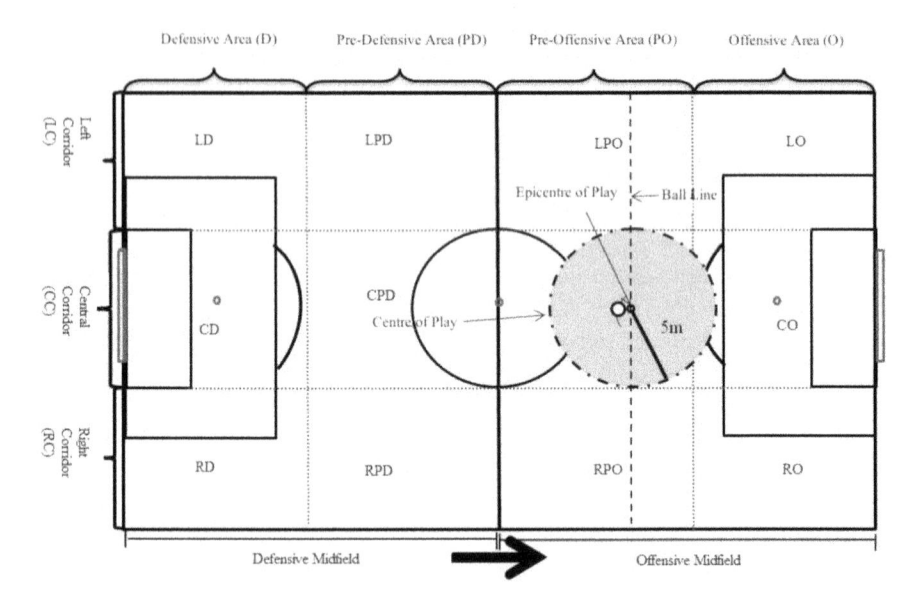

Figure 2.4 Spatial references used in the conception of the core tactical principles
Source: The authors

With respect to the dynamic spatial references, the epicentre of play, the line of the ball and the centre of play are highlighted in this grid. The epicentre of play is where the ball is located at a given instant "t" of the match. The epicentre is the point of the greatest concentration/release of energy, responsible for providing greater changes to the structures—wherever the ball is, it tends to cause modifications in the teams' structures of play and organization lines (offensive and, especially, defensive). The area around the epicentre is usually more affected, while the more remote zones generally undergo fewer changes.

From this focal point, two other dynamic spatial references are outlined: the line of the ball, perpendicularly projected between it and the side lines of the playing field; and the centre of play, a circumference established by 9.15 metres radius from the epicentre.

The centre of play is a dynamic spatial reference used to characterize the space where the game is played with greater speed and intensity. Its radius comes from physical and mathematical studies conducted in the early 1900s, which indicated that this distance hampers the direct interception of the opponent to the player in possession of the ball. Although there are no information about official records for the *International Football Association Board* meetings, reports indicate that the organization resorted to these studies to adjust the required distance of opponents at set pieces, which until the early 1910s was 5.5 metres. This change implemented and incorporated to the rules that appear to have improved the quality of the game, providing more dynamism to the individual and collective actions and, consequently, making the game faster and more attractive to the audience.

Given its radius, the transmission of the ball between teammates within the centre of play is facilitated, or, if respected, this distance also facilitates the transmission of the ball between the player in possession of the ball and the players outside the circumference.

For players inside the centre, the transmission of the ball is facilitated because the distance between the one in possession and the receiver is shorter, which allows for greater efficiency in the movements, as well as greater speed.

With the purpose of drawing some analogies about this concept of centre of play and the soccer game according to the concepts of space and time, we call upon some knowledge from the studies of Physics, particularly from the Theory of Relativity. Taking into account this theory as background, we could say that when looking at the players' actions within the centre of play, it would be as if you were watching a soccer game in miniature: the more you focus, the faster it will be. Therefore, the actions in the centre of play are much faster than those that occur in the game as a whole. However, it is important to emphasize that to ensure the "ambient pressure" remains the same, the number of particles, that is, of players, should be reduced. So, it is recommended that for small-sided games, in addition to having their dimensions adapted, a reduction in the number of participating players should also be considered.

Additionally, if we consider Astronomy, it is possible to verify that players' behaviours in a soccer game are similar to the behaviour of celestial bodies in the

28 *Understanding the Soccer Game*

stars' gravitational field, according to the relative strengths/energies within the game. The closer to the Sun, the greater the planets' angular speed: for example Mercury takes around 88 days to complete a revolution around the Sun. Neptune, on the other hand, takes around 60.225 days to complete the same revolution. If we also consider some physics and chemistry theories on the speed of electrons, it is possible to verify that when electrons change layer and get closer to the nucleus, they become much faster. By analogy, we could say that in soccer something similar occurs: when players are moving close to the epicentre of play, they need more speed; on the contrary, if they are further away from the epicentre and centre of play, they may slow down.

With respect to the connections of the player in possession of the ball with the ones positioned outside the centre of play, the transmission of the ball becomes faster if the distance from the radius of the centre of play is respected by the opponent according to the trajectory (parable) described by the ball until it reaches the receiver. Let us take as an example, a player in possession of the ball who intends to pass the ball to another teammate who is outside the centre of play, 15 metres away. In this case, we will use as reference players who are 1.80 metres tall and who can jump up to 2.20 metres. If the opponent is 9.15 metres away from the player in possession of the ball, the trajectory of the ball (angle) is facilitated and reaches the teammate faster (see trajectory 1 on Figure 2.5). On the other hand, if the opponent is closer than 9.15 metres, the angle required for the trajectory is greater (see trajectories 2 and 3 on Figure 2.5).

On the illustration it is possible to see an example of an opponent who is 5.5m away from the player in possession of the ball. This distance makes it easier for

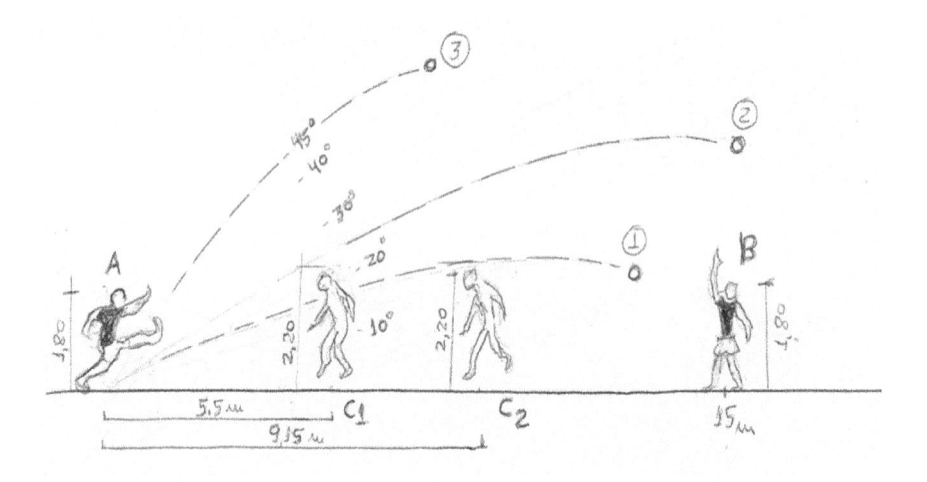

Figure 2.5 Illustration of the trajectories of the ball for a 15-metre pass, when the opponent is 5.5 and 9.15 metres away from the player in possession of the ball

Source: Antônio Walter Sena Junior

him/her to intercept the ball and to generate obstacles to the offensive play. For the player in possession of the ball to transmit the ball to his teammate, he/she would have to pass/shoot it at an angle of approximately 30 degrees to make it go over the opponent and, still, there would be a great chance that the ball goes over the player who was to receive it. Therefore, by having greater angle and trajectory, the time taken for the ball to travel the distance would also be greater, and the game would become slower, thus losing dynamics and performance.

Based on what was mentioned, the core principles were conceived according to the two phases of play. In defence, there are the principles of: (i) delay, (ii) defensive coverage, (iii) balance, (iv) concentration and (v) defensive unity; whereas in attack, there are the principles of: (i) penetration, (ii) depth mobility, (iii) offensive coverage, (iv) width and length and (v) offensive unity (Teoldo, Garganta, Greco, & Mesquita, 2009). Figure 15 schematically shows the links between the general, operational and core tactical principles, as well as their purposes in each phase of play.

Specific principles, in turn, are based on the unique characteristics of a model of play that determine the playing style of a team. They receive this designation because they are specific to a model, thus assisting in guiding and synchronizing the behaviours of all players within the field. These principles may be categorized into sub-principle and sub-sub-principle (Silva, 2007). For example, if in a model of play for the moment of defence-attack transition, the specific principle of "keep possession of the ball" is advocated, a sub-principle could be "take the ball away from the pressure zone", and the sub-sub-principle would be "try to play safely for offensive organization" or "to go deep if there is a scoring opportunity".

The conception of all specific principles and their variations are based on the interchange between the general, operational and core principles. Therefore, the development of the specifics will depend on players' game understanding about the structuring bases of these principles, and is from their combination that the team's playing style will be "born". Metaphorically speaking, it is possible to say that the relation established between the specific and the general, operational and core principles is similar to that established between music and musical notes. There are only seven musical notes, but their combination is what enables the creation of the most pleasant and wonderful melodies that one can listen to (Sun Tzu, 1996). Similarly, there are few general, operational and core tactical principles, but their combination will enable the emergence of the team's model of play, which will result in the players' and team's behaviours in the match.

2.4.1.1 The Tactical Principles and the Teaching-Training Process

Once these four categories of principles are known, the teacher/coach should then organize his/her contents for a teaching process during the different development phases of the young players. Therefore, it is recommended that

Tactical Principles of Soccer

General Principles	Seek for numerical superiority	Avoid numerical equality	Do not allow numerical inferiority
Phases	**Attack (with ball possession)**		**Defence (without ball possession)**
Operational Principles	Maintain ball possession Build up offensive actions Progress through the opponent's half Create shooting opportunities Shoot on goal		Prevent opponent's progression Decrease opponent's playing space Protect the team's goal Avoid shooting opportunities Recover ball possession
Core Principles	**Penetration** - Destabilize the opponent's defensive organization; - Directly attack the opposite player or the oppponent's goal; - Create advantageous attacking situations in numerical and spatial terms. **Offensive Coverage** - Support the player in possession by providing options to give sequence to the play; - Decrease opponents' pressure on the player in possession; - Create numerical superiority; - Unbalance the opponent's defensive organization; - Ensure conservation of ball possession. **Width and Length** - Use and enlarge the effective play-space of the team; - Expand the distances between the opponents' positions; - Make marking difficult for the opponents; - Facilitate the offensive actions of the team. - Move to a safer space; - Win time to make adequate decision for a better subsequent action; - Seek safe options through players in defensive position to give sequence to the play. **Depth Mobility** - Create actions to disrupt opponent's defensive organization; - Position oneself in a suitable space to score; - Create in-depth passing options; - Achieve ball control to give sequence to the offensive action (pass or shot on goal). **Offensive Unity** - Facilitate team dislocation onto opponent's midfield; - Allow team to attack in unity; - Make safer the ofensive actions performed in the epicentre; - Allow more players to get in the game epicentre. - Diminish play-space in the defensive midfield.	*Defence-Attack transition and/or Attack-Defence*	**Delay** - Decrease space the player in possession has for offensive action; - Direct the progression of the player in possesion; - Block or delay opponent's attack or counter-attack; - Provide more time for defensive organization. - Restrict pass possibilities to other opponents; - Avoid dribbling moves that enable the progression in own defensive midfield and towards the goal; - Prevent shot on goal. **Defensive coverage** - Act as new obstacle to the player in possession, in case he dribbles the player performing Delay; - Insure and provide confidence to the player performing Delay in order to support his initiative in blocking the offensive actions of the player in possession. **Balance** - Ensure the defensive stability in the area of the challenge for the ball; - Support teammates performing Delay and Defensive Coverage; - Block potential passing options; - Mark potential players who could receive the ball; - Chase the player in possession and make an effort to recover the ball; - Regain the ball and move it away from the zone where it was recovered. **Concentration** - Increase protection of the goal; - Drive opponent's offensive play towards safer areas; - Increase pressure within the game epicenter. **Defensive Unity** - Enable team to defend in unity; - Ensure the spatial stability and dynamic synchrony between longitudinal and transversal lines of the team in defensive actions; - Decrease the offensive amplitude of the opponent team in width and depth; - Ensure basic guiding lines that influence the players' technical-tactical behaviours positioned outside the game epicentre; - Constantly balance or rebalance the relative strengths in the defensive organization according to the playing situations; - Obstruct possible passing options for opponents that are in the epicentre of play; - Decrease the playing space using the offside rule; - Enable involvement in a subsequent defensive action; - Enable more players to get in the epicentre of play.

Figure 2.6 Phases of play, objectives and the general, operational and core tactical principles of the soccer game

Source: The authors

the general principles are taught between six and seven years of age, when children, during their processes of maturational and motor development, as well as of cognition and sociability, leave the egocentric stage and move to a stage of increased sociability (Gallahue & Ozmun, 1998; Piaget, 1993). Since these principles are based on the concepts that require the presence of other children (classmates/teammates and opponents) in order to be operationalized and comprehended, it would be unproductive to teach them during the child's egocentric stage.

Together with the general principles, the operational ones should also be taught within the first years of sports practice in the child's phase of greater sociability; this is because the action rules within these two categories of principles are responsible for facilitating the understanding of the logic of the game. Because the rules resort to concrete operations, it is expected that the students learn and develop the game in formal and informal context through the dissemination and understanding of their concepts (Gallahue & Ozmun, 1998; Piaget, 1964).

Subsequently, the core principles of the game should be introduced in the teaching process. Since these principles demand abstract thinking and hypothesis testing for occupation of space and moving in the field, they should be taught at around 12/13 years of age, when the child's stage of cognitive development is mature or is in the final stage of maturation (Gallahue & Ozmun, 1998; Piaget, 1964).

Teaching the action rules of these three categories of principles will provide young players with a solid knowledge base about the logic of the game and the movement and occupation of the playing spaces. By understanding these aspects, players will be more apt to learn and incorporate the model of play of their teams, that is, they will be more prepared to begin the learning process of the specific tactical principles.

This point in the teaching process of the specific tactical principles will coincide with the direction phase advocated by literature for the player's sportive development (Greco & Benda, 1998), and also with the sporting structure available at soccer clubs, which projects, from 14 years of age onwards, a better development organization (specific technical staff for each age group, accommodations at the clubs, social and medical staff) for the young talents.

2.4.1.2 The Core Tactical Principles of the Game

The core tactical principles of the game have characteristics and behaviours associated with the offensive and defensive principles. Therefore, the next topics of this chapter will be destined to the presentation of each one of the five principles of the offensive and defensive phases.

2.4.1.2.1 Core Tactical Principles of the Offensive Phase

The core tactical principles of the offensive phase of play help all the players to guide their technical-tactical behaviours according to the team's objective, that is to take the ball to vital areas of the field and score a goal (Castelo, 1996). The organization of these principles is established according to the players' management of the space of play, in which each one of them has its own characteristics and plays an important role in guiding the player through the field (see Figure 2.7).

The compliance to these tactical principles allows the team to obtain favourable conditions in terms of time and space to fulfil the tasks, that is, a higher amount of players in the "centre of play", greater ease to perform offensive tactical-technical

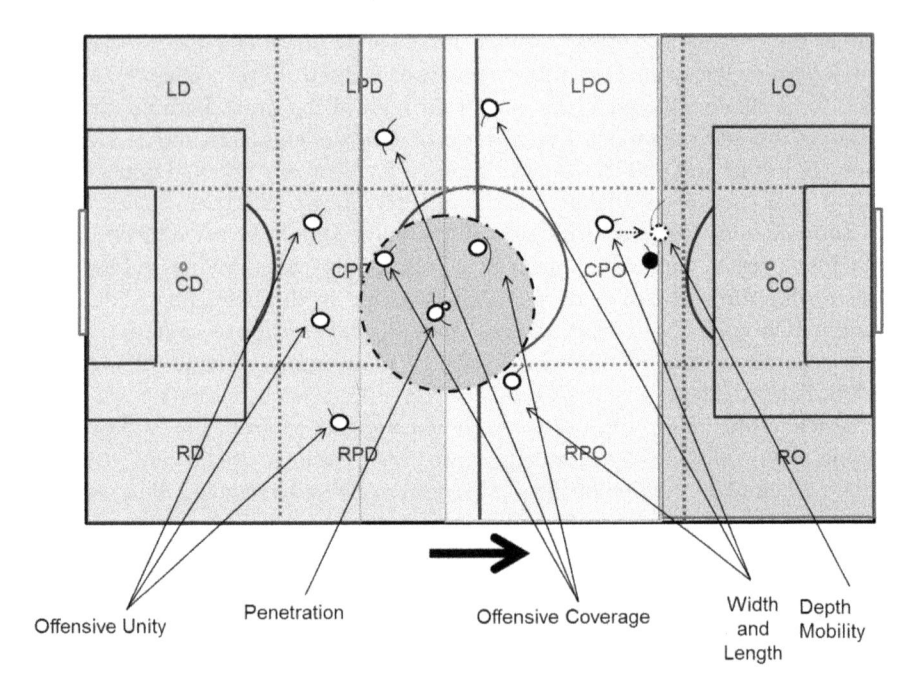

Figure 2.7 Management of space according to the core tactical principles of the offensive phase

Source: The authors

actions and greater possibility to create instability in the opponent's defensive organization (Castelo, 1994).

PRINCIPLE OF PENETRATION

The principle of penetration is characterized by the evolution of the game, in situations in which the player in possession of the ball is able to progress towards the goal or the goal line, seeking for areas of the field that are favourable for the continuity of the offensive action, to leave the opponent in a situation of risk and ultimately to shoot on goal.

The guidelines of this principle are governed by the search for the disorganization of the opponent's defence, creating beneficial situations for the attack in terms of space and numbers, thus allowing the attackers to move up to vital field zones favourable to shoot on goal.

Dribbling and carrying the ball can be considered typical penetration actions, because they decrease the space between the player in possession of the ball and the opponent's goal line, enabling crosses or displacements towards the opponent's penalty area. Dribbling opposite player(s) allows the gain of space and guides the player in possession of the ball towards the goal, or allows him/her to perform a pass/assistance to a teammate to give sequence in the play or shoot on goal.

Penetration can also be a situation of 1X0 in which the player in possession of the ball "attacks" the space towards the opponent's goal.

Chart 2.1 shows the characteristics that describe the principle of penetration and, subsequently, Figure 2.8 shows an example of the space that may be used to develop its actions.

Chart 2.1 Characteristics of the principle of penetration

	Principle of Penetration
Characteristics	Progression of the player in possession of the ball towards:
	A) the opponent's goal (convergent); or
	B) the opponent's goal line (divergent).
Spatial Reference	A) Line of the ball and opponent's goal;
	B) Line of the ball and opponent's goal line.
Purposes	• Reduce the distance between the player in possession of the ball and the opponent's goal or goal line;
	• Unbalance opponent's defensive organization;
	• Directly attack the opponent or the goal;
	• Create advantageous attacking situations in numerical and spatial terms.
Player(s) Who Perform	Player in possession of the ball.
Examples of Actions	• Carrying the ball through the available space (with or without defenders ahead).
	• Performing dribbles in search of numerical advantage in attacking situations or that enable the sequence of the play towards the opponent's goal line or goal.
	• Carrying the ball towards the opponent's goal line or goal.
	• Performing dribbles towards the opponent's goal line or goal searching for favourable conditions for a pass/assistance to a teammate to resume the play.
Performance Indicators	*Successful (+)*
	a. Enables shooting, passing or dribbling.
	Unsuccessful (−)
	a. Allows opponent's tackle / b-Force the play to an occupied space.
Description of Performance Indicators	*Successful (+)*
	b. When the movement of the player in possession of the ball enables (offensive) shooting, passing or dribbling.
	Unsuccessful (−)
	a. When the movement of the player in possession of the ball allows the opponent to recover possession.
	b. When the player in possession of the ball goes towards a space that is already occupied by other players, thus hindering his team's offensive action.

Source: The authors

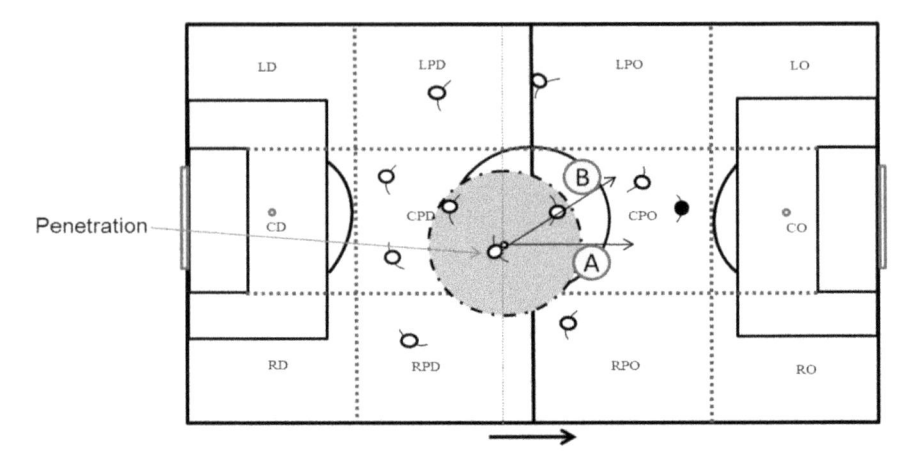

Figure 2.8 Management of space in the principle of penetration
Source: The authors

PRINCIPLE OF OFFENSIVE COVERAGE

The principle of offensive coverage is related to the teammates approaching the player in possession of the ball, giving him/her offensive options to resume the play through passing or penetrating the opposite defence.

The guidelines of this principle assume the simplification of the tactical-technical response from the player in possession of the ball to the game situation, the decrease of pressure from the opponent, the proper increase of ball possession maintenance and, in a certain way, the formation of the collective balance that benefits first defensive actions in case the player in possession of the ball loses the ball to the opposite team.

The actions related to this principle can be noticed when the teammates are positioned in order to receive the ball and proceed with the play, performing, for example, "1–2 combinations" and/or triangle passing with the player in possession of the ball. We consider that the player performed the principle of offensive coverage when he/she is positioned in the "centre of play" and facilitates a passing zone[3] to the player in possession of the ball, allowing him/her to pass the ball.

In practical terms, it is possible to verify that the distance between the player who performs the offensive coverage and the player in possession of the ball may vary according to the technical, tactical, physical and psychological characteristics of the opposite team, their strategy for the game (midfield marking, pressing, etc.), the weather conditions (wind, rain, snow, heat, cold, etc.), the field conditions (grass, gravel, irregular, etc.) and the position of the ball (defensive, offensive or midfield third). Players who perform offensive coverage have to be aware of these variables to position themselves accordingly. For example, the player performing offensive coverage can be nearer the player in possession of the ball when the ball is closer to the offensive third, as it implies more pressure from the opposite team to regain the ball, or when the weather and field conditions are poor, as greater skills to control the ball are necessary. In contrast, when the ball is closer to the defensive third, where the pressure from the opposite team is lower, or weather and field conditions are more favourable for the execution of pass, players can perform offensive coverage from further positions to encourage longer passes (Castelo, 1994).

Chart 2.2 shows the characteristics that describe the principle of offensive coverage and, subsequently, Figure 2.9 shows an example of the space that may be used to develop its actions.

Chart 2.2 Characteristics of the principle of offensive coverage

	Principle of Offensive Coverage
Characteristics	Movements of players without the ball performed:
	A) inside the centre of play; or
	B) outside the centre of play, within the area limited by the line of the ball and the line of the border of the less offensive half of the centre of play, and the touchline facing the direction of play.
Spatial Reference	A) Centre of play.
	B) Less offensive half and the playing corridor.
Purposes	• Support the player in possession of the ball by offering options to give sequence to the play;
	• Decrease opponents' pressure on the player in possession of the ball;
	• Create numerical superiority, especially in the centre of play;
	• Unbalance the opponent's defensive organization;
	• Ensure maintenance of ball possession.
Player(s) Who Perform	Players positioned within the specified spatial references.
Examples of Actions	• Offer constant passing lines/zones to the player in possession of the ball;
	• Closer supporting the player in possession of the ball, allowing them to keep possession;
	• Perform 1–2 and/or triangular combinations with the player in possession of the ball;
	• Closer supporting the player in possession of the ball, allowing for offensive numerical superiority;

(Continued)

Chart 2.2 (Continued)

	Principle of Offensive Coverage
Performance Indicators	*Successful (+)* a. Ensures passing lines/zones/ b. Decreases the pressure on the player in possession of the ball c. Allows shooting possibilities. *Unsuccessful (−)* a. Does not ensure passing lines/zones. b. Does not decrease the pressure on the player in possession of the ball. c. Does not allow shooting possibilities.
Description of Performance Indicators	*Successful (+)* a. When players' movement ensures passing lines/zones to the player in possession of the ball. b. When players' movement enables the decrease of the number of players around the player in possession of the ball. c. When players' movement allows shooting possibilities. *Unsuccessful (−)* a. When players' movement does not ensure passing lines/zones to the player in possession of the ball. b. When players' movement does not enable the decrease of the number of players around the player in possession of the ball. c. When players' movement does not allow shooting possibilities.

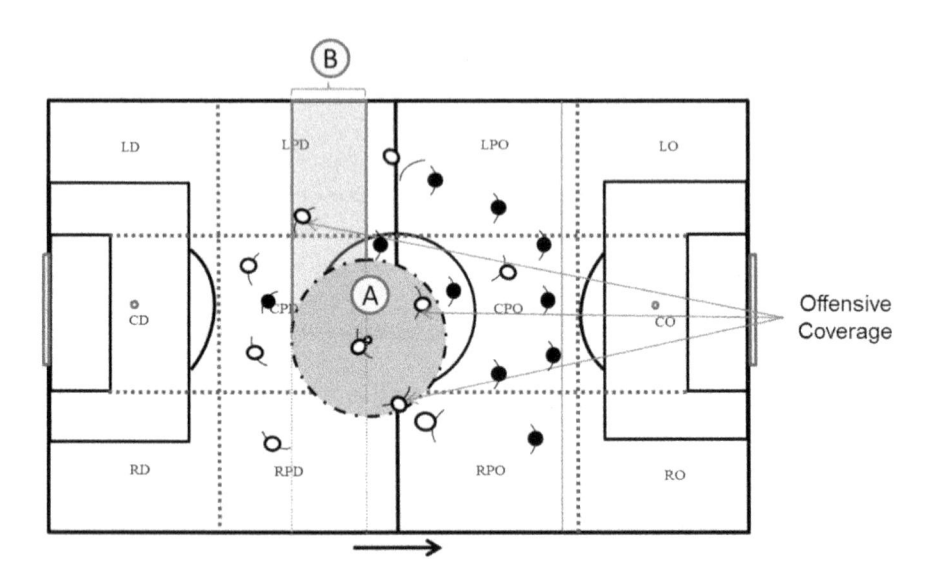

Figure 2.9 Management of space for the principle of offensive coverage

Source: The authors

PRINCIPLE OF DEPTH MOBILITY

The principle of depth mobility is related to the initiative of the attacking player(s) without possession of the ball to search for optimal positions to receive it on the back of the last defensive player in order to generate instability in the defensive actions of the opposite team, and substantially increase the number of chances to score a goal. It is also considered that these movements favour the creation of new playing spaces, which provides better conditions to the player in possession of the ball to give sequence to the offensive action towards the opposite goal and/or to enable other teammates to move in the effective play-space.

At first instance, the guidelines of this principle aim at the variability of positions, the creation of options for deep passes, hence the rupture of the opponent's defensive structure, and the increased game pace. Another important aspect is related to the difficulties generated by the attackers without possession when they perform actions of depth mobility that hamper their markers the perception of the ball and of themselves. In addition, the spaces created by these movements, when properly explored by other teammates, make it harder for the opposite players to mark their respective attackers and complicate mutual defensive coverage (Worthington, 1974).

Because of such advantages, this principle is considered to be one of the most important to be developed collectively. To do so, it requires that all players are able to comprehend the displacements of their teammates according to the position of the player in possession of the ball, which implies moving with tactical meaning and organization.

The actions related to this principle can be noticed through the players' displacements in relation to the opponent's goal or goal line. The movements towards the goal line can be designated by divergent depth mobility as it aims to create passing options, increase the width and length of the play-space, and/or destabilize the opposite defence. In contrast, there is the convergent depth mobility, which characterizes actions in which the attacker moves towards the opponent's goal, aiming to find extremely favourable conditions to score a goal.

Visually, the success of the actions of depth mobility can be observed when the player can receive the ball in a more advantageous situation and can give sequence to the attack, forcing the defender to move from his position of defensive coverage to follow him/her, or when a pass is made towards the space created by the action of depth mobility, threatening the opponent's defensive system.

Chart 2.3 shows the characteristics that describe the principle of depth mobility and, subsequently, Figure 2.10 shows an example of the space that may be used to develop its actions.

Chart 2.3 Characteristics of the principle of depth mobility

	Principle of Depth Mobility
Characteristics	Movements performed by the players without the ball behind the line of the last defender towards: A) the opponent's goal (convergent); or B) the opponent's goal line (divergent).
Spatial Reference	A) Line of the last defender and opponent's goal. B) Line of the last defender and opponent's goal line.
Purposes	• Enlarge the effective play-space in depth; • Hamper opponent's marking through arrhythmic and multi-targeted moves; • Create in-depth passing options; • Occupy a favourable space to score a goal.
Player(s) Who Perform	Players without the ball positioned within the specified spatial references.
Examples of Actions	• In-depth or wide moves on the back of the last defender towards the opponent's goal line or goal. • In-depth or wide moves on the back of the last defender aimed at gaining offensive space. • In depth or wide moves on the back of the last defender that favour ball reception. • In-depth or wide moves on the back of the last defender aimed at creating opportunities for the offensive sequence of play.
Performance Indicators	*Successful (+)* a. Enables a deep pass to a teammate. b. Enlarges the EP-S on the back of the defence. *Unsuccessful (–)* a. Does not enable a deep pass to a teammate/b-Player is "offside".
Description of Performance Indicators	*Successful (+)* a. When players' movement provides the player in possession of the ball with the possibility of performing a deep pass to a teammate in an action of disruption in relation to the opponent's defence. b. When players' movement allows the enlargement of the team's effective play-space on the back of the last defensive line. *Unsuccessful (–)* a. When players' movement does not provide the player in possession of the ball with the possibility of performing a deep pass to a teammate in an action of disruption in relation to the opponent's defence. b. When players' movement puts him/her into an "offside" situation.

Source: The authors

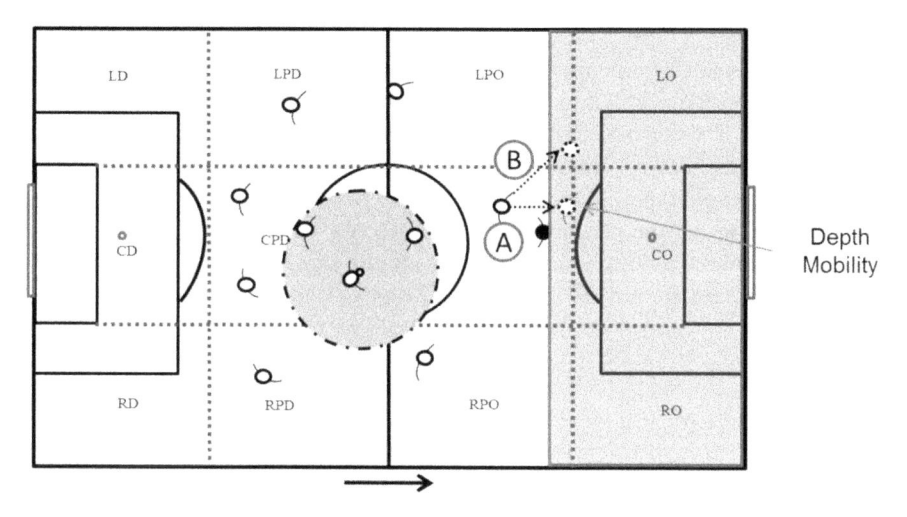

Figure 2.10 Management of space for the principle of depth mobility
Source: The authors

PRINCIPLE OF WIDTH AND LENGTH

The principle of width and length is distinguished by the relentless effort of players to take distance from the player in possession of the ball in order to create defensive difficulties to the opposition. The transverse and/or longitudinal increase of the field of play forces the opponents to choose between marking a vital space of play or the opposite player (Castelo, 1996; Worthington, 1974). This principle may also be performed by the player in possession of the ball who, when facing an unfavourable playing organization, will carry the ball towards the side line or his own goal with the aim of gaining space and time to resume the play.

The actions of this principle begin after a team has regained the possession of the ball, when all players seek for and explore positions that allow increasing the offensive play-space, based on the technical-tactical behaviours of teammates and opponents according to the position of the ball. The distance of some players from the "centre of play" creates spaces for other teammates and provides free corridors towards the opponent's goal, or facilitates the occurrence of 1X1 situations with clear advantage for the attacking player (Castelo, 1996).

The guidelines of this principle are directly associated to the theoretical knowledge that the players have on game tactics. Thus, comprehension of space, particularly for a certain offensive action, is crucial to help them occupying and exploiting key spaces, which provide greater amount and quality of deep and wide passing options, important for the generation of a better number of offensive tactical options (Solomenko, 1982).

Besides, since the space constrains the time to perform an action and to make a decision according to the transitory configuration of the match, it is vital to master the typical actions of this principle in order to achieve success in the game. In that sense, the more space a team has to attack, the more elaborated their responses to the demands of a given situation can be.

The actions of this principle can be observed when players perform dispersing movements, both in width and length, seeking to increase the effective play-space. For instance, if efficiently carried out by the team, the individual movements performed immediately after possession of the ball are regained that enable the creation and exploitation of free spaces in order to shoot on goal.

Chart 2.4 shows the characteristics that describe the principle of width and length and, subsequently, Figure 2.11 displays an example of the space that may be used to develop its actions.

Chart 2.4 Characteristics of the principle of width and length

	Principle of Width and Length
Characteristics	A) *Width and Length without the ball:* Movements of the players without the ball performed outside the centre of play, between both the line of the ball, and the line of the last defender
	B) *Width and Length with the ball:* Movements of the player in possession of the ball towards the own team's goal line (convergent) or either touch line (divergent)
Spatial Reference	A) Line of the ball and line of the last defender.
	B) Line of the ball, side line and team's goal.
Purposes	• Enlarge effective play-space in width or length until the last defender's line;
	• Expand the distances between opponents' positions;
	• Hamper opponent's marking;
	• Facilitate the offensive actions of the team;
	• Move to a safer space (less opponent pressure);
	• Gain time to make adequate decision for a better subsequent action;
	• Seek safe options with players in defensive positions to give sequence to the play.
Player(s) Who Perform	A) Players without possession positioned within the specified spatial references.
	B) Player in possession of the ball.
Examples of Actions	• Search for spaces not occupied by opponents within the field.
	• Movements of enlargement of the space of play that allow numerical advantage in attack.
	• Dribbling backwards/sideways to decrease opponent's pressure on the ball.
	• Movements that allow (re)starting the offensive process in zones far from that where the recovery of possession occurred.

Chart 2.4 (Continued)

	Principle of Width and Length
Performance Indicators	*Successful (+)* a. Enlarges EP-S in width b. Enlarges EP-S in depth c. Creates spaces for teammates' movements d. Goes to safer zones e. Decreases pressure (sideways or behind the CP)/f-Keeps ball possession. *Unsuccessful (−)* a. Does not enlarge EP-S in width. b. Does not enlarge EP-S in length. c. Does not create spaces for teammates' movements/d-Does not go to safer zones. d. Does not decrease pressure (sideways or behind the CP). e. Allows opponent to recover possession.
Description of Performance Indicators	*Successful (+)* a. When players' movement enables his team to enlarge the space of play in width, that is, enlarges the transverse limit of the effective play-space. b. When players' movement enables the enlargement of the space of play in depth until the line of the last defender, that is, enlarges the longitudinal limit of the effective play-space. c. When players' movement (even towards a zone of higher pressure) enables the creation of spaces for teammates' movements or a successful pass. d. When players' movement allows him/her to be positioned in zones with lower opponent's pressure (inside the effective play-space). e. When the movement of the player in possession of the ball (sideways or backward displacements) enables the decrease of pressure on the ball and ensures the conditions to resume the offensive play. f. When the movement of the player in possession of the ball (sideways or backward displacements) enables the team to keep possession. *Unsuccessful (−)* a. When players' movement does not enable his team to enlarge the space of play in width, that is, does not enlarge the transverse limit of the effective play-space. b. When players' movement does not enable the enlargement of the space of play in depth until the line of the last defender, that is, does not enlarge the longitudinal limit of the effective play-space. c. When players' movement (even towards a zone of higher pressure) does not enable the creation of spaces for teammates' movements or a successful pass.

(Continued)

Chart 2.4 (Continued)

Principle of Width and Length
d. When players' movement does not allow him/her to be positioned in zones with lower opponent's pressure (inside the effective play-space). e. When players' movement (sideways or backward displacements) does not enable the decrease of pressure on the ball and does not ensure the conditions to resume the offensive play. f. When the movement of the player in possession of the ball allows for the opponent to recover the ball.

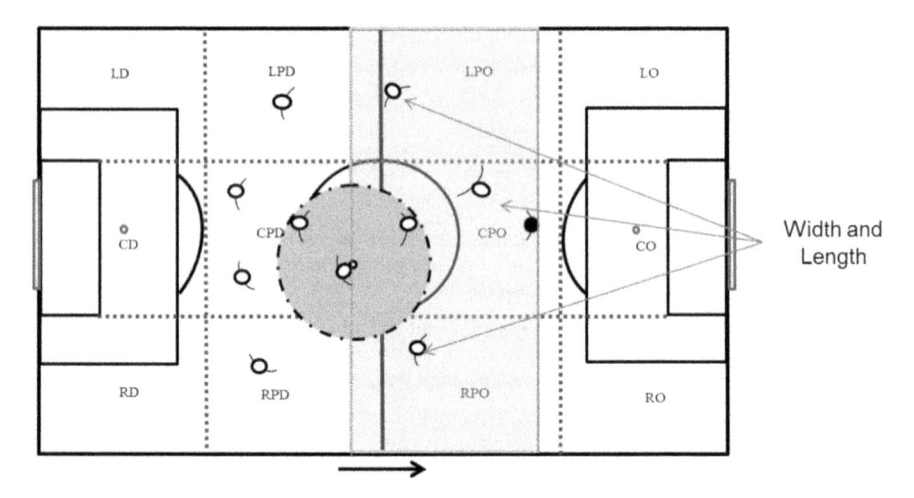

Figure 2.11 Management of space for the principle of width and length
Source: The authors

PRINCIPLE OF OFFENSIVE UNITY

The principle of offensive unity is strictly related to the comprehension the players have of the game and to the game model adopted by the team. This principle is established based on the knowledge the players have on the importance of their movements, their limitations and their position in relation to their teammates, the ball and their opponents (Hainaut & Benoit, 1979; Teissie, 1969). Players should show a high degree of tactical understanding so as not to break down the solidity of the team, hence keeping the effectiveness and the functional balance between the longitudinal and transverse lines in the offensive actions (Silva & Rias, 1998).

The guidelines of this principle assume an organization that adapts to the play-space and to the specific roles of the players, in which they should fulfil a set of tactical-technical tasks during the offensive phase that clearly goes beyond the dominant mission of each player (Castelo, 1996). Its execution is based on the cohesion, effectiveness and functional balance between the team's longitudinal and transversal lines, so as to transmit confidence and security to teammates and provide indirect intervention in the "centre of play" from the players who are further away from the zones of challenge for the ball.[4]

When considering the guidelines of this principle, the actions of a highly organized attack support preventive measures ensured by one or more players who position themselves and act in the rearguard of the attacking players. It is through such behaviours that the conception of team organization originates as responsible for making an organized transition to defence in case of unsuccessful offensive actions, and/or a temporary defence according to the situation, until all teammates return to their real positions, in agreement with their defensive system (Teodorescu, 1984).

By playing according to this principle, the team acts as a uniform block and is able to increase their lines of action without compensation, and penetrate in the opposite block in order to solve momentary game tactical situations as a whole. In practical terms, the execution of the tactical behaviours regarding this principle comes from situations in which the player feels that his/her team has basic organization that enables the occurrence of compensations or supports to the actions within the "centre of play", ensuring effectiveness and organization. In fact, by taking up another specific position or task in the game, according to a momentary game situation, a player expects another teammate to fulfil his/her tasks and position in the team's playing system (Castelo, 1996).

During a match, the representative actions of this principle can be observed through the position of the players in the field favouring a continuous, fluent and effective circulation, while avoiding its interruption (loss of ball possession) at the same time. Besides, collective actions will instil confidence and safety to the teammates within the "centre of play", allowing the creation of continuous instability and resulting imbalances in the opponent's defensive organization.

Chart 2.5 shows the characteristics that describe the principle of offensive unity and, subsequently, Figure 2.12 shows an example of the space that may be used to develop its actions.

Chart 2.5 Characteristics of the principle of offensive unity

	Principle of Offensive Unity
Characteristics	Movements of players without the ball inside: A) within the area delimited by the border of the less offensive half of the centre of play and the own team's goal line; or B) outside the centre of play and within the area delimited by both the line of the ball, and the line of the border of the less offensive half of the centre of play; and the touchline opposite to the direction of play C) the wing opposite to where the ball is, delimited by both the line of the ball; and the line of the border of the less offensive half of the centre of play.

(Continued)

44 *Understanding the Soccer Game*

Chart 2.5 (Continued)

	Principle of Offensive Unity
Spatial Reference	A) Less offensive half of the centre of play and the team's goal; B) Less offensive half of the centre of play and the side line; C) Less offensive half of the centre of ply and the playing corridor.
Purposes	• Facilitate team displacement through the opponent's half; • Allow more players to get into the centre of play; • Allow the team to attack in unity or in block; • Provide more security to the offensive actions performed in the centre of play; • Decrease the space of play in the defensive half.
Player(s) Who Perform	Players without possession positioned within the specified spatial references.
Examples of Actions	• Progression of the last defensive line, allowing the team to play as a block. • When the last defensive line moves away from the defensive zones and approaches the midfield line. • Progression of the defensive players allowing more players to take part in the actions within the centre of play. • Movements of player(s) that contribute(s) to the execution of collective offensive actions behind the line of the ball.
Performance Indicators	*Successful (+)* a. Brings the team closer to the CP b. Takes part in the subsequent action c. Contributes to offensive actions behind the line of the ball d. Helps the team to progress towards the PO area. *Unsuccessful (−)* a. Does not bring the team closer to the CP. b. Does not take part in the subsequent action. c. Does not contribute to offensive actions behind the line of the ball. d. Does not help the team to progress towards the PO area.
Description of Performance Indicators	*Successful (+)* a. When players' movement allows other teammates to take part in the team's actions or to approach the centre of play. b. When players' movement enables him/her to take part in a subsequent offensive/defensive action. c. When players' movement contributes to the execution of team's offensive actions behind the line of the ball. d. When players' movement helps the team to progress towards the offensive half.

Chart 2.5 (Continued)

Principle of Offensive Unity

Unsuccessful (−)

a. When players' movement does not allow other teammates to take part in the team's actions or to approach the centre of play.

b. When players' movement does not enable him/her to take part in a subsequent offensive/defensive action.

c. When players' movement does not contribute to the execution of team's offensive actions behind the line of the ball.

d. When players' movement does not help the team to progress towards the offensive half.

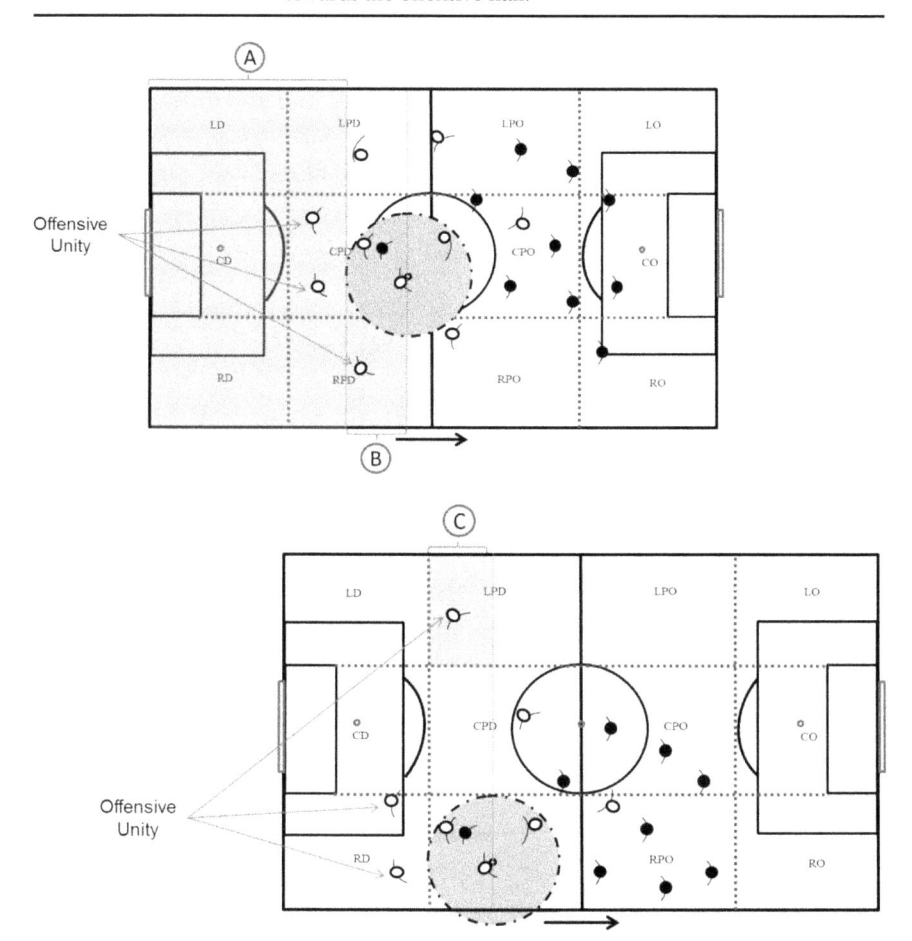

Figure 2.12 Management of space for the principle of offensive unity
Source: The authors

46 *Understanding the Soccer Game*

2.4.1.2.2 Core Tactical Principles of the Defensive Phase

The specific tactical principles of the defensive phase help all players, both distantly and directly involved in the "centre of play", to coordinate their actions and their tactical-technical behaviours according to the logic of movements proposed for the team's defensive method. This collective logic essentially seeks for rapid and effective execution of actions that lead to the achievement of both defensive objectives: protect the team's own goal and regain possession of the ball (Castelo, 1996; Worthington, 1974). The organization of these principles is also established according to the management of play-space performed by the players, in which each one of the principles has its own characteristics and assumes an important role in guiding the player throughout the field (see Figure 2.13).

The fulfilment of these principles will help players to guide their behaviours and positions in relation to the ball, their own goal, their opponents, their teammates and the dynamic events of the match. This allows the defence to send opponent's attacking actions to less vital areas and also to limit the space and time available for their execution (Bangsbo & Peitersen, 2002; Castelo, 1994).

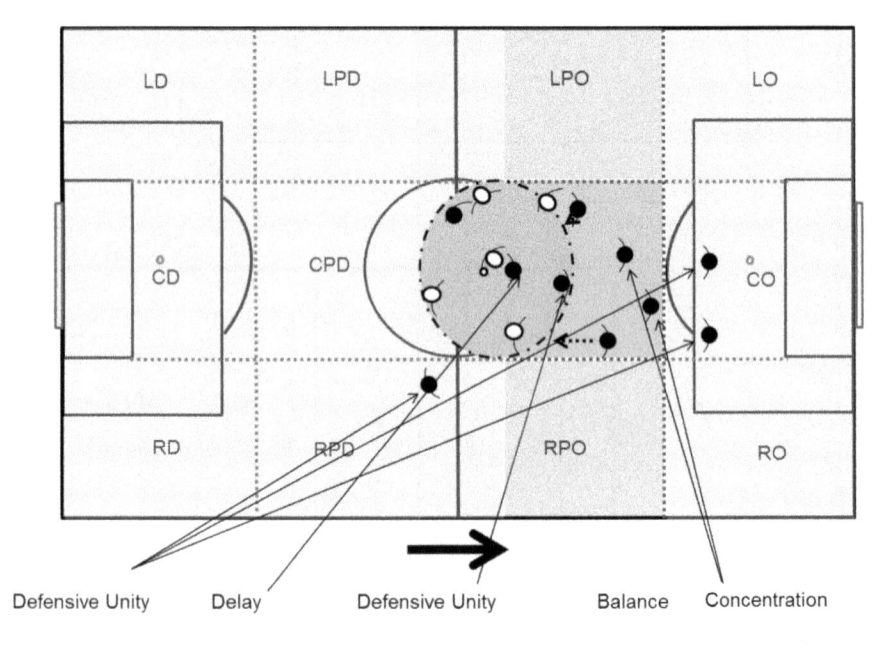

Figure 2.13 Management of space according to the core tactical principles of the defensive phase

Source: The authors

PRINCIPLE OF DELAY

The principle of delay essentially refers to an action of opposition held on the player in possession of the ball by a defensive player to decrease the space of the offensive action. It consists in restricting passing options to another attacking member or impeding dribbling moves that favour the progression, consequently, preventing a shoot on goal (Castelo, 1996).

The guidelines of this principle advocate to rigorously marking the player in possession of the ball, to stop or delay the opponent's offensive action, to restrict passing options and shots on goal. Delay also prevents the longitudinal progression through the field of play, directs the attack towards a given side and grants time for the defence to organize in order to increase the probability of protecting effectively and regaining the ball (Garganta & Pinto, 1994; Worthington, 1974).

The typical actions of this principle are present in the frontal approach that usually occurs in the central corridor of the field of play and/or closer to the defensive area, where the defender should be positioned between the ball and his own goal. In another approach that usually occurs in situations closer to the sideline, the defender is positioned according to the ball, his own goal and the attacker, with the intention to drive the actions of the opponent's attack to this side/direction.

Chart 2.6 shows the characteristics that describe the principle of delay and, subsequently, Figure 2.14 shows an example of the space that may be used to develop its actions.

Chart 2.6 Characteristics of the principle of delay

	Principle of Delay
Characteristics	Movements of the defensive player nearest to the player in possession of the ball that are performed inside the more offensive half of the centre of the play between the ball and the own team's goal.
Spatial Reference	Defending goal and the more offensive half of the centre of play.
Purposes	• Decrease the space of the player in possession of the ball for offensive actions; • Block or delay attack or counter-attack of the player in possession of the ball; • Provide more time for defensive organization; • Reduce pass possibilities to other opponents; • Prevent dribbling moves that enable progression in own defensive midfield and towards the goal; • Prevent shooting on own team's goal; • Constrain the progress of the player in possession of the ball
Player(s) Who Perform	Player nearest to the player in possession of the ball and positioned within the specified spatial references.

(Continued)

Chart 2.6 (Continued)

	Principle of Delay
Examples of Actions	• Marking the player in possession of the ball, preventing the action of penetration; • Protection of the ball preventing the opponent to reach it. • "Double mark" the player in possession of the ball. • Perform technical fouls to hold the opposite progression when the defensive system is disorganized.
Performance Indicators	*Successful (+)* a. Prevents shooting. b. Prevents progression. c. Delays opponent's action. d. Forces the player in possession of the ball to safer zones. *Unsuccessful (−)* a. Does not prevent shooting. b. Does not prevent progression. c. Does not delay opponent's action. d. Does not force the player in possession of the ball to safer zones.
Description of Performance Indicators	*Successful (+)* a. When players' movement /opposition prevents the player in possession of the ball to shoot at goal. b. When players' movement prevents the player in possession of the ball to progress towards the goal. c. When players' movement delays the opponent's offensive action, allowing his/her team to be defensively organized. d. When players' movement forces the player in possession of the ball to go to safer zones. *Unsuccessful (−)* a. When players' movement /opposition does not prevent the player in possession of the ball to shoot at goal. b. When players' movement does not prevent the player in possession of the ball to progress towards the goal. c. When players' movement does not delay the opponent's offensive action, and does not allow his/her team to be defensively organized. d. When players' movement does not force the player in possession of the ball to go to safer zones.

Source: The authors

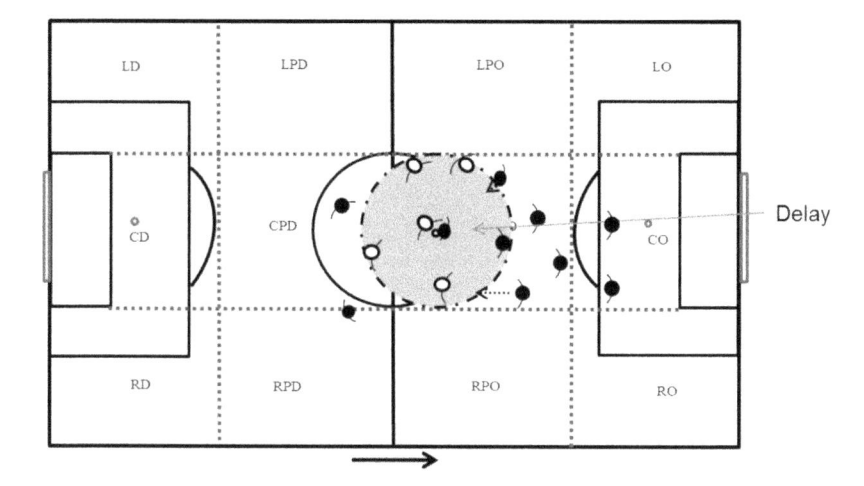

Figure 2.14 Management of space for the principle of delay
Source: The authors

PRINCIPLE OF DEFENSIVE COVERAGE

The principle of defensive coverage refers to the supporting actions of a player behind the first defender with the intention of strengthening defensive marking and avoiding the progression of the player in possession of the ball towards the goal. By taking a position that avoids defensive imbalances opening favourable spaces for the progression of the opponent, the player who executes the actions of defensive coverage has to behave as a new obstacle to the player in possession of the ball in case he/she overtakes the defender performing delay. The defensive coverage player can also guide the player performing the delay through the opponent's tactical-technical actions, in order to stimulate him/her to take the initiative of opposing the offensive actions from the player in possession of the ball (Bangsbo & Peitersen, 2002; Castelo, 1996). This facilitates the opposition against the attacking actions and also makes the first defender feel safer and more confident (Worthington, 1974).

When performed in a situation of defensive numerical superiority (e.g. 2X1), defensive coverage facilitates the actions of support of the player who performs it, because the action is focused on the player in possession of the ball. In contrast, the defensive coverage performed in situations of numerical equality (e.g. 2X2) requires the player in position of coverage to pay attention to the player in possession of the ball, the teammate performing the delay, and also to the movements executed by the attacker in offensive coverage.

Some factors related to the extrinsic and intrinsic aspects of the game should be considered by the players when performing defensive coverage due to their influence on the distance and the angle between them and the player in delay, thus determining the efficiency of the actions performed. These include the zone of the field where coverage will be performed, the field and weather conditions, the communication between the players and the tactical, technical, physical and psychological skills that their teammates and opponents possess and display during the game (Bangsbo & Peitersen, 2002; Castelo, 1994; Worthington, 1974).

The distance and angle of the coverage will vary according to two very important concepts implied and gradually stabilized according to the position of the ball: the meaning of risk to goal and the allowance of space to offensive actions. Therefore, the closer the "centre of play" is from the defensive sector and the central corridor, the more risk there is for the ball to be shot on goal and less space should be available for the attacker to perform offensive movements. When the "centre of play" is within the central corridor and close to the goal, the player responsible for defensive coverage should approach the player in delay in order to reduce the chances of finishing from the opponent and provide more safety to the defensive sector of his own team. When the ball is played in the side corridors and far from the defensive sector, the player in coverage should stay far from the player in delay, since the player in possession of the ball, granted with more velocity, can pass both markers at once. Also, the risk to goal is minimized on the sides of the field in comparison to other areas of the field of play, as shown in Figure 2.15.

In relation to the field and weather conditions, the player in defensive coverage should keep a shorter distance from the player in delay as adverse as conditions are

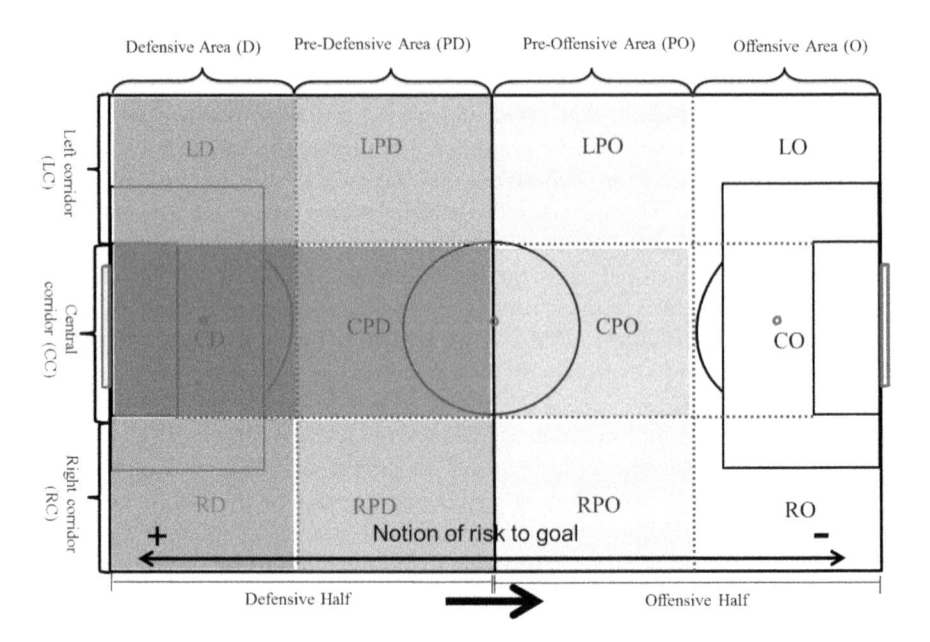

Figure 2.15 Representation of the idea of risk to goal: the darker the area, the greater the risk it provides

Source: The authors

for the attacking team.[5] The adoption of this kind of behaviour will discourage the player in possession of the ball to execute dribbling, as it will be harder for him/her to maintain possession, and will facilitate the defensive action. Besides, defensive balance will also be facilitated, in case the player in possession of the ball executes a pass to a teammate who performs the offensive coverage, since, in case of unfavourable weather conditions, they may be positioned farther away, which increases the time of ball trajectory and demands more time for reception and control.

The communication between the players is another factor that also determines the success of the defensive coverage since it may act as guide to create harmony between all defensive movements. Communications may be verbal and non-verbal. The verbal forms are essentially expressed through the instructions provided by the players with respect to their own and their opponents' positions. On the other hand, non-verbal communications, noticed essentially by the visual system and sometimes by the tactical system, are expressed through body signs from teammates and opponents. It can also be said that the degree of rapport and mutual confidence in communication is determining in the success of defensive actions.

Last but not least is the factor related to the tactical, technical, physical and psychological skills that players present during the match (Castelo, 1996). It is related to the previous acquired knowledge and to the game awareness of the player performing defensive coverage. Therefore, establishing a similar line of thinking for all situations in which there is prevalence of skills, it may be stated that if the player performing defensive coverage is aware that the player in delay is weak in any of these skills, he/she should approach him/her. On the other hand, if the player in delay displays superior skills, the coverage can be performed at greater distance, as there will be more possibilities for the player in delay to regain the ball, so the one performing defensive coverage becomes an offensive option to resume the play.

As an example of such variability of positioning in soccer, it is possible to highlight a situation of technical dominance in which the player in possession chooses to dribble or pass. In such case, if the player performing defensive coverage has observed that the player in possession of the ball is a skilled dribbler, he/she should approach the player in delay, because the chances of the latter being passed are higher. In contrast, if a player is aware that he/she is performing the action of coverage towards one who possesses better skills of passing the ball to dangerous zones in the field, he/she should keep a distance, because the probability of the execution of a pass is higher than those of a dribble. Moreover, if the player in coverage is aware that the player in possession of the ball is not well developed in any of these skills, he/she can stay further away from the player in delay, being able to support a new configuration of play if possession is regained by his/her team.

The characteristics of the actions of defensive coverage in game situations can be noticed when the position of the player in defensive coverage, ideally between the player in delay and his/her own goal, provides support and safety to the later.

Chart 2.7 shows the characteristics that describe the principle of defensive coverage and, subsequently, Figure 2.16 shows an example of the space that may be used to develop its actions.

Chart 2.7 Characteristics of the principle of defensive coverage

	Principle of Defensive Coverage
Characteristics	Movements of the defensive players behind or beside the defensive player nearest to the player in possession of the ball that are performed inside the more offensive half of the centre of play
Spatial Reference	Player in delay, defending goal and more offensive half of the centre of play.
Purposes	• Act as a covering defender in case the player in possession of the ball dribbles past (beats) the first defender; • Ensure defensive stability inside the more offensive half of the centre of play; • Reduce pass lines to other opponents; • Provide assurance to the first defender in order to support his initiative of blocking the offensive actions of the player in possession of the ball.
Player(s) Who Perform	Players within the specified spatial references.
Examples of Actions	• Actions of coverage to the player in delay. • Positioning that allows the obstruction of potential passing lines/zones to opposite players. • Marking opponent(s) who may receive the ball in advantageous attacking situations. • Adequate positioning that allows to mark the player in possession of the ball whenever the player in delay is beaten.
Performance Indicators	*Successful (+)* a. Is positioned between the player in delay and the goal/ b-Enables 2nd delay action/c-Obstructs passing lines/zones. *Unsuccessful (−)* a. Is not positioned between the player in delay and the goal. b. Does not enable second delay action. c. Does not obstruct passing lines/zones.
Description of Performance Indicators	*Successful (+)* a. When players' movement allows positioning between the player in delay and the goal, within the more offensive half of the centre of play. b. When players' movement allows him/her to be a new obstacle to the player in possession of the ball, in case the player in delay is beaten. c. When players' movement enables the obstruction or interception of passing lines/zones from the player in possession of the ball to other opponents.

Chart 2.7 (Continued)

Principle of Defensive Coverage
Unsuccessful (−)   a. When players' movement does not allow positioning between the player in delay and the goal, within the more offensive half of the centre of play.   b. When players' movement does not allow him/her to be a new obstacle to the player in possession of the ball, in case the player in delay is beaten.   c. When players' movement does not enable the obstruction or interception of passing lines/zones from the player in possession of the ball to other opponents.

Source: The authors

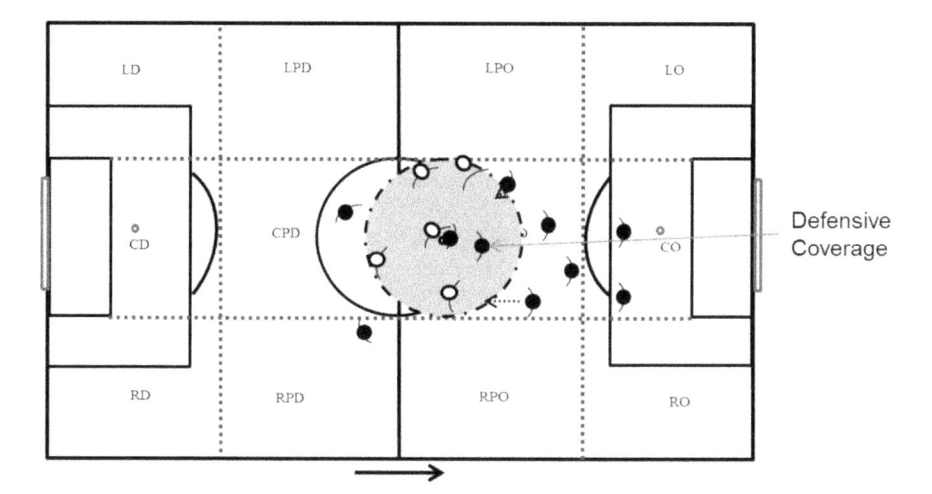

Figure 2.16 Management of space for the principle of defensive coverage
Source: The authors

PRINCIPLE OF BALANCE

The principle of balance is assured the moment the players grasp the notions inherent to their structural and functional aspects. The first is the premise that the team's defensive organization should possess numerical superiority, or at least equality of defensive players in the "centre of play" positioned between the ball and own goal. The second is associated with the actions of readjustment of defensive positioning in relation to opponents' movements.

The purpose of these ideas is to ensure defensive stability in the "centre of play" by supporting teammates who perform actions of delay and defensive coverage. By taking an adjusted position in relation to other teammates, the player who performs the balance is in better conditions to make teammates feel safer in creating unfavourable conditions to the player in possession of the ball and other opponents. As a result, this increases the predictability of the opponent's offensive play and the possibility of regaining possession (Castelo, 1996).

Therefore, the guidelines of this principle include the coverage of spaces and the marking of free players without possession, the coverage of eventual passing options and, in some cases, the decrease of game velocity, forcing the opponent to cope with an adverse game pace.

The actions of the principle of balance can be essentially detected through the equalized configuration of defenders between the ball and their own goal, while marking opponents without possession and supporting other teammates who are in charge of performing actions of delay and defensive coverage.

Chart 2.8 shows the characteristics that describe the principle of balance and, subsequently, Figure 2.17 shows an example of the space that may be used to develop its actions.

Chart 2.8 Characteristics of the principle of balance.

	Principle of Balance
Characteristics	A) *Defensive Balance*: Movements of the defensive players performed in the lateral zone(s) in relation to the location of the more offensive half of the centre of play, delimited by the line of the ball and the border of the next area of the game. B) *Recovery Balance*: Movements of the defensive players performed in the less offensive half of the centre of play
Spatial Reference	A) More offensive half of the centre of play, zones and areas of play; B) Less offensive half of the centre of play.
Purposes	• Ensure defensive stability within the lateral zone(s) in relation to the location of the more offensive half of the centre of play; • Reduce pass lines to other opponents; • Mark potential players who could receive the ball; • Support teammates who perform actions of delay and defensive coverage; • Increase pressure on the player in possession of the ball; • Perform defensive recovery towards the centre of play
Player(s) Who Perform	Players within the specified spatial references.
Examples of Actions	• Movements that ensure defensive stability. • Movements of defensive recovery performed behind the line of the ball. • Positioning that enables the obstruction of potential passing lines/zones. • Marking opposite players who support offensive actions of the player in possession of the ball.

Chart 2.8 (Continued)

	Principle of Balance
Performance Indicators	*Successful (+)* a. Stabilizes lateral zones of the CP. b. Obstructs passing lines/zones. c. Stabilizes CPO zone. d. Pressurizes the player in possession of the ball within the CPO zone. e. Obstructs passing lines/zones. *Unsuccessful (−)* a. Does not stabilize lateral zones of the CP. b. Does not obstruct passing lines/zones. c. Does not stabilize CPO zone. d. Does not pressure the player in possession of the ball within the CPO zone. e. Does not obstruct passing lines/zones.
Description of Performance Indicators	*Successful (+)* a. When players' movement allows for the creation of defensive stability in the relations of opposition within the lateral zones in relation to the centre of play (through marking opponents who may receive the ball or obstructing passing lines/zones), preventing the opponent's offensive progression. b. When players' movement allows for the obstruction or interception of passing lines/zones of the player in possession of the ball to another opponent positioned in the lateral zones in relation to the centre of play. c. When players' movement allows for the creation of defensive stability in the relations of opposition within the less offensive half of the centre of play, by marking opponents who may receive the ball or by obstructing passing lines/zones. d. When player's defensive recovery movement (less offensive half of the centre of play) interferes in the action of the player in possession of the ball generating difficulties for the opponent's offensive sequence or facilitating ball recovery by own team. e. When players' movement allows for the obstruction or interception of passing lines/zones of the player in possession of the ball to other opponents within the less offensive half of the centre of play. *Unsuccessful (−)* a. When players' movement does not allow to create defensive stability in the relations of opposition within the lateral zones in relation to the centre of play (through marking opponents who may receive the ball or obstructing passing lines/zones), and does not prevent the opponent's offensive progression.

(Continued)

Chart 2.8 (Continued)

	Principle of Balance
	b. When players' movement does not allow to obstruct or intercept passing lines/zones of the player in possession of the ball to another opponent positioned in the lateral zones in relation to the centre of play. c. When players' movement does not allow to create defensive stability in the relations of opposition within the less offensive half of the centre of play, by marking opponents who may receive the ball or by obstructing passing lines/zones. d. When player's defensive recovery movement (less offensive half of the centre of play) does not interfere in the action of the player in possession of the ball generating difficulties to the opponent's offensive sequence or facilitating ball recovery by his team. e. When players' movement does not allow to obstruct or intercept passing lines/zones of the player in possession of the ball to other opponents within the less offensive half of the centre of play.

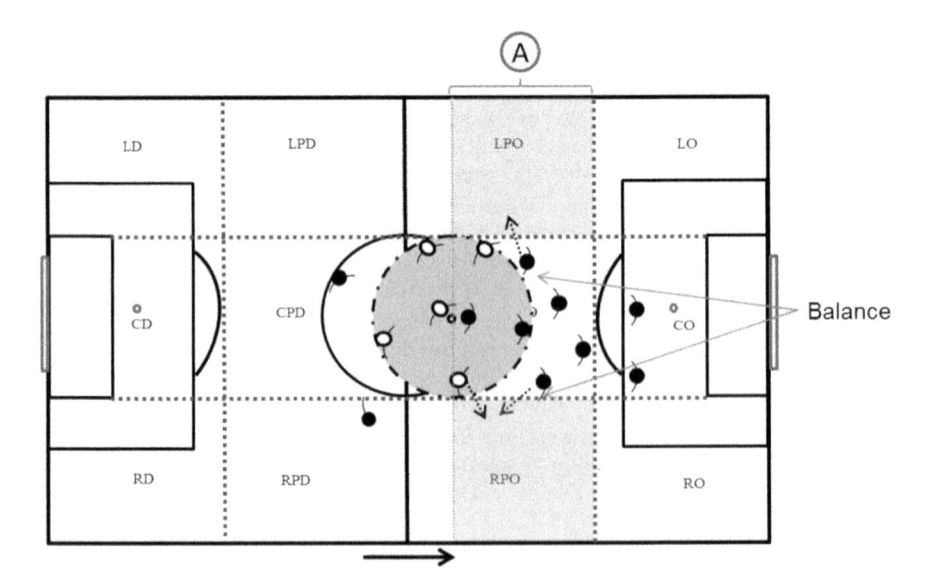

Figure 2.17 Management of space for the principle of balance
Source: The authors

PRINCIPLE OF CONCENTRATION

The principle of concentration is based on players' movements towards the zone of the field with higher risk to goal, aiming at increasing defensive protection, reducing the space available to the player in possession to perform offensive actions and facilitating the regain of ball possession (Bangsbo & Peitersen, 2002).

The guidelines of this principle are intended to direct opponent's offensive play to less vital zones and to minimize the offensive amplitude in width and length, avoiding the creation of free spaces, especially on the back of players who perform delay, coverage and defensive balance.

Therefore, the actions of concentration can be performed in any zone of the field, as long as all players who are involved are aware of the importance of their movement to reduce space and increase pressure in the "centre of play".

During the match, the typical actions of this principle can be observed when defenders positioned further away from the player in possession of the ball are able to gather in order to limit the offensive options of the attack to a certain zone of the field.

Chart 2.9 shows the characteristics that describe the principle of concentration and, subsequently, Figure 2.18 shows an example of the space that may be used to develop its actions.

Chart 2.9 Characteristics of the principle of concentration

	Principle of Concentration
Characteristics	Movements of the defensive players performed in the zone where the more offensive half of the centre of play is, delimited by the border of the more offensive half of the centre of play, the border(s) of the wing(s), and the border of the next area of the game
Spatial Reference	More offensive half of the centre of play and zones of the playing field.
Purposes	• Increase protection of the goal; • Force opponent's offensive play towards safer areas; • Increase pressure within the centre of play
Player(s) Who Perform	Players within the specified spatial references.
Examples of Actions	• Movements that enable defensive support within the zone of lower risk to the team. • Marking opposite players who search for the enlargement of the offensive play-space. • Movements that enable an increased number of players between the ball and the goal. • Movements that force the opponent's attacking actions towards the sides of the field.

(Continued)

58 *Understanding the Soccer Game*

Chart 2.9 (Continued)

	Principle of Concentration
Performance Indicators	*Successful (+)* a. Reduce opponent's depth/b-Force opponent's play towards safer zones. *Unsuccessful (−)* a. Does not reduce opponent's depth/b-Does not force opponent's play towards safer zones.
Description of Performance Indicators	*Successful (+)* a. When players' movement s help the team reduce the opponent's offensive amplitude (or effective play-space) in its depth. b. When players' movement s help the team force the opponent's play towards safer zones. *Unsuccessful (−)* a. When players' movement s do not help the team reduce the opponent's offensive amplitude (or effective play-space) in its depth. b. When players' movement s do not help the team force the opponent's play towards safer zones.

Source: The authors

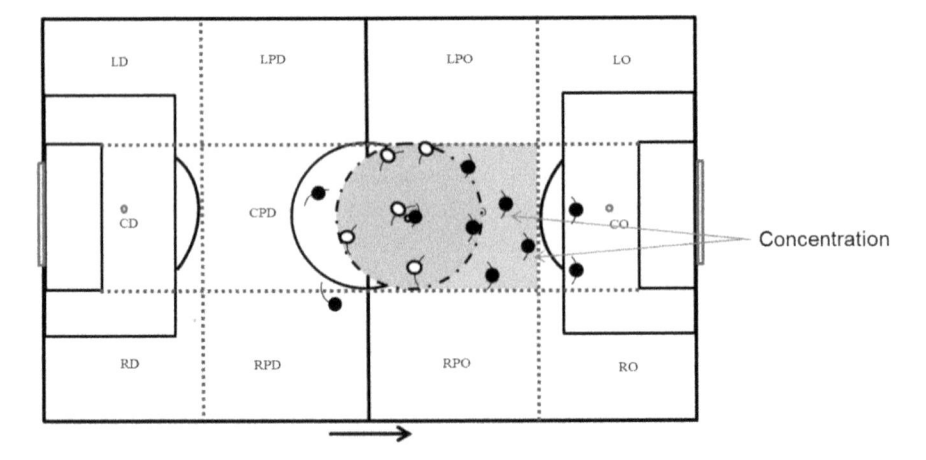

Figure 2.18 Management of space for the principle of concentration
Source: The authors

PRINCIPLE OF DEFENSIVE UNITY

The principle of defensive unity has a strong relation with the tactical understanding of the game and with the concept of functional unit of the team. The concept of unitary defence of a team goes through the awareness of all players in respect to the importance of their movements, their limitations, their capabilities and their positions in relation to their teammates, the ball and their opponents (Hainaut & Benoit, 1979; Teissie, 1969).

The guidelines of this principle aim to ensure the coordination of attitudes and tactical-technical behaviours of the players positioned outside the "centre of play". They also allow the team to constantly and automatically balance and rebalance the distribution of power of the defensive method according to the momentary configurations of play (Castelo, 1996). Therefore, the execution of the typical behaviours of this principle provides better conditions for the players who are directly involved in the actions near the ball to press the opposing team. However, it is necessary that, besides being aware of the playing surface, their limits and basic specific tasks, players are also attentive to their teammates' tasks and ready to help them in any game situation, providing support or taking up their tasks.

In this context, the offside rule is an important ally of the defending team, since the last defensive line, when effectively explored and executed, is able to decrease the opposite effective play-space and exert more pressure within the "centre of play", as shown in Figure 2.19, in relation to the movement from situation A to situation B.

Therefore, by performing effective movements that suit the offside rule, and considering the characteristics of the principle of defensive unity, the team is able to pressure the player in possession of the ball and the teammates who help him/her in their offensive actions. Pressure and reduction of space decrease the time available for decision-making and execution to the offensive players and can lead them to tactical or technical mistakes that benefit players getting ready to directly intervene in the "centre of play" at any moment either through displacement

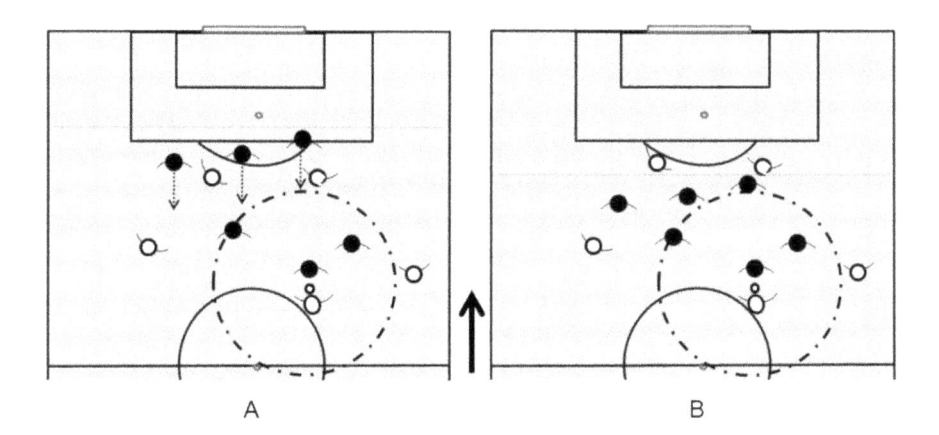

Figure 2.19 Reduction of the effective play-space through the use of the offside rule
Source: The authors

60 *Understanding the Soccer Game*

towards the ball or through the fluctuation of the "centre of play" towards them (Tavares, Greco, & Garganta, 2006).

However, to ensure cohesion, effectiveness and functional balance between the team's longitudinal and transverse lines in defensive actions, the players responsible for executing the principle of defensive unity need to be aware of their displacements, and their teammates' skills and possible movements to recognize appropriate moments to act according to the variability of the momentary game situations (Pinto, 1996).

During the match, the typical actions of this principle can be observed through the coordination of the movements of the players outside the "centre of play" in line with the position of the ball. This allows the development of a more harmonious and efficient play between the team's longitudinal and transverse lines, as for example the movement of the side player towards the centre of the field to help on team compaction when the game action is being developed in the opposite side.

Chart 2.10 shows the characteristics that describe the principle of defensive unity and, subsequently, Figure 2.20 shows an example of the space that may be used to develop its actions.

Chart 2.10 Characteristics of the principle of defensive unity

	Principle of Defensive Unity
Characteristics	Movements of the defensive players performed outside of the centre of play and within the area delimited by the line of the ball and the opponent's goal line or the next area(s) in relation to the zone where the more offensive half of the centre of play is; or the wing opposite to where the ball is, delimited by the line of the ball and the border of the next area of the game.
Spatial Reference	A) the line of the ball and the opponent's goal line;
	B) the next area(s) in relation to the zone where the more offensive half of the centre of play is;
	C) the wing opposite to where the ball is, delimited by the line of the ball and the border of the next area of the game;
Purposes	• Allow the team to defend as a unity or block;
	• Ensure spatial stability and dynamic synchrony between the team's longitudinal and transverse lines in defensive actions;
	• Decrease the opponent's offensive area in width and/or depth;
	• Ensure guiding lines that influence the technical-tactical behaviours of the players positioned outside the centre of play;
	• Constantly balance or rebalance the relative strengths of the defensive organization according to the playing situations;
	• Reduce pass lines to other opponents who are outside of the centre of play;
	• Decrease the space of play through the offside rule;
	• Enable involvement in a subsequent defensive action;
	• Allow more players to move to the centre of play.

Chart 2.10 (Continued)

	Principle of Defensive Unity
Player(s) Who Perform	Players within the specified spatial references.
Examples of Actions	• Organization of defensive positioning after losing possession, with the purpose of recreating the defensive lines. • Players' movements, particularly full-backs and wingers, towards the central corridor when playing actions are developed in the opposite side. • Defensive packing within the zone of the field that represents higher risk to goal. • Movements of players who make up the last defensive line so as to reduce opponent's play-space (through the "offside" rule).
Performance Indicators	*Successful (+)* a. Reduces opponent's amplitude. b. (Re)balances defensive organization. c. Contributes to defensive actions behind the line of the ball. d. Approximates the team to the CP. e. Takes part in subsequent action. *Unsuccessful (−)* a. Does not reduce opponent's amplitude. b. Does not (re)balance defensive organization. c. Does not contribute to defensive actions behind the line of the ball. d. Does not approximate the team to the CP. e. Does not take part in subsequent action.
Description of Performance Indicators	*Successful (+)* a. When players' movement promotes the reduction of opponent's offensive amplitude in width and/or depth. b. When players' movement allows to constantly balance or rebalance the distribution of forces of the defensive organization according to the momentary game situations (subsequent area in relation to the more offensive half of the centre of play). c. When players' movement contributes to the execution of defensive actions behind the line of the ball (by marking opposite players who may receive the ball or by obstructing passing lines/zones). d. When players' movement allows other defensive player to take part in the actions within the centre of play. e. When players' movement allows him/her to take part in a defensive/offensive subsequent action.

Chart 2.10 (Continued)

Principle of Defensive Unity
Unsuccessful (−)   a. When players' movement does not allow the reduction of opponent's offensive amplitude in width and/or depth.   b. When players' movement does not allow to constantly balance or rebalance the distribution of forces of the defensive organization according to the momentary game situations (subsequent area in relation to the more offensive half of the centre of play).   c. When players' movement does not contribute to the execution of defensive actions behind the line of the ball (by marking opposite players who may receive the ball or by obstructing passing lines/zones).   d. When players' movement does not allow other defensive player to take part in the actions within the centre of play.   e. When players' movement does not allow him/her to take part in a defensive/offensive subsequent action.

Source: The authors

2.5 The Tactical Principles and the Teaching-Learning Process

The development of the cognitive and tactical skills that lead to a better understanding of the game can be done from the child egocentric phase to the adult phase, taking four stages into consideration: (1) Me+Ball+Space, (2) Me+Ball+Space+Teammates, (3) Me+Ball+Space+Teammates+Opponents and (4) Me+Ball+Space+Teammates+Opponents+Conditionings. As a rule, in all phases and formats, the contents are directed based on the practitioner's (child, teenager, adult) latent phase of development, looking to emphasize those that fit in better with the developmental characteristics of each age group, always with the main objective of intelligence and creativity being able to manifest themselves in a game context.

Considering the first stage *Me+Ball+Space* and as a way to start up the comprehension of game space in the first years of life, it is important that the child dominates, still in the egocentric phase, a few important contents related to their perceptions, namely the bodily, spatial and directional perceptions. The bodily perception is related with the child's ability to discriminate accurately his/her body parts, developing genuine and detailed knowledge about his/her body, therefore knowing what each part can do and how to move efficiently. The spatial perception is related to the child's ability to identify himself/herself in space and know how much space that body takes up, and from that, project that body effectively in open space. Finally, the directional perception relates to the ability to give dimension to objects that are in open space through laterality and directionality,

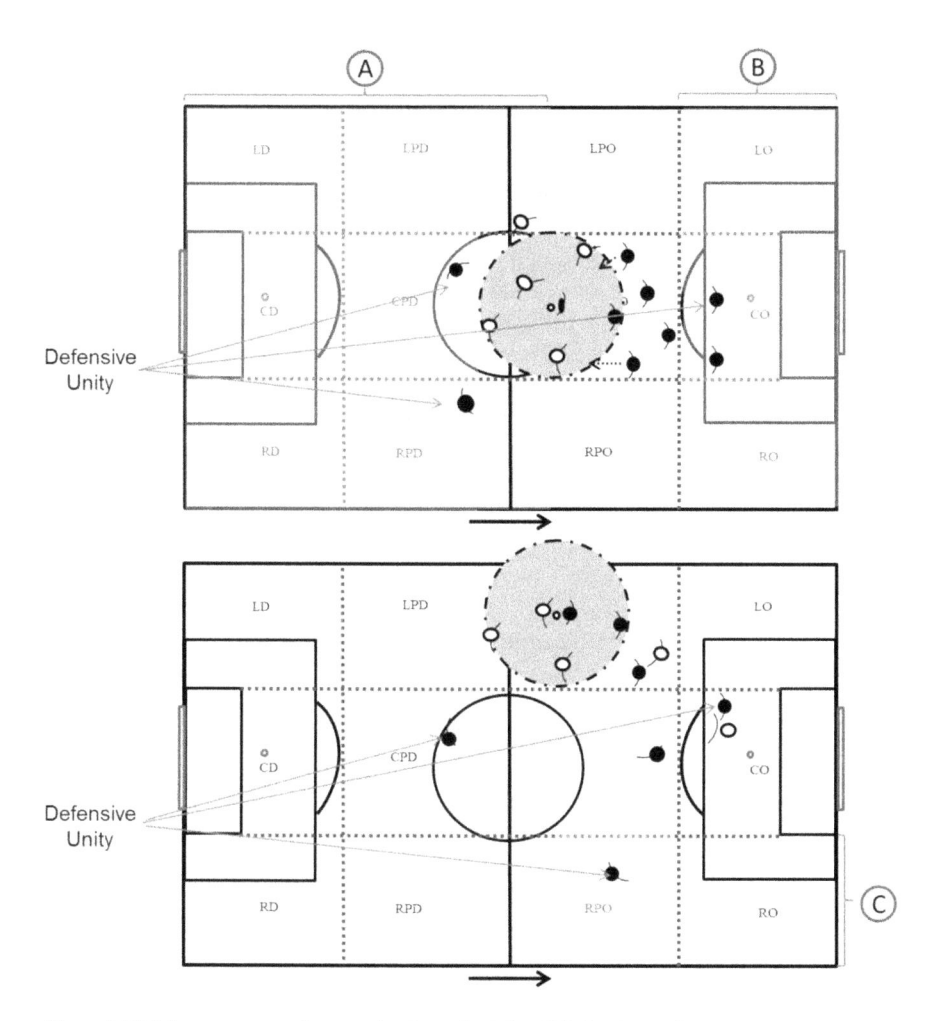

Figure 2.20 Management of space for the principle of defensive unity
Source: The authors

that being: (i) laterality, the internal perception of the multiple body dimensions as their location and direction (right-left, up-down, in-out, forward-backward, etc.) and (ii) directionality, the external projection of laterality, giving dimension to objects in space, such as the letters b, d, p and q, which, due to the positioning of their constituent parts, have different meanings. In case this triad becomes difficult to comprehend to some children, early on the professor can use the following relationships: Me+Ball and Me+Space. When performing some exercises with these binomials and ensuring basic learning, later, he/she will be able to introduce Me+Ball+Space.

The full development of the three perceptions (bodily, spatial and directional) will allow the child to develop a more adequate body orientation to the game and have the important synergy between the cognitive and motor development in order to play soccer. In this context, good body orientation on the field will allow a greater utilization of all human senses responsible for receiving information (visual, auditory, tactile and vestibular) and, consequently, lead to development optimization of individual tactics associated with the tactical principles. Based on this information and respecting the latent phases of human development, the motor part is also enhanced, once good body orientation will allow better positioning of the feet and other body parts (torso, hips, etc.) and a better use of the head (checking before receiving the ball). All these elements if well combined will allow, from the child's socialization phase, a better quality and speed in the search for information within the game, better recognition of space and time to play, ability to anticipate movement, better positioning to receive the ball (using the foot that is more distant to the opponent or better feet coordination), better movement and search for open spaces, among other factors.

The second stage of development *Me+Ball+Space+Teammates* must start after the end of the child's egocentric phase and the start of the socialization phase, which occurs around the age of 6 (J. Piaget, 1964, 1983; Jean Piaget, 1993). From that, the situations of simple understanding of group tactics must be explored and, with the evolution of the child, the third stage *Me+Ball+Space+ Teammates+Opponents* begins gradually and concomitantly. In that moment, teaching the general tactical and operational principles also becomes extremely important once its rules of action are responsible for facilitating the comprehension of the game logic and its understanding. As these are rules that use concrete operations and because of the fact that the child up to the age of 9–10 is in a cognitive process that limits the uptake of a large number of information found in the game environment, it is recommended that the space and the relations of cooperation and opposition that are established within the game are the easiest to assimilate by the children. Thus, up to the third stage the 4 × 4 relationships are the ones that best suit the children's development phase in terms of perceptual elements to game-space management, since in this configuration each child has a specific space to understand and fill, in both box and diamond shapes. The triangular shape, originating from the games with three players, makes players play in a "space crisis" and have to think in an abstract and hypothetical way about the management of this game space. See that in Figure 2.21, the positions of the ball and/or opponents represented by the letters A, B and C would require that players in black move to these points and manage "the space crisis" that would happen due to these movements.

In this moment, as mentioned before, children, due to their stage of cognitive development, would have more difficulty in having a more assertive and fast behaviour to this demand, which would, consequently, cause a greater difficulty in understanding and a greater number of positioning and movement errors on the field (tactics) and also mistakes in motor response (technical gesture). Thus, in

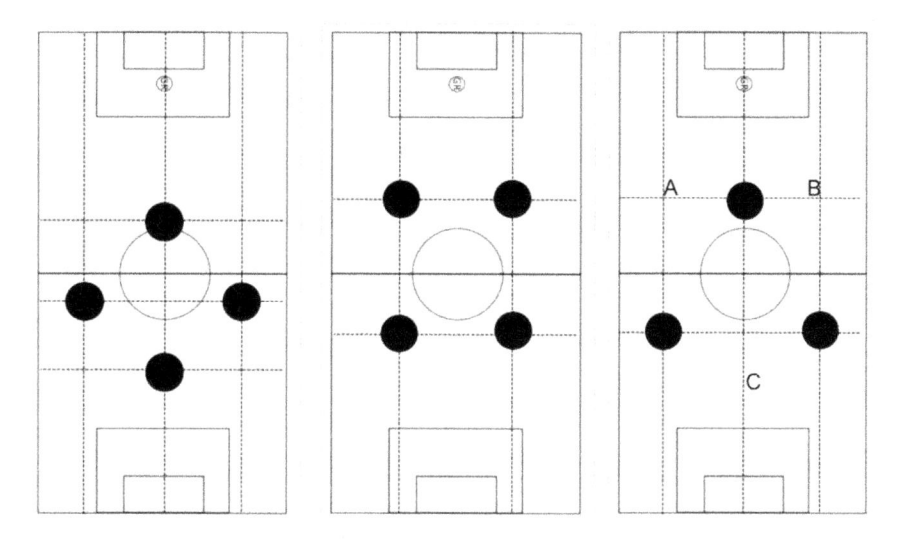

Figure 2.21 The layout of the players in three geometric configurations: diamond, box (square) and triangle
Source: The authors

the development of these stages and seeking to optimize the understanding of the game, the core tactical principles must be introduced from the interaction relationships that are established from the game centre to its exterior.

As the child evolves, the fourth stage *Me+Ball+Space+Teammates+Opponents+ Conditioners* should start being developed, since changes in the structure and/or in the functionality of the game influence the space-time demands that, in their case, modify the actions of players and teams. The changes that will be promoted will encourage the players to self-organize and self-transform, therefore, enabling the adaptation of the cognitive processes to the conditions of the environment, the opponent and the other elements that are part of the game.

At this stage the conditions must explore the contents that are present in the general and operational principles and emphasize three essential aspects to the development of game comprehension: field size, the dynamic space of the game and the frequency of actions/movements. At this point, it is important to specify the dimensions of the field and organize the elements of the game so that the environmental context can facilitate and adapt to the children's learning and development process. Chart 2.11 presents a proposal for spatial organization and adaptations for the game by age, which takes into account the maximum and minimum measures allowed for a soccer field by the International Football Association Board, the ratio of use of playing space and the density of players per square metre.

Chart 2.11 Proposal for spatial organization and adaptations for the game

Phase (Age Group)	Number of Players	Field Dimensions	Dimension of the Goals	Ball Size	Playing Time
6–8 years old	GK+4×4+GK GK+3×3+GK	36 m × 20 m	2.0 m to 3.0 m × 1.3m to 2.0 m	N° 4	3 × 12' × 5' (int.)
9–10 years old	GK+7×7+GK	52.5 m × 34 m	6 m × 2 m	N° 4	3 × 15' × 5' (int.)
11–12 years old	GK+10×10+GK	68 m × 45 m	6 m × 2 m	N° 4	3 × 20' × 5' (int.)
13 years old	GK+10×10+GK	105 m × 68 m	7.32 m × 2.44 m	N° 5	2 × 30' × 10' (int.)

Source: The authors

It is important to note that these measures proposed in the previous table were tested in scientific studies which indicated that this type of adaptation makes it easier for the child to play the game with all the elements of a formal game (11×11), but adapted to the age and developmental phase needs (Teoldo & Silvino, in press; Teoldo, Silvino, & Sarmento, in press). The results of these two studies indicate that the use of these adaptations and game configurations exacerbates the more individualized game and with a greater number of shots once the reduction of spaces and the number of players also lead to a smaller number of elements involved in the game. The reduced space also increases the opponent's pressure, which implies that the players must circulate the ball with more speed and use better the width and length of the field. Offensive sequences become shorter, leading to a more fragmented game with more transitions between phases. In this context, there is a need to maintain the attention levels and changes in the interactional mind-set (attack and defence) with greater frequency, which are enhanced by the greater number of actions performed in the game centre and closer to the goal, which, in turn, brings an even greater emotional involvement (Andrade, Machado, & Teoldo, 2016; Gonzaga, Albuquerque, Malloy-Diniz, Greco, & Costa, 2014).

In addition, the results of these researches also showed that these field and game formats stimulate the speed and width/length of ball circulation, the amount of shots and the amount of dispossessions due to errors and tackle in a compatible and corresponding way to the numbers/values that can be found in professional- and academy-level games (Teoldo & Silvino, in press; Teoldo et al., in press). These results show that paying attention to the adaptation of rules and spaces in younger ages is extremely relevant to facilitate the learning of these essential elements in order to play better soccer and adequately stimulate the development of all tactical-cognitive and technical-motor competencies in line with the learning and development stages of all young practitioners (children and teenagers).

In this context, the core principles of the game should be widely taught, starting from those more related to the behaviours close to the ball and, gradually, expanding to other principles related to the behaviours in spaces farther from the ball, providing a transition from group tactics to collective tactics. As these principles require abstract thinking and hypothetical testing to fill space and movement on the field, we recommend that its teaching-learning process gets consolidated by the age of 12 or 13, when the child's cognitive development stage is already mature or in the final phase of maturation and will allow to incorporate all these concepts and apply them on a collective/macro interaction scale (collective tactics).

The teaching of the three categories of principles (general, operational and core) will allow young players to have a solid knowledge base about the logic of the game and about the movements and space filling within the game. From understanding these aspects, players will be better able to learn and incorporate their teams' game models, that is, they will be better prepared to start the learning process of the specific tactical principles. This moment of the teaching process of the specific tactical principles will coincide with the guidance of the player development phase and also with the facilities and sports structure available in soccer clubs that provide, from under 14 and on, a better training structure (specific coaching staff for each age group, dorms in the club, medical and social staff) to the young talents.

From this development stage there is a greater emphasis on stimulating the synaptic channels related to game schemes that favour more complex and combined movements, to game systems with well-defined phases and transitions, and to the game model that must guide the developmental process up to the last years of academy youth soccer. In this context, the game model becomes extremely important and must be understood by everyone involved in the process: head coaches, players, members of the coaching staff, directors, coordinators and other professionals. Due to the importance of this theme in this stage of player development, we will deal with tactical modelling in a special and detailed way in the next chapter of this book, and in Chapter 4 we will address information about soccer training for this stage of development, addressing its conceptual and operational plans.

In this regard, it is important to emphasize that the variability of tasks and environments can and should continue to be stimulated in this stage of player development. Therefore, the next two chapters will show that we must not only vary the tasks and environments randomly, but instead think about this variation in a progressive way and based on the contents and demands of game spaces. The difference is how often that will be done, once in the specialization phase we must provide an increasingly specific space like the one soccer players will find in a high-performance environment, just as it is in the formal and professional game.

Before moving on to the next chapters of this book, we would like to emphasize that in the Brazilian reality, especially in grassroots soccer, futsal is incorporated inside the soccer player development process; in some clubs, the futsal and soccer departments already operate in an integrated manner with the goal of providing a unique development to the player, starting at futsal and transitioning to soccer. In this context, it is essential to comprehend the benefits of this integrated work and, especially, according to the subject we are dealing with in this book.

2.6 Futsal as an Important Element for Player Development

During the explanations of the children development process, especially regarding the playing space understanding, we highlight in Chart 2.11 the first configurations that should be used with the children, that is GK+4×4+GK and GK+3×3+GK in spaces of 36 metres in length by 20 metres in width, and with goals that are from 1.3 to 2 metres tall and 2 to 3 metres in length. You don't need to be an expert in the field to quickly realize that these measures are met by physical spaces and materials already used in futsal. Because of this convenience and once futsal is extremely present in the context of grassroots soccer, especially in the Brazilian scenario where it is widely practiced in schools and it is easier to organize the game—less players and less space necessary to play—the sport becomes an asset in the process of athletic evolution and development, especially in the early ages.

The first significant point of contribution of futsal during the player development process is the fact that its own practice provides flexibility for game variation in regard to space dimensions, number of players and playing surface. It is worth remembering that the playing surface must, whenever possible, be switched between cement court, dirt, grass, turf and even the street, as it was more common in the past, because just like alternating the ball size and type, the number players and playing space, this variation in the type of floor also allows for different synaptic records throughout the nervous system during the teaching-learning process.

Another important issue is the greater spread of the practice of the sport in school and public environments, once it is easier to structure the game in smaller spaces and with a smaller number of people. In addition, because of urban growth, it is easier to find courts and spaces where futsal can be played when compared to spaces with grass and/or soccer fields. In this sense, futsal fits perfectly in the idea of contributing to player development. In fact, futsal contributes to the learning of specific elements of soccer and the reverse can also happen, especially regarding the technical and tactical aspects of the two sports.

In regard to the tactical part (focus of this work), it is important to highlight that although soccer and futsal are two different sports and, hence, present different demands in game reading, movement and decision-making during games, there is also a range of similarities between the two sports that make them complementary and important in the developmental process. The main similarity is in the tactical and strategic essence, once in both sports cooperation and opposition relations happen at all times, putting teams in opposite phases of the game against each other, with players and teams trying to reach, amongst several possible objectives, two that are intrinsic to the internal logic of the game, which are scoring a goal (attack) or avoiding being scored on (defence). In order to reach the goal, it is necessary to know how to move and position yourself, that is to manage the playing space according to a strategy and a collective plan. In addition to these tactical and strategic aspects, the technical and physical components are similar in essence, differing in a few cases due to the demands imposed by specific contexts.

Due to these similarities, we can also take advantage of contents developed for soccer, such as the tactical principles, to be used in futsal and in all other adapted spaces during the teaching-learning process. Regarding the tactical principles, some studies analysed the tactical behaviours of futsal players, according to the core tactical principles of the game (Muller, Garganta, Santos, & Teoldo, 2016; Muller, Teoldo, & Garganta, 2018). In these studies, the authors observed that futsal players performed more actions close to the player with the ball and/or to the game centre, unlike soccer players, who perform more actions distant from the game centre. Furthermore, the authors indicate that in the game of futsal there is a better defensive performance and easier control and circulation of the ball. In the study of Muller et al. (2016), for example, in addition to futsal players presenting a better defensive tactical performance, the mistakes in these actions were smaller. According to the authors, in futsal's environment, all players are highly active in the defensive and offensive phases, facilitating the alternation of the attention and concentration levels that are specific to each one of these phases, and also because they have greater control and circulation of the ball because several characteristics of the sport, such as the type of surface, the dimensions, the number of players, the speed and intensity of the game, the more stable environmental conditions, the type of footwear and even the type of ball—will be covered in more detail later.

Of all the results and information derived from these studies, one of them is of vital importance to the player development process, which is the performance of more actions close to the game centre and to the player with the ball. This information is important because the actions closer to the ball and the game centre, even due to space limitations, imply that players must perform movements at a higher speed and intensity, in a greater proportion than in the soccer environment. This is, in fact, one of the main elements that make the game of futsal very important to the player development process and in the perspective of space progression, once the speed and intensity of the game influence the development of the tactical, technical and physical aspects, and especially the player's cognitive skills, once they are driven to read the game and make quicker decisions. In addition, in a futsal game a permanent tactical attitude is required, in both phases of the game, favouring the development of the defensive and offensive performance, through actions of delay and defensive coverage, and penetration and offensive coverage, respectively (Müller; Garganta; Teoldo, 2010).

Regarding the speed and intensity of the actions that are typical of the game in the futsal environment, it appears that these are the products of various elements in interaction. Let's look at a few examples: flat surface and flat soled shoes that allow greater stability and balance, facilitate the transmission of the ball (pass and reception) and, consequently, make the actions of the players faster. The weight of the ball influences its trajectory (closer to the ground), facilitating the actions of receiving the ball using the sole of the foot, allowing better ball control, which, in the end, allows greater speed and intensity in the actions during the game. Other aspects could be highlighted here from the items mentioned previously, and how that culminates in the speed and intensity of the game. However, we will highlight how an environment with a higher proportion of actions closer to the game centre strongly influences the cognitive aspects, from the perception of the information in the environment to the motor execution resulting from decision-making.

In this context and as stated previously in this chapter the ball, as the game epicentre, is the point that can bring more changes in its structure and in the players' organizational lines. Thus, the player with the ball can make these changes based on his/her actions. Consequently, the zone around the game epicentre is more affected by the actions of the player with the ball. This zone called game centre, with 9.15 metres radius from the ball, is the place where the game takes place with greater speed and intensity. In Chapter 5 of this book, we provide a table with the calculation and the measures of the game centre determined by the ratio of game space usage by the players. Therefore, in a GK+10×10+GK game, with official dimensions, the game centre has a radius of 9.15 metres. In futsal's case, in which a GK+4×4+GK game is played, in spaces of approximately 40 m × 20 m, the measurement of the game centre has a radius of 5 metres.

These dimensions and organizational dynamics involved in these spaces have direct implications in the players' perceptual field and, consequently, in their performance. Therefore, playing games in environments with smaller dimensions and smaller number of players, such as futsal, becomes important for the extension of the perceptive field to be done gradually, starting from a more ball-centred vision to a more game-centred vision. This factor is even more important in terms of the fact that players have a greater difficulty in controlling the ball and perceiving a greater amount of information in the initial stages of the player development process and, because of that, the games of smaller structure (smaller number of players and smaller spaces) offer a less complex environment, where the comprehension of the elements that make up the game becomes better adjusted to the latency phases of the human and athletic development of the young practitioner (children and teenagers).

Because of this reason, the specialized literature in the area has repeatedly suggested that the variation in the practice environment during the player's development stage is an important factor since it gives young players different experiences during their development stages (Garganta & Pinto, 1994). However, it is important to emphasize that it is not just a matter of varying spaces and environments in isolation just so the players find different spaces and stimuli, but to think how to make a progression and variation of these spaces, as shown in Chart 2.11, providing a contextualization of the contents covered in each space, its specificity for the teaching-learning process and, above all, to the evolution of the young practitioner (Muller et al., 2016; Muller et al., 2018).

In terms of progression, it is important to note that recent researches have shown that less experienced players tend to focus more their central attention on performing actions closer to the ball and the game centre (Américo et al., 2016; Assis, Costa, Casanova, Cardoso, & Teoldo, 2020; Machado, Cardoso, & Teoldo, 2017; Muller et al., 2016; Muller et al., 2018). Thus, as previously mentioned, regarding the need for the progressive development of the perceptual field, we must begin the progression of game spaces, starting from environments that provide more actions inside the game centre. In sequence, we must gradually expand them, adding more players and increasing spaces so that they can comprehend the tactical principles and the rules of game space management as they develop the cognitive and motor aspects necessary to play soccer.

Regarding the cognitive aspects, the attention and concentration are fundamental to the perception of information in the environment and, consequently, for game reading (Andrade, González-Víllora, Casanova, & Teoldo, 2020; Gonçalves, Gonzaga, Cardoso, & Teoldo, 2015). In this process, the memory and information processing are crucial to the assertiveness of decision-making and its qualification in terms of creativity and intelligence. Given this, once the futsal context has more actions performed closer to the ball and inside the game centre, it potentializes the development of the cognitive aspects in this stage of development. At this stage and as the process develops, especially after 9–10 years of age, the ability to perceive information further away from the game centre and the ball improves and allows the players to observe more the opponents and free spaces and, thus, manage to occupy, physically and mentally, larger spacer.

Therefore, firstly we must think about the development of the players in environments with more actions performed close to the game centre so that players can have knowledge and skills to solve problems in these spaces. Secondly, other game structures can be incorporated to the teaching-learning process. In this case, if the learning of the structures GK+4×4+GK and GK+3×3+GK has been well consolidated, it will be easier to move forward to the GK+7×7+GK and GK+10×10+GK structures once these are products of the interaction of the two first structures [GK+4×4+GK (diamond and/or box) + 3×3 (inverted triangle or regular) = GK+7×7+GK (junction of the interactions) and [GK+7×7+GK (junction of interactions + 3×3 (inverted triangle or regular)]. It is worth mentioning that in a teaching-learning process based on the integral athletic development of the young practitioner, these first interactions of game structure will build the foundation for the expansion of the existing relationships and communication channels between players, in organizational structures where these interactions overlap (see Figure 2.12 of this chapter).

In this development process, the futsal environment is a strong ally, once the game space facilitates the child's development and his/her enjoyment for the game through active participation (they touch the ball more often and participate more in the game without the ball) and the cement space that is commonly found in schools and public spaces can effectively substitute the grass space to the evolution of the player's learning. When evolving in the development process reaching the under 10s, futsal can or should keep being part of the players' development, in order to bring the same benefits already listed regarding the speed and intensity of the game. As of 12/13 years of age, due to the cognitive maturation of the player and the sports specialization phase (Côté & Erickson, 2015; Greco & Benda, 1998), a better direction for the practical experiences related to the sequence of the development of these young practitioners becomes necessary, with greater specificity to the sport in which he/she intends to continue playing and try to become a professional at.

Therefore, and to summarize the ideas we developed so far, we will list a few aspects that are favourable to the development of children from experiences that can also be provided by futsal. The aspects we will list at the end of this paragraph are based on the innumerable differences of the game in the futsal environment, which makes it unique and, at the same time, important to the development of players, exactly because these differences provide, in a few moments, simpler actions and, in others, the difficulty that is important for the teaching-learning processes and player development. Those are:

> Flat game surface—facilitates the actions of controlling the ball, dribbling, and passing, once the flat surface offers less variation in the ball trajectory.
> Ball type—in futsal, the ball is smaller (circumference) and heavier, it bounces less and also becomes a facilitating aspect in controlling the ball, dribbling and passing;
> Type of footwear—in futsal the sole of the shoes used to play is flat, facilitating the stability, balance and speed actions, in addition to influencing the actions of controlling the ball, that are mostly done using the sole of the foot.

Environmental conditions—in futsal, normally, there is no exposure to the sun and rain, to dew, to wind interferences and also to holes in the field and/or an uneven floor that, consequently, also makes it easier to control the ball, to dribble, and to pass.

Characteristics of technical actions—these actions differ in the biomechanical aspects (positioning of the body during passes, shots, ball control and dribbling). The passes are shorter due to the dimensions of the playing space and passes on the floor predominate, with less long balls and crosses in the air being performed. The positioning of the supporting foot also changes depending on the strength that is desired to make a shorter pass or a medium/long distance with the ball at a medium height.

Using the feet for throw-ins and corner kicks—this point is combined to the facility in ball control and the fact that the actions are performed predominantly with the ball closer to the ground.

Goal size—more adequate to children's sizes.

Speed/intensity of the game—this is a fundamental factor, if not the most important one, because it characterizes the game of futsal and makes it relevant as a home for player development.

Player interaction—in futsal it is possible to try out all game configurations suggested for the early ages: GK+4×4+GK (diamond and/or box) and 3×3 (inverted triangle or normal).

Notes

1 Chance is referred to as "luck" when it is in our favour and as "bad luck" when it is not (Eigen & Winkler, 1989; Garganta & Cunha e Silva, 2000).
2 Chaotic variables are circumstances through which one can achieve the purpose (goal) in an unplanned, casual or unpredictable manner (Werner, 1995).
3 The concept of passing zone goes beyond the well-known one of passing line, since the former does not necessarily require the player to be in line with the player in possession of the ball, or demands that there are no opponents between them. It demands from the player who offers a passing option to analyse/reflect about the skills of the one with the ball and those of his direct opponent(s), that is, in case they offer a passing option to a player who is both tactically and technically limited, they will position themselves in a particular way. However, in case they provide an option to a more tactically and technically skilled player (such as Ronaldinho Gaúcho, Ganso or Neymar), they will be able to position themselves differently, even allowing for a defender between them, since those players possess superior passing skills and will be able to find another solution to the play.
4 The team's longitudinal and transverse lines originate from the position of the players in the field of play. It is based on imaginary lines outlined between players' positions that, if conceived perpendicularly to the goal line, are designated longitudinal, while if conceived alongside this same referential are designated transverse.
5 In case of wind, this relation is inverted. If the attacking team has the wind in their favour the coverage should be closer, while if the wind is against them, the distance between the players in coverage and delay should be increased.

3 Tactical Modelling in Soccer

3.1 A Means to Understand and Map Out the Game

The identification and interpretation of the dynamics of soccer matches demand the use of references that allow to characterize the contents and the logic of the game through the dimensions deemed essential.

Soccer is really a game that consists of a random set of several sequences that are developed from the chain of actions performed depending on many polarities, for example global polarity between opponents, attack-defence polarity and polarity between cooperation and opposition. These characteristics, among others, make it impossible to predict from an initial state the outcome of an action or sequence, which means that we are in the presence of open-ended dynamical systems.

Indeed, many of the actions performed by the players, despite being in accordance with the regulation and complying with the logic regarding the action principles and rules of playing management, constitute sudden changes that occur in a context of ambiguity. A modification, such as the variation of the pace of execution of an action or performing a long pass in a given zone of the field, may cause significant effects in other zones, which explains the sensible dependence on the initial conditions experienced by the system (Garganta, 1997, 2008). Therefore, subtle differences in the initial conditions may, in certain circumstances, lead to major changes in the system's behaviour, that is a micro fact may result in macro consequences at match and final score levels. In order to seize these fluctuations it is more important to observe the organization of actions with respect to the interaction of constraints than to dissect the individual behaviour of the performers (Garganta, 2008).

In highly complex dynamical systems, the artificial separation of constraints that contribute to sports performance proves itself to be useless. Effective reasoning seems to be above all related to the possibility of generating relevant information and knowledge that lead to an appropriate mapping of the game(s). Thus, understanding the intricacies of performance demands inclusive ideas and concepts that grant comprehension on how behaviours are organized according to game constraints.

Within this domain, the so-called chaos theory provides knowledge on how complex dynamical systems cease to be totally predictable, even if their initial stages are known in great detail. Under the influence of multiple constraints, teams tend to embrace preferential behaviours, which, within the dynamical systems domain, are called "attractors".

Although soccer matches include several phase transitions between states of stability and imbalance, the phases and moments of play (attack, defence and transitions) occasionally comply with a process of gradual change, which is not separated by sudden or abrupt boundary lines, but rather by dissipating or diluting into each other (Garganta, 2013).

Teams' global movement is likely to evidence a geometry of actions, in search for stability or imbalance. Quite often, this pattern is only perceptible on the macro level, that is with respect to the collective network, given that on the micro level (in the centre of play) behaviours seem to comply with a different logic. In fact, as referred by Ball (2004), although order and patterns are often associated to symmetry, and randomness to its absence, perhaps randomness has its own kind of organization.

Hence, the process of modelling needs to be context-dependent, which demands an increase in the power of the observational "conceptual lens" and a refinement of the tools to operationalize it (Garganta, 2008). More than focusing on the game actions, it is important to shift perception to the interactions between the players and their involvement. It is in its articulations that system weaves its identity, and it is also through them that it creates conditions to keep or change this character, according to the circumstances (Garganta, 2005).

Given the increasingly effective tendency to demand indicators of individual, group and collective tactical effectiveness, the ideal methodology to approach the game is the one that allows to consider the phenomenon as a unity, without neglecting the specificity of the match in its different organizational levels (Garganta, 2008).

For the teams have mutable anatomies and features, which are set up as the game is put together, the interpretation of match events stems, mostly, from the substantial information that one obtains based on the meaning attributed to players' and teams' typical and atypical behaviours (Garganta, 2009). This assumes the existence of a meta level that governs players' and teams' dynamics and that encompasses the respective decisions and interactions (Garganta, 2008). This level is what we call "model".

In this context, the concept of "model" is mainly linked to the processes that allow to describe and understand the phenomena, presenting them as an information summary. As Le Moigne (1990) refers, the models, despite functioning as an anticipatory creation based on an existing reality, are not established by a presumably accurate and objective analysis of the positively observable phenomenon, but rather by the "projection" of the modeller's design, which is named "conception".

According to Durand (1992), one can say that a model: (1) resembles the reality that it is supposed to represent, although it should not be mistaken by it; (2) is pertinent to the extent that it incorporates the dynamics of the phenomenon upon which it is intend to act and (3) occupies an intermediate position between the real object and the scientific theory.

Therefore, the model includes the principles and conditions that govern players' and teams' performances, among others, so that they tend to the chosen way of play and take on a given identity. Thus, models are important tools in the relationship between the observer and the observed (Bouleau, 2002), playing a transitory role of heuristic catalysts (Cohen-Tannoudji, 2002) and of instruments of visibility and intelligibility (Utaker, 2002).

In the context of soccer, resorting to models that act as references to sports performance and to coaches' intervention has enabled the access to increasingly congruent training processes, with respect to what one expects players and teams to perform in competitive settings.

The Romanian León Teodorescu, one of the most emblematic theorists of sports games, had already referred in 1975 that the analysis and interpretation of the contents of sports competitions and team functionality through the prism of modelling assured the possibility of using more effective methodologies on training plans, player selection, opposition scouting, selection of playing tactics and of coaches' and teams' activities in general.

Tactical modelling, regarded as the configuration and explanation of systematized information and knowledge with respect to the principles of management and action rules that guide the behaviour of players and teams, reveals a paramount importance for the build up of the training process, for learning and for the regulation of the competitive performance.

Considering that tactical modelling is an expression of an idea, a conception about the game, among many possible others, the observation and recording or notation of the most significant match events, as well as the analysis of the resulting data, play an important role.

Some experts (e.g. Hughes & Franks, 1997) have indicated as preferential strategies for a higher development within this domain: (1) computing and video technology progress; (2) expansion of databases in order to increase knowledge about the sports being researched and (3) improvement of mathematical methods for data analysis.

However, the key issue regards the awareness of how tactical modelling can support the comprehension of the present state and the evolution tendencies of dynamical system (team/game), so as to allow training adaptations and greater effectiveness in competition, the decision of which information is important and how it can be used to improve performance becoming essential (Carling, Reilly, & Williams, 2009; Perl, 2004).

Being aware that the limitations of reducing the game to a sum of punctual actions and/or to statistical data results on the lack of information to understand it, we hold the position that it is necessary to know not only "where", "when" and "how" game events take place, but mostly "why" and "for what purpose" they occur (Garganta, 2013).

We admit that, in the context of soccer, each team shares an "action grammar", a "language" that enables a group of players to become collectively organized according to principles, intentions and meanings. This "language", which should promote a combination of consistency and versatility, standardization and variability, is the expression of an identity. In this line of thought, it is not convenient that tactical modelling results in the standardizing of methods or playing styles of players and teams. Instead, it is important that it encourages diversity and development, taking into account the upgradeable characteristics of sports players, by resorting to insights that are able to provide important information to improve training and play.

Thus, it seems desirable that match and training modelling are carried out so as to develop players who are capable of influencing the course of game events, rather than just reacting to them.

3.2 A Way of Mapping the Ideas to Play

You have your way. I have my way. As for the right way, the correct way, and the only way, it does not exist.

F. Nietzsche

The conceptual and methodological pillars that guide research and thinking within soccer have been largely based on paradigms that demand an excessive segmentation of the constraints that contribute to sports performance in training and competition.

However, in complex systems that function in random contexts, such as soccer teams, the separation of constraints that contribute to sports performance and the intention to assign them different weights regarding their respective influence have proved ineffective in understanding and explaining the impact of learning and training on the development and application of knowledge and playing skills (Garganta, 2013).

As referred by McGarry, Anderson, Wallace, Hughes, and Franks (2002), it is not plausible that the collective behaviour of a complex system may be explained by the properties of its constituent parts. Accordingly, rather than being reduced to the properties of its components, the system should be understood and envisaged in its entirety (Kelso & Tuller, 1984).

Because it stems from a network of relations that incessantly changes its conditions, the game of soccer represents a phenomenon of strong situational implications. Since it is an activity of technical and tactical features, the training process consists of the implementation of a "playing culture", which translates into a dynamic state of readiness with respect to concepts and principles (Garganta, 2008). For that matter, it is possible to say that the tactical performance represents a nuclear functional instance in the management of the playing behaviour of players and teams.

The prevalence of constraints of tactical nature stems from a reference framework that includes: (1) the type and relation of forces (conflict) between the opposing teams; (2) the variability and randomness of the context in which the match actions occur and (3) the required skills to act in specific contexts (Garganta, 2005).

Thus, understanding the purposes of teams' performance demands inclusive ideas and concepts that allow understanding the way players and teams organize and coordinate their behaviours with respect to the typical and atypical scenarios of the game.

Provided that soccer is clearly a situational sport of tactical prevalence, performers must learn to deal strategically with the demands of the game, so as to induce advantageous changes. Hence, it is important to promote the development of "game intelligence" in its intimate dependence with the constraints of perceptual and decisional nature so that players are encouraged to evolve groups of "skills" that constitute effective ways of dealing with blocks of significant information (Marina, 1995; Garganta, 2005).

Gerd Gigerenzer, a German scientist who has been dedicating himself to the study of human decision-making in several domains, states that most of the experts' skills are based on unconscious aptitudes and highlights the importance of intuition, in particular with respect to the "recognition heuristic" and the "gaze heuristic" (Gigerenzer, 2007). By recognizing some details in the game, the expert player converts them into a series of intuitions that act as a shortcut, that is a concise expression of the experience of several years (Lehrer, 2009), which allows him to save time and to be more effective when acting.

Although it is desirable that players are aware of their resources, since the idea they have of themselves influences their ability to act, the know-how relative to the game is learned, largely, as if it was a language. However, as tacit knowledge, it is not expected that players are able to describe the capital of technical and tactical solutions they possess, particularly because they come from the interaction with scenarios provided by the game. In addition, the complex behaviour does not necessarily involve more intricate mental strategies from the players (Gigerenzer, 2007).

The term "intuition" should not therefore be understood as an innate quality, but rather as a consequence of the way the individual organizes the different levels of its relation with the phenomena and how it weaves and upgrades its conceptions and experiences *hic et nunc* (Garganta, 2008). Thus, it is possible to assume that the "good intuitions", characteristics of experts in a given activity, are learned and continuously upgraded (Gigerenzer, 2007).

3.3 The Compatibility of the Functional Organization of the Team and Players' Positional Roles

The consummate player never moves the piece his opponent expects him to, and, less still, the piece he wants him to move.

Baltasar Gracián

In modern soccer, the designation of the players according to their position in the playing field (defender, midfielder, forward) has been preserved. However, this classification is only used to describe their dominant role (Kacani, 1982), as, given the current demands of soccer, the activity performed by the players during the game widely transcends the limit imposed by such categorization (Garganta, 1997).

Current soccer increasingly demands that the player is able to fulfil various tasks in addition to the space he/she predominantly covers in the playing field, so that the notion of position has overlapped the notion of function.

However, the identification of tactics with the "tactical systems" has caused the importance assigned to the so-called playing systems to be overrated, with respect to the assessment and interpretation of playing styles in soccer. Indeed, two teams may use the same "tactical system", for example 4–3–3, and play in completely different styles (Boulogne, 1972; Hughes, 1973), which means that knowing the positional apparatus does not imply knowing how it works (Gréhaigne, 1989).

Soccer players seek to perform actions during the game that, as a whole, contribute to: (1) achieve harmony of behaviours that grant stability and allow an effective organization of one's team and (2) break or unbalance the organization of the opposing team, with the purpose of destabilizing it with respect to its positioning and functioning.

In this context, the organization of players' actions stems from systems that are not limited to a base structure, that is a fixed share of forces in the playing field, but are rather mainly configured by the evolution of tasks (Mombaerts, 1991; Godik & Popov, 1993). It is possible to say that the elements of a team (system) operate from teleological[1] and teleonomic[2] perspectives, to the extent that the activities that contribute to the success of the process are organized with a purpose that may be achieved through various ways (Bertalanffy, 1968). The system presents an equifinality, that is a specific target, or final state, that may be achieved by different means, through different working conditions (Epstein, 1986).

The concept of system is then closely linked with the concept of organization, to the extent that the latter stems from an array of relations between components, resulting in a new unit (wholeness) with qualities that transcend their elements, when isolated.

According to Gréhaigne and Guillon (1992), in the team sport of soccer, three main categories of problems coexist: (1) at the spatial and temporal level, during the offensive phase, individual and collective problems with ball handling in the attempt of overcoming non-uniform moving obstacles (opponents); during the defensive phase, problems related to the production of obstacles, with the purpose of obstructing or stopping the movement of the ball and the opposing players, aiming to recover possession; (2) at the informational level, problems related to the generation of uncertainty to opponents and certainty for teammates and (3) at the organizational level, problems related to the integration of the collective project in individual actions and vice versa.

It is noticeable that opposing teams operate collectively, organized according to a particular logic, following rules, principles and prescriptions. The actions of players within the same team may differ in style, but tend to converge, as individual strategies and actions are aimed at achieving mutual ends and goals. Facing a game situation, each player favours certain actions over others, thus establishing a hierarchy of relations of exclusion and preference, with implications for the global team behaviour.

In addition, a soccer team behaves as a system capable of displaying behaviours that, although not predetermined, may be potentially anticipated. Thereby, despite being conscious that the content of the game is uncertain and unpredictable, we understand that there is the need to identify and register characteristics or quality indicators from the qualitative and quantitative analysis of the behaviours displayed within the game. Once systematized, this kind of information allows rationalizing the so-called playing patterns and, consequently, the models of play (Garganta, 1997).

According to Garganta and Cunha e Silva (2000), top-level soccer teams seem to operate in non-equilibrium states, interacting with the environment so as to generate the conditions and situations that are more advantageous for them, that is imposing their playing style, mainly through the variation of type of passing, spaces of ball circulation and control of the pace. This implies that players are in conditions to invent new games within the game, being in the zones of uncertainty that the critical phases of the match are played. There is a shared game and players who devise strategies, without which there is no competition.

In this context, the Model of Play works as a reference that for a while has allowed to frame and operationalize the process of training and competition; that is it is what grants the configuration of the process with some coherence and, by extension, enables a higher or lower transfer to the game one intends to play. From this, it is possible to understand that, in the context of team building, there is no abstract soccer, but a rather concrete one.

As it turns out, the model of play is what frames the concepts and gives them meaning. If the soccer game is played through concepts, it is the model of play that gives and takes away the purpose from these concepts, that gathers or separates them.

However, we propose a distinction between "model of play" and "conception of play".

The model of play, also described as ideal model of play, comprises a set of transversal tactical references, which translate the tendencies of the game played at the highest level. On the other hand, the conception of play, also called adapted model of play, corresponds to the way of conceiving a playing style for each team in particular.

Hence, it is possible to infer that the conception of play is influenced by the ideal model of play and, simultaneously, conditioned by several constraints, such as players' characteristics and skills, the culture and history of the club/city/country, the goals defined for the team and the players, the context of the competition, how one intends to manage the phases and moments of the game and the facilities available at the club.

The playing conception remains a model. However, it is a situated model, and, as such, it is adapted and adjusted to particular conditions.

In fact, in 1989 Pinto and Garganta published a paper in which they sought to systematize information relative to this subject (Pinto & Garganta, 1989). Yet, it was observed that there are often abusive uses and some misinterpretations related to the concept of "Model of Play". In those cases, it is assumed that the model of play explains, justifies and legitimates the early making of the game, mainly with respect to the predetermination of players' and teams' behaviours. In our opinion, this is a mistake. Indeed, the model acts as an attractor of the behaviours/attitudes that are intended to emerge from the game, but does not define them as to their sequence nor anticipates the respective intermediate and final shapes.

For that matter, it is crucial to relate at all times the process of training to the acquisitions that one intends to foster on players and teams. The importance of training well rather than training too much must be noticed. Quality training demands intensive sessions, with greater commitment, focus, attention and concentration. This leads to higher quality due to the commitment one seeks to establish between the identity relative to the model of play and the integrity of the players and the team to express themselves at the highest level.

Above all, what counts is that the player and the team understand what is intended to be implemented, with regularity and consistency. The starting point is the conception of play. Ultimately, it is the approximation to the conception of play that should guide the readjustment and fine-tuning of the other constraints to play and train. The quality of performance is a product of the commitment between the ability to play, according to the conceived conception, and the possibility for players to express themselves at a high level of sport performance.

Therefore, everything that is done should be in accordance to that reference as much as possible. In fact, the process of training control includes, above all, comparing what we do and what we obtain to what we envision to do and obtain. One trains to play and, accordingly, it should be noted that training is a process that intends to free the player from the limitation of the mere personal experience, but that simultaneously uses it to maximize its effects. Hence, training is not about cloning players, but rather making room for each one to express their individuality while respecting the collective project (Garganta, 2004).

Like that, training is about the improvement and development of competencies, maximizing potentialities and minimizing limitations. It is about seeking the development of "healthy" behaviours for quality play. It is turning action patterns into habits and resulting in a reduction of response time to stimuli within the match and increase the likelihood of an assertive decision-making. It is approximating the realities of training and game, surpassing the old saying of soccer—Training is Training, Game Time is Game Time—in favour of: Training is Game Time and Game Time is Training, if we really want to see the influence of training on the qualification for the game.

Good soccer is played according to good ideas, whereas bad soccer is played without them or with poor ones. Soccer played with superior quality is, above all, a game of concepts, regarding how two collectives organize themselves and manage opposition and cooperation in dynamic situations. We acknowledge that whenever soccer is not envisaged as a game of concepts and principles, which guide its

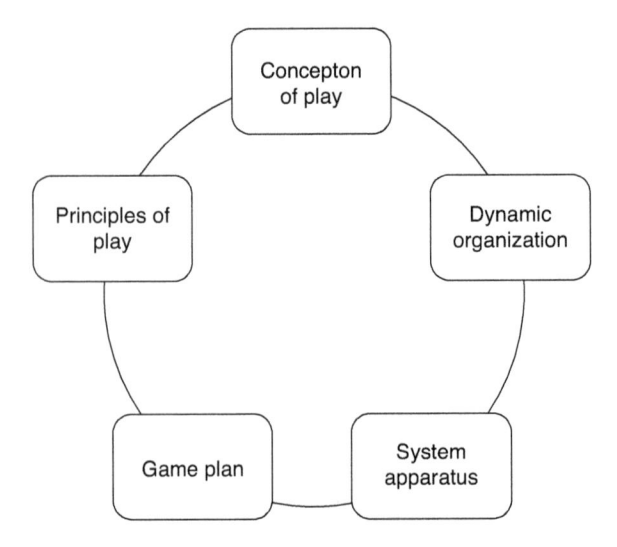

Figure 3.1 Inseparability of conception, principles, organization, systems implemented and respective game plan

Source: The authors

dynamical organization, there are increased risks of being subject to overly compartmentalized, restrictive and, not rare, blurred perspectives (Garganta, 2012).

According to this interpretation, we state that the model of play is neither on the top nor at the bottom, but rather in the centre of the process. All things must emerge from it and all things must converge to it. More than hierarchical, it is a heterarchical plurality of variable priorities and, to this extent, behaviours that influence and are influenced by performance are manifested either centripetally or centrifugally in relation to the model (Figure 3.2)

The aim of the coach is to make the process happen so as to support the accomplishment of the model and its permanent improvement.

According to Garganta (2005), the soccer game is an active construct, to the extent that its development stems from the affirmation and updating of players' choices and decisions, performed in an environment of various constraints and possibilities. Facing a game situation, each player favours certain actions over others, thus establishing hierarchical relations of exclusion and preference, with implications for the behaviour of the team as a system.

As mentioned earlier, the elements of a team operate in a teleological perspective, to the extent that the activities that contribute to the success of the process are organized according to an end, which may be achieved through different working conditions. Nonetheless, there is the need of detecting and interpreting invariants, as well as significant variations. These variations, because they lead to important

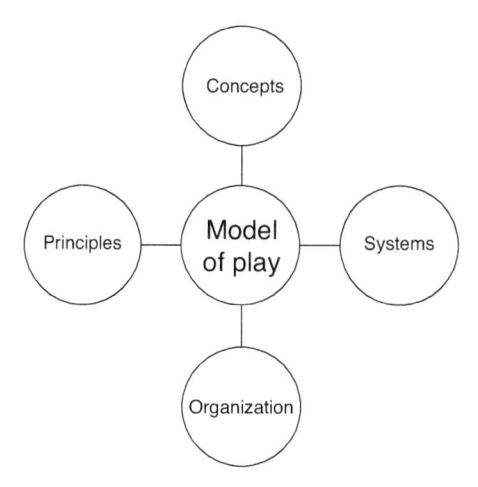

Figure 3.2 The model of play as meta level of tactical behaviours, both in competition and training

Source: The authors

imbalances, are phase transitions or critical phases of the game, which are crucial to the effectiveness of the game dynamics, in particular with respect to defence/attack and attack/defence transitions.

It is not, however, about reducing the game to an abstract idea of system, but rather trying to understand principles that guide behaviour and define the organization of the systems involved. This might be done through the identification of management and functioning rules of players and teams, and the description of regularities and variations that occur during the game. The teams, as complex systems, display properties that allow us to develop a more specific training process, therefore more adjusted to the demands of the sport and to the characteristics of the model(s) of play and of the players who seek to interpret it (them).

From such properties certain features emerge with clear implications to the mapping of the game(s) and, therefore, to the design of training drills that correspond to them. We refer to three principles we consider central to the organizational dynamics: (1) the non-linearity, related to the fact that the identity of the systems of play does not result in a superposition of effects or of elementary behaviours; (2) the interdependence, that is the characteristic that makes every behaviour of one of the systems' elements reverberate in the behaviour of the others and (3) the emergence, which stems from the creation of collective properties qualitatively different from the competencies and attributions of each player.

The following examples aim at illustrating the expression of these principles in the specific context of soccer (Garganta, 2005):

(1) Non-Linearity

Sometimes the prevailing idea is that, in soccer, in order to achieve offensive effectiveness it is advisable to play the ball quickly and directly towards the opposing goal, thus attempting to get there as quickly as possible. Although, it is possible to notice that most of the time one may be more successful when choosing paths that, although metrically longer, are more accessible because they do not display as many, nor as difficult constraints. The most important, then, is not the metric distance, but rather the issues one experiences in order to overcome it until the opposing goal.

(2) Interdependence

The type of defensive organization assumed by a team may be decisive to the way this team attacks the opposing goal and to the final score. Given that the game is about continuity and fluidity, it does not seem feasible that a team is closely linked to an attacking behaviour if it is not linked to the search for the ball. Consider as an example the notion of "docking", much discussed to ensure the defensive effectiveness. According to a systemic and dynamical understanding, such strategy is negative, due to the fact that the team, when "docking", is subjecting to the opponent's will. Instead of acting, it only reacts.

A major advantage of effective teams when not in possession of the ball is the survival of a dynamical balanced structure, an aspect that ensures the coordination of the players and the functioning of the block. The defensive references are areas, surfaces, zones and not so much the opponents, occasionally put in perspective.

The achievement of a more balanced, more efficient defence, which allows to make better use of the values within the group, is related to the fact that the players are not focused on marking physical targets, but rather on marking spaces and the ball, assuming that some spaces are more important than others. Marking is about players, space, ball, timing and, therefore, about reading the situation. More than physical marking, it is related to a meaning attributed to the situation, depending on the force lines and the probabilities of evolution of play, considering the respective interdependence, according to the different moments.

(3) Emergence

Inducing convulsions in the flow of the opponent's game is key to obtain more fluidity in one's own game, so as to ensure higher scoring probabilities.

According to the principles of play, when a team loses ball possession, it should try to restrict the effective play-space[3] (make the field smaller), so as to remove opponent's space, time and initiative; on the other hand, the opposite team tends to expand the play-space and ensure fluidity, continuity of actions, in order to circulate the ball and create favourable spaces to score.

From the so-called dark game to the "light" one, there is a certain abrupt change in the flow of actions. Those who adapt best will be able to impose their game, something that is easily observed in some top-level teams. One of the assumptions for playing effectively has much to do with the issue of the first defensive moment, that is immediately after the ball is lost. This moment is crucial, given that it is not advisable that players approach their direct opponents either individually or by waves. In this case, it is convenient to have one or two players who, being closer to the location where the ball was lost, immediately hold the opponent's attack and allow their teammates to regroup.

This means that a seemingly individual behaviour may induce the resulting defensive coverages and the blocking of key passing lanes/passing zones, the balance and the spatial concentration, thus generating emergent dynamics that meet the purposes of the collective organization.

Experience has demonstrated that quality of play cannot succeed based on the mechanical application of tactical combinations learned and repeated in training. On the contrary, it is important that players are challenged with the evolution of offensive, defensive and transitional configurations, considering distinct organizational levels, from 1X0 to 11X11. For this reason, we assume that resorting to reasoning based on the dynamical systems' perspective seems to be the most suitable way to successfully deal with the problems posed by the specific interaction between the two teams (Garganta, 2005).

By fine-tuning through the pitch of the dynamical approach to the tactical action, it is possible to emphasize the importance of the specific training, based on opposition and unpredictability as evolution factors. This understanding has provided meaning to the use of soccer training drills that trigger an important mobilization of perceptive and decisional skills in contexts with varied constraints and possibilities. This intervention strategy induces the development of more adaptable behaviours, broadens the variety of responses and prepares players to deal with unconventional situations. It is an approach that, by favouring the opposition and the management of unpredictability as a source of evolution, restores the game as key element for learning and allows to envisage training as an opportunity for autonomy. In summary, it "gives back the game to the players" (Garganta, 2005).

Notes

1 Teleological—what serves a purpose or an end.
2 Teleonomic—what is regulated according to a purpose or an end.
3 Polygonal surface configured according to the lines that link the players located in an instant t at the periphery of the space occupied by the two opposing teams, except for the goalkeepers (Mérand, 1976; Buono & Jade, 1977).

Section II
Improving Quality Play
Training and Assessment as Key Elements for Intelligence and Creativity

4 Periodization of Tactical Training

In soccer, training periodization is related to the time necessary to build a style of play, that is splitting the training process into more or less extended periods with specific aims that facilitate the build-up and evolution of the practice, the game and the player and, simultaneously, allow the control of this process.

The structured training process came with the main objective of improving the athletes' and teams' different skills and competencies so that the quality of performance could match the required competitive demands.

These concerns are not recent, having appeared from the moment when improvement of performance started to be held as an important aspect. In a study conducted by Martins, Feitosa, and Silva (1999), the authors refer to the possibility of describing the evolution of training theory in three separate steps. The first happened until the 1950s, and it was characterized by the attempt to systematize and organize some ideas that arose from individual experiences. The second, held between 1950 and 1970, featured the onset of training methodologies that were supported by the scientific knowledge of that time. The third step, which arose in the 1980s, was characterized by an attempt to overcome previous models due to three aspects: new scientific knowledge related to sport activities that were flourishing, new competitive models that had begun to emerge, with reduced preparation periods and long competitive ones, and as a way to adapt to the increasing demands of team sports.

Throughout these steps, knowledge about training was reproduced, having been responsible for the exponential development of quality and results in various sports. Much of the patented evolution was based on knowledge from various fields, including physiology, biology, biomechanics, anatomy, sociology, psychology and pedagogy, among others. Nevertheless, training theory throughout its history has always sought to be unifying, that is attempted to create a knowledge network that allowed to respond, simultaneously, to the problems and burdens from different sports, thus aiming at designing a General Training Theory.

However, as development and the resulting demands from the different sports increased, it started to be noticed that each sport displayed its own characteristics and should be studied and developed according to its particularities. At an early stage, it was thought that separating individual and collective sports would suffice to contextualize these different scenarios, yet, it is admitted that each sport has

DOI: 10.4324/9781003223375-6

its own characteristics and should be studied and understood in specific contexts (Tschiene, 2001). Hence, we understand that training theory should increasingly cease to be unifying and general, in order to have specific expressions.

Considering these ideas we do not intend to deny the importance of Training Theory, nor of the various fields in which it is based, we only deem essential to acknowledge the existence of different contexts with their own particularities, and that Training Theory and its respective supporting fields might generate specific ramifications. The particularities of soccer training will be certainly distinct—in the various parameters we may find—to those from handball, volleyball or basketball training. Nonetheless, we recognize that there may exist methodological, didactic, pedagogical and other principles that may have some resemblance, but even those also carry their characteristic features.

4.1 Soccer Training

Throughout the years, soccer training has followed the evolution of Training Theory; however, it is currently also looking for ramifications from different fields so that knowledge can grow and generate a specific body of expertise.

Until the 1960s, soccer training was under the responsibility of former players, whose education was related to their experience and respective empirical knowledge (Tani, 2002). Therefore, training focused, above all, on the tactical and technical aspects. Yet, as referred previously, the 1950s and 1960s were revolutionary with respect to the ideas of play and, as consequence, to the players' tasks. As we have seen, this is the stage in which the dynamics of play emerge. Although this characteristic revolutionized the game, it also had profound implications in the training process (Guilherme, 2004). For the dynamics of play to be evident, training process needed to be reconfigured, with different scientific fields being born to support the new course. Thus, the new professionals, called physical coaches, started to play a major role in training management (Tani, 2002).

In the sixties, different training ideas were developed, driven by the opening of new playing horizons, the emergence of players with broader tasks, knowledge arising from different scientific fields that were needed, the onset of new careers related to training and the adaptation of training methodologies from other sports whose physical component was more developed.

Martins (2003), in a study about periodization and soccer training, identified three tendencies: one originated from Eastern Europe, another from Northern Europe and North America, and a third from Latin America, or Integrated Training.

The tendency from Eastern Europe, strongly influenced by Matvéyev's ideas, conceives the training process from the acknowledgement of the existence of four distinct dimensions in the game: tactical, technical, physical and psychological. The supporters of this concept believe that, by splitting these dimensions during training, it is possible to maximize their development independently, so they can be expressed with superior proficiency in the game. Because these ideas came from adaptations of training methodologies from other more studied and well-developed sports, in which the physical dimension is key to the respective performance, this measure has taken on the coordination of the entire training process, namely of the decisions of what to do, the amount of what is done and the moment it should be done (Guilherme, 2004).

The tendency originated from Northern Europe also acknowledges the existence of the four dimensions in the game; however, it considers that there may exist a connection between them and that, in certain moments of the training session, they should be stimulated together. Although this conception also regards the physical dimension as coordinator and manager of the training process, it does not acknowledge it as abstract, assuming that it is entangled in soccer specificity. In other words, it considers the existence of a relation of proximity between the physical and the other dimensions that, in certain moments of the training session, should be stimulated through sport-specific drills. Another characteristic of this tendency is the importance given to individualized training. The reason for this lies in the distinct physiological demands that are required from the players, according to their specific positions. Because of these highlighted aspects, the supporters of this methodology award great relevance to the specific effort of the sport and to the assessments of physical fitness as a means to control and drive the entire training process, both at team and player levels (Guilherme, 2004).

As it can be seen, there are differences between these two conceptions. The first is more analytic, having the separation and management of training within the different dimensions as an important aspect. The second, although acknowledging the existence of distinct dimensions, identifies the dominance of the specificity that the different elements should display in relation to the sport. As such, it becomes important that these measures are also stimulated through specific drills. However, not undervaluing the others, the physical aspect takes on the process of coordination of training planning, periodization and management due to the reasons mentioned earlier.

The Latin American tendency, or Integrated Training, vindicates a training process manifested by the integration of these four aspects of the game. By this conception, they manifest themselves at the same time and by consequence, the training should take it into account. From this logic, the concept of specificity plays an important role. It is a qualifying concept of a relation between different variables (Gibson, 1979), that is the dimensions of the game, which represent the specific information from a certain context (in this case, soccer). Therefore, the dimensions are only considered specific if their informational and consequent involvement relations are able to predict each other (Beek et al., 2003). For these reasons, the supporters of this methodology believe that specific training simultaneously develop tactical, technical, physical and psychological skills. In case tactical dimension is to be focused on during training, the physical and technical elements are also demanded. Likewise, if greater focus on the physical dimension is required, the tactical and/or technical elements will also be needed. In other words, whichever aspect the training is concerned with, the others will also be requested (Guilherme, 2004).

This conception is based on different assumptions in relation to the previous ones. The specificity of the sport takes on an effective role and the entire training periodization, planning and management process evokes this ground.

As mentioned, the understanding of the soccer game and its training process goes through moments of certain dichotomy of opinions. On the one hand, there are people who attempt to perceive, analyse and intervene in the game by separately studying the different constituting parts: the different dimensions, the game, the player and the distinct moments/phases of play, among other aspects. On the other hand, there are those who understand the game in its complexity and do not conceive the possibility of its separation. Studying the game in its entirety or in parts, it is verified that the inherent complexity can never cease to exist, since the part influences the whole as the whole has implications for the part. The interactions must always be considered.

Through this perspective Vitor Frade created a conception called "tactical periodization", which intends to possess a logic of comprehension and operational intervention that differ from others. The name comes with a provocative nature, not negative, but with the purpose of effectively emancipating itself from other conceptions. To perceive the theoretical and operational assumptions of this methodology, an interpretation of reality is needed with ideas from the predecessor rather than with the ideas and concepts established in other designs and/or in the sport training theory.

The word "periodization" arises from the conclusion of the need for a certain length of time to build up something, in this case, a specific team culture of play that has to be "incorporated" (Maciel, 2011) by the team and the respective players. This idea of periodization is defined by the initial concept of dividing a sports cycle in three distinct stages: preparatory, competitive and transitory, and these stages in substages, with different goals, contents and training methods. The creation of a particular context, originated by the interactions of the different participants, is what allows the team to display an identity and generate its own specificity. From this point a unique identity is created and expressed by a particular style of play, which Vítor Frade calls tactics. Thus, tactics is not only the dimension related to the organizational aspect of the team and the players, but is also mainly a culture that is developed and that will enable the existence of a specific informational context that allows the "incorporation" of principles of play and their respective interaction, which manifest themselves by a *sui generis* form with a dynamic of spiralling development. As such, tactics will bring together the other dimensions, mutually influencing each other, and take on the roles of manager and coordinator of the entire process of training periodization, planning and management. The other dimensions do not play a secondary role; they are fundamental for the tactical one to express itself. The construction of tactics is conceived by respecting a conceptual framework and by fulfilling specific methodological principles.

The training conceptions presented here regard a sequence of different interpretations of the same reality. We do intend neither to judge them according to each other nor to highlight its fragilities or virtues. Throughout the years, all of them proved to be important for several achievements. However, we also acknowledge that some of them are a result of the evolution of others, whilst others are alternative proposals that may open horizons to new insights.

4.1.1 Fundamentals to Consider

As referred previously, there are conceptions with different perspectives about the same reality. In order to perceive the direction of ours, it is necessary to understand our point of view.

Literature is unanimous when considering that players' and teams' performance is associated with the interaction of cognitive, perceptual and motor skills (Garganta, 2006a; Tavares, Greco, & Garganta, 2006; Williams, 2000; Williams, Davids, & Williams, 1999; Williams & Hodges, 2005).

The analysis of these skills leads us to the studies that distinguish the quality of performance of players from opposite proficiency levels, that is between experts and novices (Anderson, 1987; Chase & Simon, 1973; Chi & Glaser, 1992; Eysenck & Keane, 1994; French & Thomas, 1987; McPherson & Thomas, 1989; Rezende & Valdés, 2003; Williams et al., 1999). The core ideas from these studies highlight that expert participants display certain characteristics that:

- they are quicker and more precise in recognizing patterns of play and detecting and locating relevant aspects that occur within their visual field;
- they are effective at anticipating teammates' and opponents' actions, relying on visual cues and specific game knowledge;
- they display superior knowledge regarding situations that are more likely to happen;
- they have the ability to distinguish significant from less relevant information, and are not distracted by the latter;
- they make efficient use of cognitive skills, usually as a result of the automation of core abilities;
- they adopt more suited decisions according to game events;
- they display a specific technical development, which in association with cognitive and perceptual skills, allow them to respond effectively and efficiently to the decisions made.

Briefly, it is possible to consider that experts display higher specific knowledge, which allows them to intervene in a more appropriate, effective and efficient way (Williams et al., 1999). The specific knowledge, among other constraints, is related to the interaction between declarative and procedural knowledge (Eysenck & Keane, 1994).

Declarative knowledge is defined as that which is possible to be expressed, declared or transmitted through verbalization (Cohen & Squire, 1980). It is associated with information, *facts*, concepts, existing specific knowledge and the cognitive processes that promote rationalization (Cohen & Squire, 1980; Ennis, Mueller, & Zhu, 1991; Eysenck & Keane, 1994).

In turn, procedural knowledge is linked with the accomplishment of actions. It is transmitted, essentially, through actions rather than words (Cohen & Squire, 1980), and related to the sensory memory—perceptual and procedural representation—that is to the implicit or procedural memory. It is not consciously expressed and it is related to the execution of an action to solve a certain situation. It is acquired through specific experiences (Cohen & Squire, 1980; Eysenck & Keane, 1994).

Although a distinction is established between these two kinds of knowledge, each with their own expression, there is, in practical terms, a permanent and concomitant relation between both as they interact, improving one another and generating specific knowledge. Thus, specific knowledge is related to the interaction between declarative and procedural knowledge, which are related to the ability to intervene in a given context (Allard, 1993). In other words, specific knowledge is related to the skills one displays when performing particular tasks within an equally particular context. In different circumstances, the interaction between declarative and procedural knowledge and the evidence of one over the other take particular shapes. Therefore, players from a same given sport also display distinct specific knowledge, as does a coach, and a player from a different sport. Further detailing, we can assume that the specific knowledge of a centre-back is different from that of a centre forward. These dissimilarities exist due to the contextual differences and, also, the distinct specific tasks they represent within these contexts (Guilherme, 2004).

Eysenck and Keane (1994) highlight that the role of knowledge for problem solving is critical and suggests that the problem solving methods may be categorized according to the amount and specificity of knowledge domain. They present four scenarios:

- the first occurs in situations of reduced specific knowledge, in which there is limited specific experience that might be useful. In this scenario, it is possible to find novices in a given context, in which the difficulties to solve problems are many due to the lack of declarative and procedural knowledge that allow one to intervene properly;
- the second occurs when the problem raised is familiar, but there are no specific plans for solving it. In this scenario, the players are undergoing a developmental stage of their specific knowledge, thus requiring the experience of multiple situations within the context of intervention;
- the third takes place when the problem raised is familiar and there are specific plans for solving it. Under these circumstances, participants have knowledge to solve the problem that may arise. In this scenario, it is possible to identify experts in a given domain;
- the last occurs when, faced with a certain problem, there are no specific or general plans for its respective solution. In this context, it follows that the problems are solved by analogy, that is previous experiences will be used and applied in order to solve the problem at hand. This scenario demands creative solutions, the ones displayed by experts who attain the highest level.

These four scenarios display, as proposed by the researchers, how different kinds of knowledge are related, created and developed.

Considering them, the importance of specific knowledge for excellent performances and for the quality of their respective cognitive, perceptual and motor skills is quite relevant. The question arises as to understand which characteristics of the training process better suit the development of such skills.

4.2 The Importance of Training Configuration for Playing

The purpose of training, regardless of the conception to which it is associated, is the search for qualitative and quantitative improvement of collective and individual performance. Therefore, the team's and players' training, preparation and development, takes on a significant preponderance. Consequently, there is unanimity in considering training as the structured and systematized process through which ideas, knowledge, skills and abilities are conveyed and developed so as to allow players to express themselves within the game (Bangsbo, 1998; Bompa, 1999; Garganta, 2002; Matvéyev, 1986; Tschiene, 2001).

Considering that experts differ from others due to the interaction between their cognitive and motor skills, that is their superior specific knowledge, we believe that the operational training process should be mainly concerned with presenting a configuration that allows, essentially, to promote their acquisition and development.

Considering that procedural learning is mainly acquired through experience, training needs to be a place in which players and teams experience the game in the multiple variations that may exist within the context of intervention. The intention is to highlight that, during training, one must design scenarios that reproduce the problems posed by the game, with the purpose of experiencing them and thus building up knowledge and, as consequence, specific cognitive, perceptual and motor skills. Within this perspective, the training, despite being a place for practising, is, mainly, a context for learning with the purpose of creating a repertoire of skills that allow players and teams to effectively and efficiently solve many and varied problems that arise during play and, in several circumstances, to be able to do so through analogies between the game and training experiences (Eysenck & Keane, 1994).

As referred by Garganta (1996), the essential problems of the soccer game evolve from the strategic plan, which emerges from the tactical dimension. Evoking the concept of tactics we have presented, a complex dimension, catalyst of a specific informational context, that is of a unique identity, we highlight the importance of driving the learning process with the purpose of guiding the way problems in the game should be solved. In this respect, the configuration of the training process should encompass characteristics that ensure that these procedures are addressed, that is enable the creation of specific model of play through its inherent complexity.

As mentioned in Chapter 3, the models are anticipated creations based on an interpretation of reality by those who create them (Le Moigne, 1990). Therefore, the creation of a specific model of play implies the organization of a body of knowledge one possesses about a given reality, which may also be called conception of play (Le Moigne, 1990).

In soccer, the model is dynamic, following the mutations that the interactions between the team and the players promote through the convergence of a more predictable dimension, induced by the rules and by the principles of play, with a less predictable one, embodied through the autonomy of players, who introduce the diversity and singularity of events.

Thus, understanding the soccer game and, consequently, training as a complex phenomenon, demands intervention tools that enable the comprehension and manipulation of this complexity without distorting or dismantling it. For this reason, we deem pertinent to resort to the notion of "fractal" in order to explain how we understand that the training process should be designed in order to create a Specific Model of Play.

A fractal is an invariant or regular part of a chaotic system that, due to its structure and functionality, is able to represent the whole, regardless of the scale in which it can be found (Mandelbrot, 1991; Stacey, 1995). Its properties allow, on the one hand, to identify the irregularity of a chaotic system and, on the other hand, to acknowledge the regularities or invariances of this irregularity. Another rather relevant characteristic of fractals is their being representative of the whole, that is a fractal always possesses a "genetic" constitution identical to the whole it represents or where it was observed. The structural and functional regularity presented throughout the different scales is another trait, called scale invariance, that describes them. It occurs because in chaotic systems with fractal organization there is a characteristic named internal homothety, that is the interactions between agents of this system, throughout different scales, have similar morphologies (Cunha & Silva, 1995; Mandelbrot, 1991; Stacey, 1995).

With the purpose of creating an analogy to better perceive the idea we are trying to convey, let us imagine a chocolate cake. Suppose the ingredients necessary to bake this cake are flour, sugar, yeast, eggs and chocolate. Depending on the quantity of the different ingredients, the particular way we mix them, the cooking temperature and time and several other variables that may be taken into account, the cake will have a specific shape and flavour according to numerous possibilities. The cake represents the whole, while a fractal is represented by a part of this cake, that is half of it, a big or small slice, or even a minuscule crumb. Any of these parts, named scales, whether they are big or small, represent this cake rather than another one, hence, are fractals of it. In the event of existing several chocolate cakes and their respective slices are mixed, they will always represent the specificities of their wholes, and their different specific characteristics can be identified. Through this analogy we aimed at highlighting that the fractals are not the ingredients, but the result of the specific interactions which these ingredients were subjected to. On the other hand, regardless of the size of the slice, that is the scale, a fractal has the property of representing the *sui generis* specificity of the whole, both in terms of texture and flavour.

We believe that the training process, both in conceptual and operational levels, should represent this characteristic of fractal organization. If that is the case, we will be sure that the concomitance of the desired interactions will be in constant creation and demand, which will support the quantitative and qualitative control of the entire process being generated within the inherent complexity of a soccer team (Guilherme, 2004).

The fractal organization of the training process emerges from the didactic and methodological necessity of fracturing the game and the training so as to more easily control and guide the intervention. As we have found, fracturing a whole, regardless of the scale, involves preserving the complexity of its essence and, also, analysing the part non-separately, but with all the connections it has with the whole.

The game and the respective training process that generates it, by didactic and pedagogical reasons, need to undergo interventions that take into account its whole and its parts. If there is still a concern in building up and analysing the game based on fractal organization, this will enable higher informational connectivity and reciprocity between the whole and its parts, between the parts themselves, and between the parts and the whole.

This perspective must be reflected transversely throughout the entire conceptual and operational processes of training. At the conceptual level, as mentioned, the coach's ideas of play and, consequently, the respective principles of play he/she expects the team to display during the different moments/phases are an assumption. At the operational level, the proposed drills and the respective sequence are the tools for the creation of the team's Specific Model of Play to be displayed.

4.3 Conceptual Level

The unpredictable and random nature of soccer generates a number of problems to the teams and their respective players, which can be overcome through distinct configurations. These different possible solutions are related to the ideas the coaches present to the teams, through principles of play, about how they want the team to act during the different moments/phases, which, in interaction, allow the emergence of the team's Specific Model of Play.

The principles of play mentioned here directly refer to the specific ones. The others (general, operational and core) covered in Chapter 2 are action rules that the different teams and players must evidence so that their game displays some organization, and should be transversal with respect to all teams. The specific principles now presented are patterns of tactical action, specific intentionalities and regularities that the team and the players should display, that is distinguished means to solve the problems posed by the game during the different moments/phases of play and in the various scales[1] of expression. When incorporated by the teams and players, they give them identity, working as fingerprints and bringing out a unique personality.

These specific principles should show some particular characteristics. A first aspect to take into account is that they should be considered as the start of a proposal of a pattern of intentionalities rather than an end in itself, taking on a rigid morphology. This feature is important because each player has a history of experiences that allow them to possess their own skills, characteristics and knowledge about the game. So, when a principle is presented to a player, he/she will interpret it according to his/her own experiences, which are not necessarily similar to those of his/her colleagues or to those of the coach who proposed it. Therefore, the individual interpretations of the same principle by the different players, when in interaction, will enable the emergence of a principle with *sui generis* features. To better express this idea, let us resort to the analogy of the colours, mentioned previously. For this, suppose that a principle presented by the coach to the team is represented by the colour blue. The interpretation of this idea by the different players will depend on the particular relations each one had with the colour blue, thus allowing to acknowledge as many shades as the number of players. When players interact, such as in a palette, the shades are mixed, and the final product is a new one; yet, it will always represent the colour blue. With respect to the principles, the same holds true. The various interpretations of the principle, when in interaction, will enable the emergence of an identifiable principle—blue—but with its very own characteristics—shade.

A second characteristic to be considered is the adaptable nature that the specific principles must display. As we found, the principles are proposed by the coach and the interaction between the different interpretations by the players will allow it to be expressed in a certain way. However, through the training process there are dialectical relations between the principle and the interpretations by the players that influence each other mutually, thus enabling the former to have individual and collective interpretations previously inexistent, that is there is a spiralling development distinguished for its reciprocal influence and non-linear dynamics. Therefore, adaptability allows for the collective and individual evolution to be always present and the players' characteristics and creativity to always be involved in the development of principles.

The characteristics mentioned point to the fact that the principles are expressed in two distinct, yet intersecting, levels: the collective or macro and the individual or micro. The first provides the team with predictability and identity; it is the colour blue. The second makes the predictability of the game unpredictable; they are the shades of blue. This relation allows the teams the ability to deal with the problems posed by the opponents, both in organized and creative ways, thus always preserving their identity and maximizing the possibilities for response of each player.

Despite being quite relevant, the characteristics presented lose some consistency in the case the principles are not expressed as fractals of the team's game. The intention is to highlight the importance of the relation of interaction and representativeness reciprocity that the different principles must have with one another, whether they are from the same or different moments/phases of play, that is a team's game is expressed through the respective specific principles. In a given moment/phase of play a principle might be more evidenced than others, however, the contextual information generated by the interactions between them will allow the ones that are not directly on demand to also be represented, that is the specific principles of play of a team must show a fractal organization so that the harmony and fluidity of the team's style of play are more evident and consistent.

For further elucidation on this subject let us examine this example: during defensive organization we intend to have as principle the team closing spaces both in width and length, thus creating a solid block with the intention of taking time and space from the opponent, consequently recovering possession. In turn, during offensive organization we expect the team to have as principle the circulation of the ball among players with the purpose of finding or creating spaces in the opponents' defensive structure in order to score a goal. When we are in training and operationalizing these principles through drills, they will interact permanently, and the way in which each of them appears is related to the informational reciprocity that one has over the other. Therefore, during defensive organization, we are being influenced by the way we are going to attack and, in turn, during offensive organization, we are also being influenced by the way we are going to defend. These interactions should be permanently taken into account and explored; however, they should never cease to express fractal characteristics.

Following what we have said, the different moments/phases of play should also display a fractal organization. This characteristic should occur at two distinct levels: the interrelation of the different moments/phases of play and the organization of the breakdown of the principles of each moment/phase.

With respect to the interrelation between the different moments/phases, those must enable, in all circumstances, the identification of the singularity of the whole. Therefore, regardless of the moments/phases and the scale in which they might express themselves, they should display the invariance that describes these moments/phases, their interactions and be representative of the team's style of play. The example previously presented about the principles illustrates what we have just referred.

In relation to the organization of the decomposition of the principles of each moment/phase, the same fractal characteristic is also a factor of particular importance. A principle of play from a given moment/phase is supported by a number of interrelated sub-principles. These are patterns of intentionalities of lower complexity that embody the principle when in interaction. Regardless of the complexity these principles might display, they should always assume a fractal organization, since it is the characteristic that will allow the sub-principle that one is focusing on to have positive effects on its supporting principle and on the others that comprise the whole envisaged by the Specific Model of Play.

Let us consider the following example: during defence/attack transition we intend to have as principle that, after the team has regained the ball, it should be taken out of the pressure zone, avoiding that the player and, consequently, the team, loses it again, so as to: (a) give depth and then counter attack, taking advantage of the opponent's defensive disorganization or (b) start the offensive process if the opponent is defensively organized. For this principle to be feasible, there are some sub-principles that should also be taken into account, such as: (i) change from a defensive to an offensive attitude; (ii) take the ball away from the pressure zone to an area in which the opponent cannot keep pressing and (iii) expand the team in terms of width and length, among others. The fractal organization, that should underpin any of such sub-principles, must allow, regardless of the one being demanded, the others to be represented as well. It is the interaction of these intentionalities that grants the Specific Model of Play to emerge and, as a result of these assumptions, the players to decide according to the collective and strategic plan.

For these reasons it is said that the specific principles of play from a team should display two kinds of fractal organization: a transversal one and another in-depth. The transversal fractal organization is related with the interrelation of the different moments/phases. The in-depth fractal organization regards the breakdown of principles' complexity from the same moment/phase into sub-principles (Guilherme, 2004).

The interactions of the assumptions mentioned project the conceptual level; however, there is the need to edify them in a way that the expression of the Specific Model of Play is an evidence. This construction is achieved through the operational plan that is materialized, essentially, by the dynamical presentation of the drills proposed by the coach, as well as by his/her intervention.

4.4 Operational Level

The drills are unanimously acknowledged as the main means through which the operationalization of teaching and training is promoted (Castelo, 2002; Matvéyev, 1986; Mesquita, 1998; Oliveira, 1993; Queiroz, 1986; Teodorescu, 1984). Regardless of the importance that has been attributed to their purposes, contents, functions, characteristics, implications and organization, there are two characteristics that, when in interaction, according to our perspective, are the foundations of all the others—the singularity of the process and the fractal organization.

The singularity of the process is linked with the idea that all drills created and proposed should be in complete harmony with the informational context the team generated and that is managed with its specificity. As we have mentioned, the specificity is a characteristic associated with a number of interacting variables that generate an informational context that allows them to predict themselves (Beek et al., 2003; Gibson, 1979; Laughlin, 2008), creating concomitant and dynamic relations of complicity that enable the emergence of a Specific Model of Play.

For these reasons, the drills proposed should always be specific, with the purpose of creating adaptations and, consequently, the specific knowledge and the necessary skills so that the different players may express themselves supported, as a team, by the principles of the Specific Model of Play.

According to what was mentioned, a drill at a given moment might be entirely suitable for a team, as it systematically demands behaviours that the respective model encompasses, thus generating specific and knowledge adaptations to the team and the players. On the other hand, if a drill repeatedly stimulates behaviours that do not fit the model, the adaptations generated will prove harmful to the development of the intended specific knowledge, both for the team and the players.

As an example, let us imagine that one of the defensive principles of a team is zone defence, whereas one of the offensive principles regards the circulation of the ball among the different players with the purpose of generating and taking advantage of spaces in the opponent's defensive structure. With the main goal of developing the offensive principle, the coach proposes a 7X7 drill, each team including a goalkeeper and six outfield players in a limited area. The coach instructs the team in possession to circulate the ball among all players and across the entire area with the purpose of finding or generating space to score. On the other hand, he/she advises the players of the defending team to hamper, as much as possible, the opponents' action, marking them man-to-man.

Despite the main purpose being the fulfilment of the offensive principles, in the event the defensive instructions are accomplished, the behaviours performed by the team and the players diverge from the purposes of the defensive principle established. Therefore, during the course of the drill, inappropriate adaptations and knowledge are being generated, hindering the improvement of the quality of the team and, consequently, the players. Hence, the proposed drill is not specific to the team, since it is forcing players to perform actions that were not intended by the principles of the Model of Play (Figure 4.1).

The example presented aims at clarifying the importance of the relation of the drills with the Model of Play and its respective specificity. However, it is also worth mentioning that the specificity is a dynamic concept and what is deemed specific today for the team may not be so after a few weeks. Let us focus on the principles of the previous example. The purpose of the coach is still the development of the offensive principle presented. To carry it out, the coach proposes the

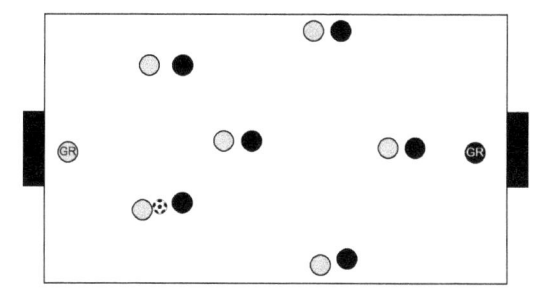

Figure 4.1 (Gk+ 6) versus (6+Gk) drill with man-to-man marking
Source: The authors

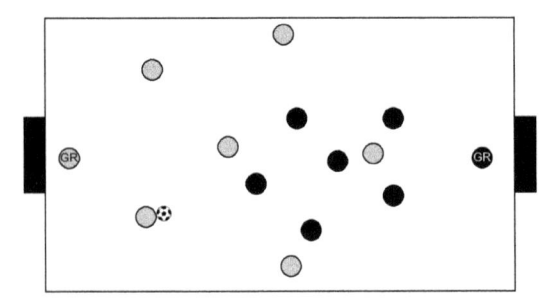

Figure 4.2 (Gk+ 6) versus (6+Gk) drill with zone defence organization
Source: The authors

same drill, a 7X7 game. In offensive terms, it demands that players display the same purposes; however, defensively, he/she instructs the players to perform zone defence (Figure 4.2).

As the drill progresses, the coach notices that none of the teams are able to achieve the intended purposes. There are constant losses of possession, players are not able to perform a passing sequence without losing possession, cannot create spaces, that is the intended purposes to develop the proposed principle are not being reached. These problems mean that the drill proposed is not specific for developing the principle the coach intends to, and there is the need of an alternative drill that allows the evolution of what is proposed. Therefore, the coach presents a 4X4 drill with two extra players who always play for the team in possession so that this team always has numerical superiority of 6X4 (Figure 4.3). By observing the drill, the coach notes that the intended purposes are beginning to be achieved and that there is learning on the part of the team and the players with respect to the principle presented, which means that this drill is specific for what is intended. However, with the course of time and the evident evolution displayed by the players, the drill becomes too simple, thus losing its potential to develop the proposed principle, and is no longer specific, since it does not generate positive adaptations for the evolution of the team and the players anymore. The next step includes the search for a new specific drill.

Another aspect to be taken into account in the creation of drills that aim to be a fractal of the style intended is its structural and functional configuration (Guilherme, 2004). Let us imagine the previously presented offensive principle of circulation of the ball in the entire width and length, with the purpose of creating spaces in the opponent's defensive structure. One of the important sub-principles for this principle to be contemplated is the positioning among the different players of the team. We advocate that the players should run, as often as possible, diagonally between themselves (Figure 4.4).

This positioning favours passing both for maintaining possession and progressing with the ball. If the players are positioned on the same line, in depth, the pass has low probabilities of success, due to the eventual intervention by the opponents,

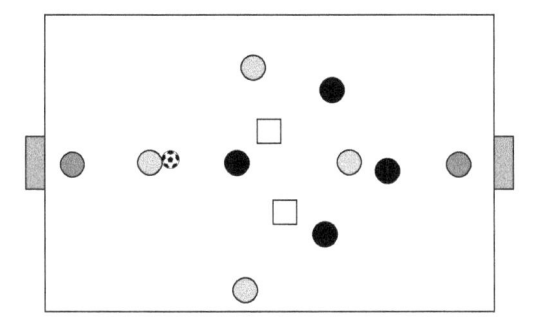

Figure 4.3 (Gk+ 4) versus (2+Gk) drill + 2 floaters
Source: The authors

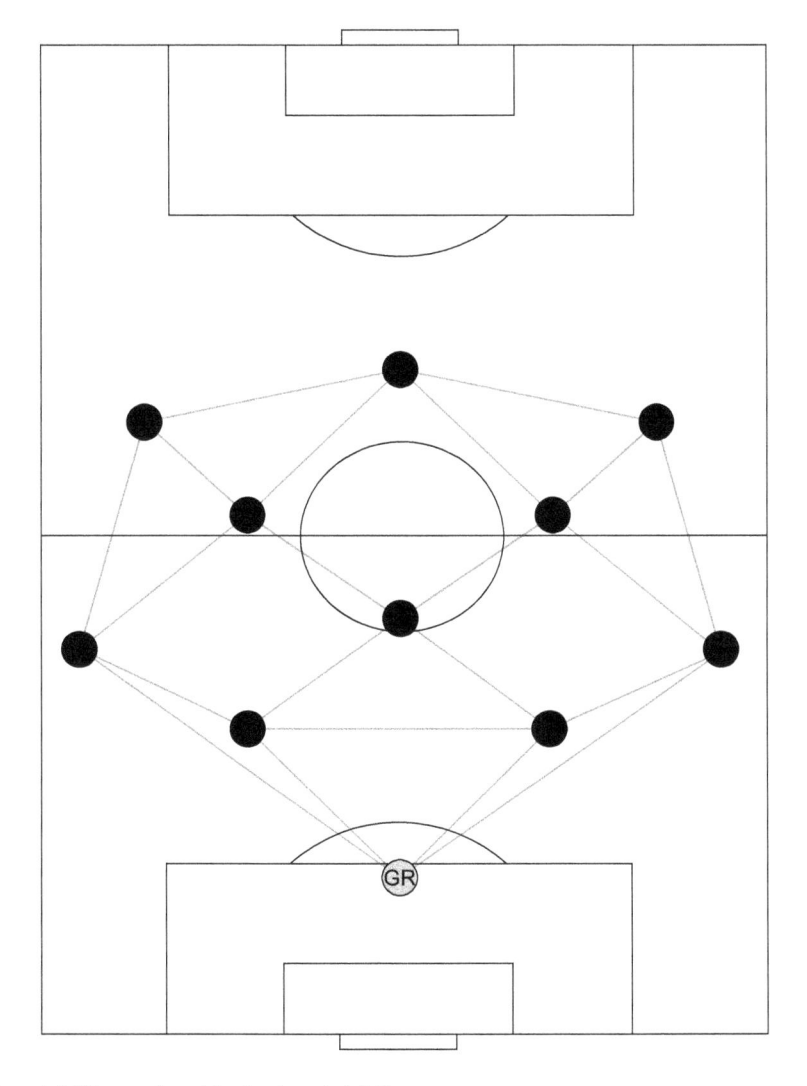

Figure 4.4 Diagonal positioning in a 1-4-3-3 structure
Source: The authors

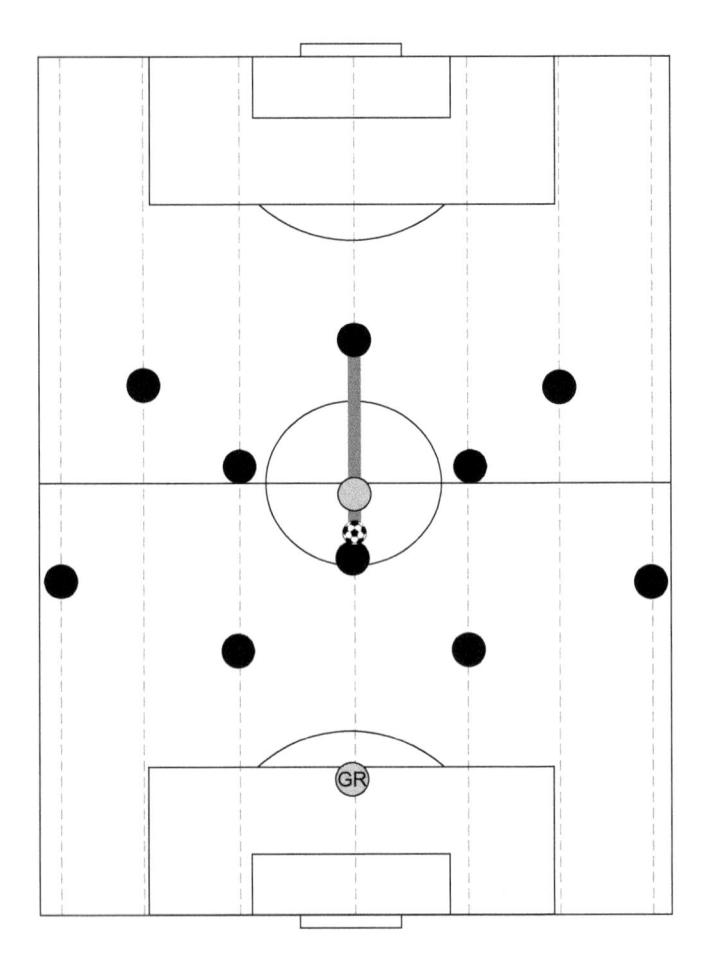

Figure 4.5 Lines in depth in a 1-4-3-3 structure
Source: The authors

who, usually, are positioned between the ball and the goal (Figure 4.5). However, if players are positioned on the same line in width, the possibility of interception is great, and a disadvantage for the respective team, since both intervenient players are immediately overcome, generating a clear positional disadvantage (Figure 4.6).

For these reasons we advocate that players' positioning in diagonal lines, adjustable to the dynamics of game situations, is a vital and facilitating condition of the collective and individual offensive organization. Therefore, if we intend to develop the coordination of ball circulation between the three midfield players and the centre forward, we may create a 4X4 possession drill with two side floaters, with the purpose of scoring in both goals positioned at the bottom line. If the configuration of the drill follows the structure displayed in Figure 4.7, such as intended for the game, the generated adaptations will

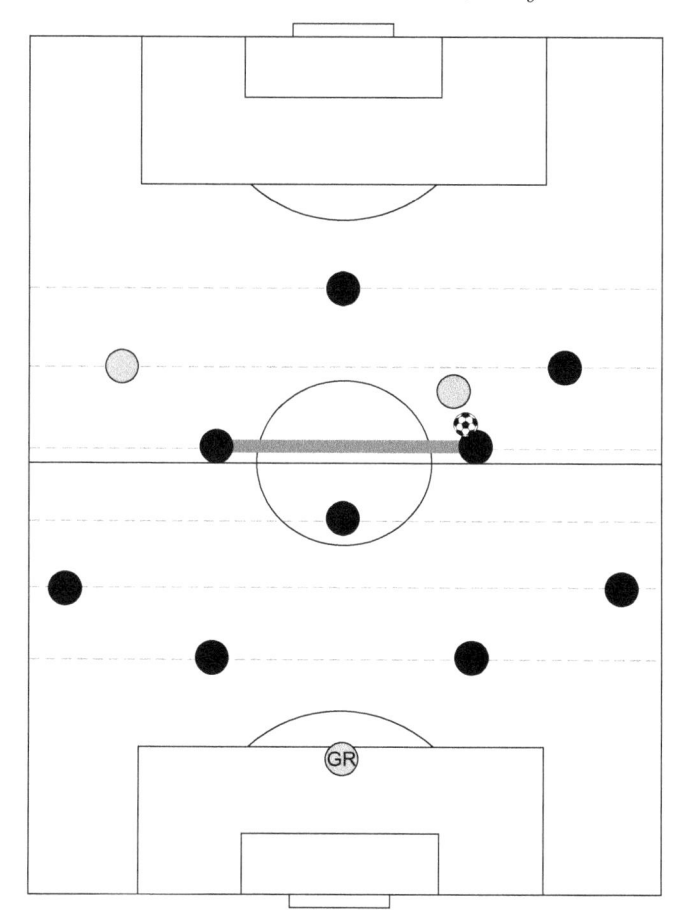

Figure 4.6 Lines in width in a 1-4-3-3 structure
Source: The authors

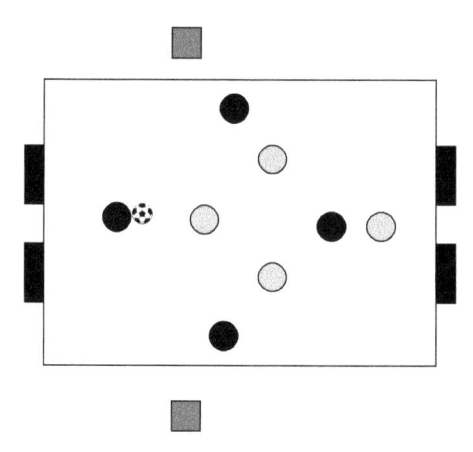

Figure 4.7 (Gk+4) versus (4+Gk) drill + 2 side floaters in a diamond shape

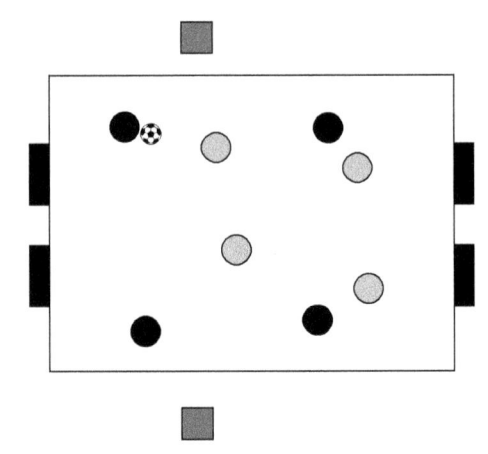

Figure 4.8 (Gk+4) versus (4+Gk) drill + 2 side floaters in a square shape
Source: The authors

address what was intended for the principle. However, if the players' arrangement is different at first, for example in a square shape (Figure 4.8), there will be many moments in which the relations between players will face different interactions from those intended for the envisaged principle, thus hindering the intended adaptations.

These examples attempt to clarify the importance of the relation between the drills and the specificity of the Model of Play, and the respective dynamics which they are subject to. However, sometimes drills entirely suit the intended principles, yet, due to inadequate or no intervention from the coach, they may become inappropriate, that is not specific. Consider the following scenario: one of the team's offensive sub-principles is to start play building up from the goalkeeper or the defensive block. The drill proposed to develop it is a game, in an area divided into two parts, between two teams made up of one goalkeeper, four defenders and three forwards each, and both teams will be supported by three midfielders who will play for the team in possession (Figure 4.9). The purpose of the drill is, after the goalkeeper plays the ball to one of the defenders or these defenders regain possession, the team in possession should coordinate their actions so that the players are able to pass the ball to one of the three midfielders who, after having received the ball, passes it to the offensive half, thus generating 6X4 situations. When the defending team regains possession, they should follow the same procedures. The goalkeeper and the four defenders coordinate their actions so as to overcome the three opposing forwards and throw the ball towards the midfielders who will pass it to the opposing half.

The dynamics of this drill aims at stimulating the relation between the different players so as to create action patterns suitable to the one intended by the coach

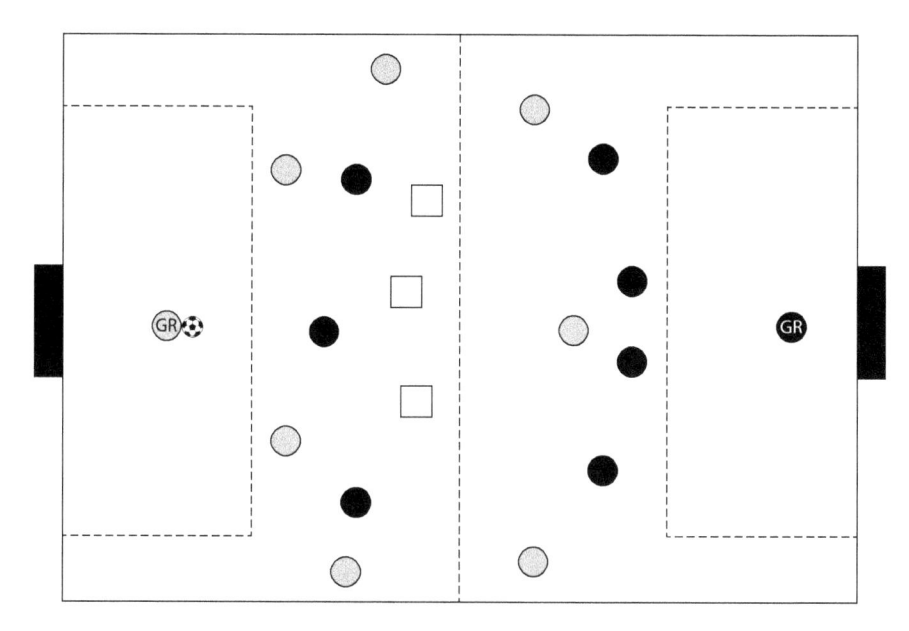

Figure 4.9 Example proposed to demonstrate the importance of coach's intervention in the drill
Source: The authors

through the mentioned offensive sub-principle. However, the drill is only potentially appropriate. The coach's intervention is what will enable the drill to be, or not, specific. Consider the situation: the goalkeeper puts the ball into play by passing it to one of the defenders, who, pressed by an opposing forward, inadvertently kicks the ball forward, without trying to play with his/her teammates, defenders and midfielders, who immediately provided him/her with passing lanes/zones. Given this situation, if the coach does not possess a pedagogical intervention of correcting the decision made and the action performed, he/she is not going to encourage specificity, thus allowing the incidence of attitudes that contradict the team's Specific Model of Play and that, when repeated regularly, will become harmful habits in relation to the intended principles. On the other hand, if the drill allows to encourage the intended principles and if the coach's intervention is a catalyst of these patterns of intentionalities, the adaptations created are much more relevant for achieving the intended purposes.

These assumptions highlight the idea that the drills may be potentially specific; yet, the way they are operationalized through the coach's intervention is what will allow them to reach the highest level so that the principles of the Specific Model of Play may be understood.

The fractal organization of the drill emerges from the fractal logic which the building up of the process should be subjected to. Regardless of what one intends to teach or train through a drill, and regardless of the scale, whether it is a principle or sub-principle of the Model of Play, the drills created and proposed to the team should consider the singularity of the whole so that the internal homothety is always in evidence. If that does not occur, the suggested drill may generate harmful adaptations for the interaction between the different players, for the creation and development of the intended specific knowledge and, consequently, for the build-up of the Specific Model of Play.

With these ideas we intend to highlight that the drills proposed by the coach to the team, when operationalized, should be expressed as fractals of the idealized game, regardless of the scale in which they are presented.

4.5 Practical Examples

In order to better elucidate the ideas that we have been presenting, in the following pages we intend to create a hypothetical scenario in which we expose some principles and sub-principles from the different phases/moments and some drills that may be important for developing them. The drills and the principles and sub-principles suggested to hold a fractal organization to facilitate the understanding of this content.

4.5.1 Offensive Organization

During offensive organization we intend that the team respect the principle of circulating the ball between the players with the purpose of finding or creating spaces in the opposite defensive structure and, consequently, exploiting them to score a goal. So that this principle can be contemplated, there are some sub-principles that should also be considered, such as (i) expansion of the team, both in width and length; (ii) variability of circulation both in width and length; (iii) players' mobility without the ball in order to find or create spaces; (iv) dynamics of circulation with different paces and (v) variability of passing: short and long.

DRILL 1

DESCRIPTION AND ORGANIZATION OF THE DRILL

3X3 drill + 2 floaters; in each half of the field there must be only two players from each team. The aim is that the team in possession, through players' mobility, coordinates the actions so as to successfully pass the ball to the floater on the opposite side. Whenever the purpose is achieved, the same team maintains possession, but must change the direction of play, hence attempting to pass the ball to the opposite side.

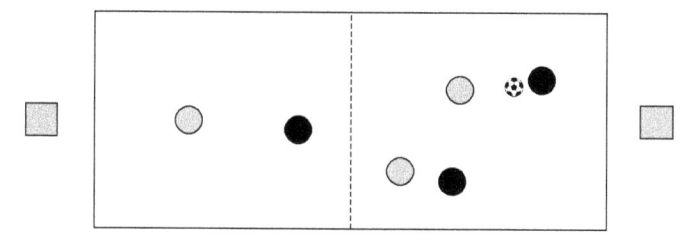

PRINCIPLES AND SUB-PRINCIPLES INVOLVED

Scale: group

- Players positioned in depth.
- Variability of circulation, both in width and length.
- Mobility of players without possession in order to find or create spaces.

DRILL 2

DESCRIPTION AND ORGANIZATION OF THE DRILL

2X2 drill + 4 (2 side and 2 in depth) floaters. The purpose is that the team in possession, through players' mobility, coordinates actions so as to successfully pass the ball to the in-depth floater on the opposite side, being allowed to use the side floaters. Whenever the purpose is achieved, the same team maintains possession, but must change the direction of play, hence attempting to pass the ball to the opposite side.

PRINCIPLES AND SUB-PRINCIPLES INVOLVED

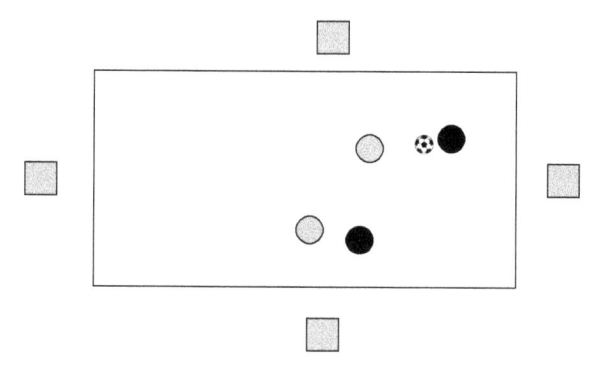

Scale: group

- Mobility of players without possession in order to find or create spaces.
- Variability of circulation, both in width and length.

110 *Improving Quality Play*

DRILL 3

DESCRIPTION AND ORGANIZATION OF THE DRILL

(GK+4) versus (4+GK) drill + 6 (two side and four in-depth) floaters. The aim is that the team in possession, through players' mobility and with the support of floaters, creates permanent spaces to shoot.
Principles and Sub-Principles Involved

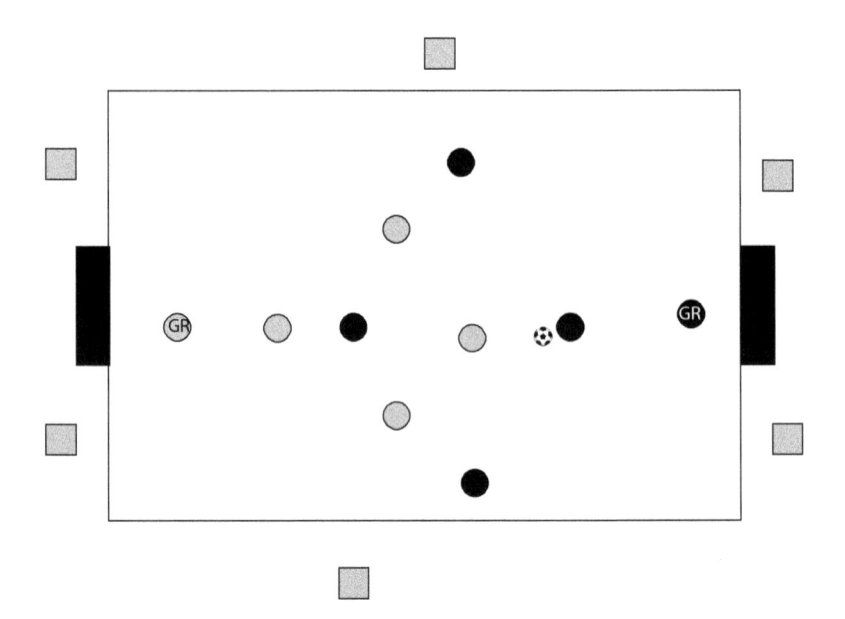

Scale: sectorial

- Mobility of players without possession in order to find or create spaces.
- Variability of circulation, both in width and length.
- Circulation dynamics with different paces.
- Shooting attempts at suitable moments.

DRILL 4

DESCRIPTION AND ORGANIZATION OF THE DRILL

(GK+8) versus (8+GK) drill. The playing field is divided into five areas. In the first area, there must be a goalkeeper and one defender; in the second area, two defenders; in the third, two midfielders; in the fourth, two forwards and in the fifth, one forward. The intention is that the team in possession, through players' action and mobility, should pass the ball from their rearmost area up to the opposite goal area, with the purpose of scoring. The drill has the particularity of the team in possession being allowed to have an extra player inside the area in which the ball is being played, a player who goes one area up or down. As such, the team in possession has permanent numerical advantage.

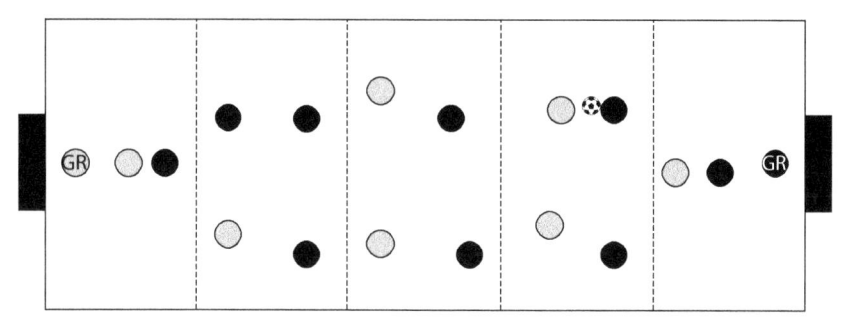

PRINCIPLES AND SUB-PRINCIPLES INVOLVED

Scale: sectorial e intersectorial

- Mobility of players without possession in order to find or create spaces.
- Players positioned in depth.
- Circulation dynamics with different paces.

DRILL 5

DESCRIPTION AND ORGANIZATION OF THE DRILL

(GK+6) versus (6+GK) drill + two floaters. The playing field is divided into two areas: defensive and offensive. In the first area, there should be a goalkeeper and three defenders; in the second, three forwards. Both floaters—always for the team in possession—take on the position of midfielders and may play in both areas. The game starts in the defensive midfield of one of the teams, as the ball is in possession of the goalkeeper and his/her purpose is to play it to the defenders, while they jointly coordinate their actions to create spaces to score. Whenever defenders regain possession the teams exchange tasks, and, with the floaters' support attempt to pass the ball to the offensive half, whereas the three opposite forwards attempt to block them.

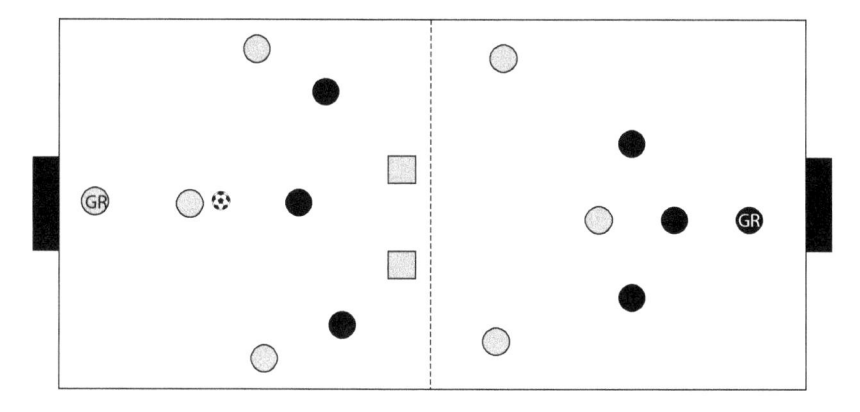

PRINCIPLES AND SUB-PRINCIPLES INVOLVED

Scale: intersectorial

- Players positioned in width.
- Restart plays with short build-ups.
- Mobility of players without possession in order to find or create spaces.
- Circulation dynamics with different paces.

DRILL 6

DESCRIPTION AND ORGANIZATION OF THE DRILL

(GK+10) versus (10+GK) drill. The playing field is divided into five areas. In the first area, there should be a goalkeeper and one defender; in the second, three defenders; in the third, three midfielders; in the fourth, three forwards and in the fifth area, there should be only one player of the team who protects this goal. The proposal is that the team in possession, through players' action and mobility, should pass the ball from its rearmost area up to the opposite goal with the purpose of scoring. The drill has the particularity of the team in possession being allowed to have an extra player in the area in which the ball is being played, a player who goes an area up or down. As such, the team in possession has permanent numerical advantage. Three forwards are allowed to go inside the fifth area; however, no defender can join in.

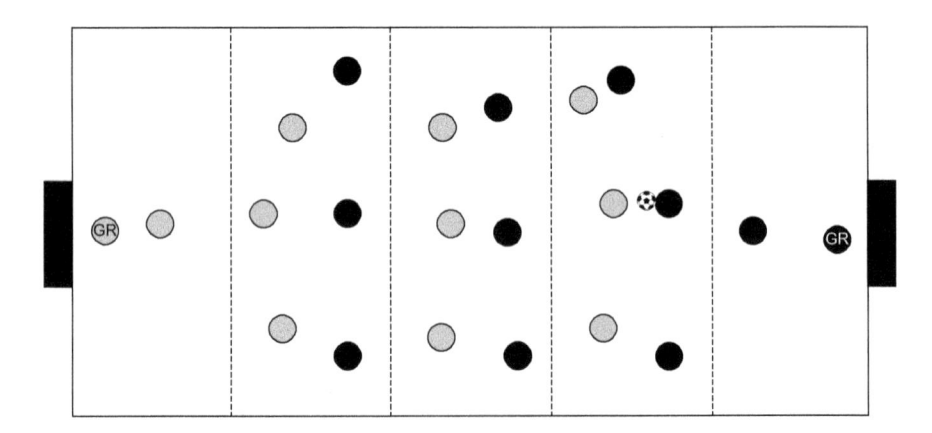

PRINCIPLES AND SUB-PRINCIPLES INVOLVED

Scale: sectorial, intersectorial and collective

- Mobility of players without possession in order to find or create spaces.
- Players positioned in depth.

- Circulation dynamics with different paces.
- Speed of coordination and conclusion of the offensive action with an attempt on goal

DRILL 7

DESCRIPTION AND ORGANIZATION OF THE DRILL

(GK+10) versus (10+GK) drill. The playing field is divided into two parts. In the defensive half, teams have one goalkeeper, three defenders and one midfielder. In the offensive half, teams have three midfielders and three forwards. The intention is that the team in possession, in their offensive midfield, coordinate players' actions with the purpose of creating spaces to go into the opponent's defensive structure and score. In turn, the defending team attempts to gain possession and, after doing so, to pass the ball to the midfielders and forwards located at the offensive half.

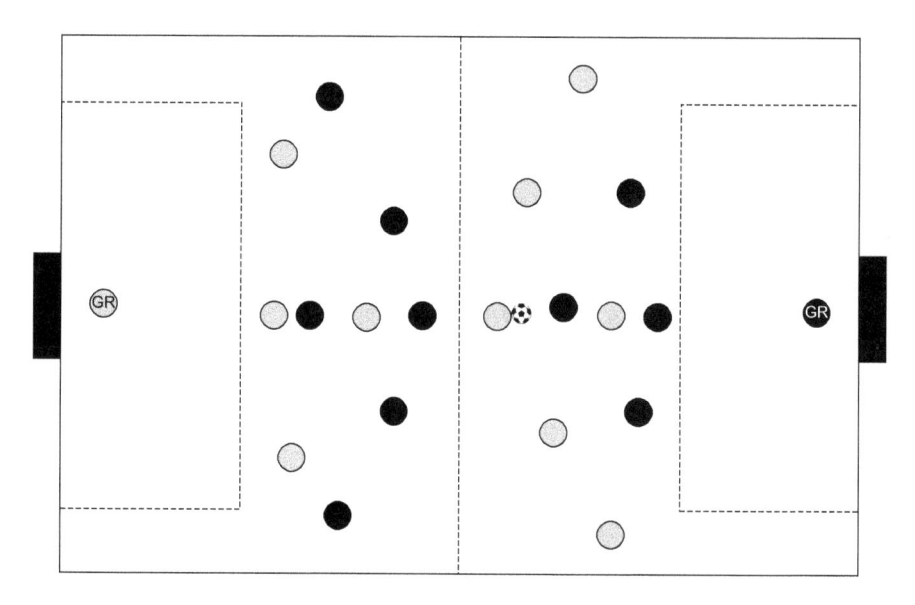

PRINCIPLES AND SUB-PRINCIPLES INVOLVED

Scale: sectorial and intersectorial

- Players positioned in width.
- Variability of circulation, both in width and length.
- Circulation dynamics with different paces.
- Mobility of players without possession in order to find or create spaces.
- Variability of passing: short and long.

DRILL 8

DESCRIPTION AND ORGANIZATION OF THE DRILL

(GK+7) versus (7+GK) drill + two floaters, with the purpose of permanently playing (GK+9) versus (7+GK). Each team is made up of one goalkeeper, three defenders, one midfielder and three forwards. The two floaters play as offensive midfielders. The proposal is that the team in numerical superiority should coordinate players' actions so as to create spaces to go into the opponent's defensive structure and score.

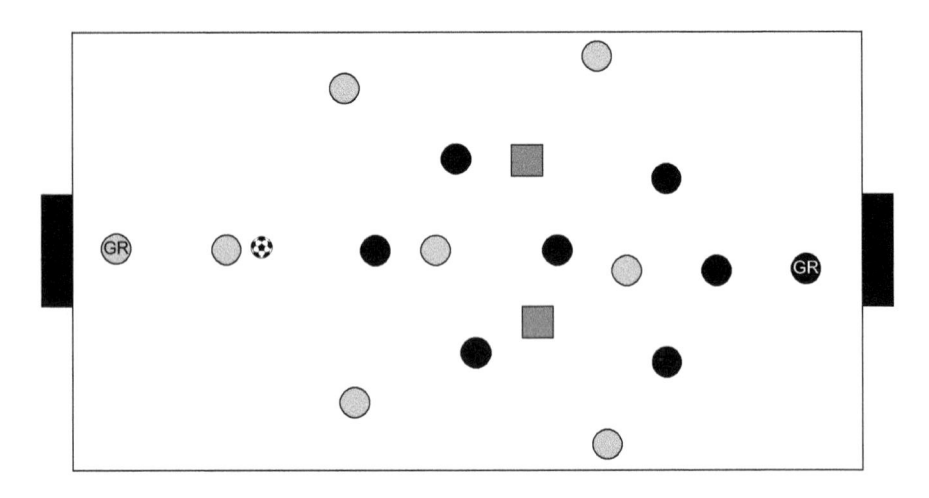

PRINCIPLES AND SUB-PRINCIPLES INVOLVED

Scale: collective

- Players positioned in width and depth.
- Variability of circulation, both in width and length.
- Mobility of players without possession in order to find or create spaces.
- Circulation dynamics with different paces.
- Variability of passing: short and long.

DRILL 9

DESCRIPTION AND ORGANIZATION OF THE DRILL

(GK+10) versus (8+GK) drill. The intention is that the team in numerical superiority coordinate players' actions so as to create spaces to go into the opponent's defensive structure and score.

PRINCIPLES AND SUB-PRINCIPLES INVOLVED

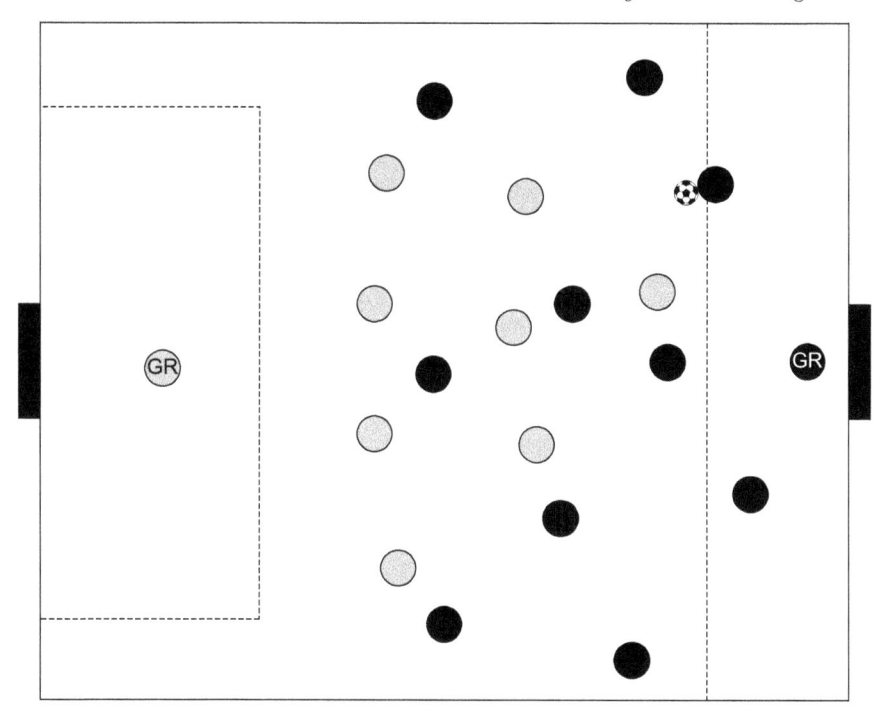

Scale: collective

- Players positioned in width and depth.
- Variability of circulation, both in width and length.
- Mobility of players without possession in order to find or create spaces.
- Circulation dynamics with different paces.
- Variability of passing: short and long.

4.5.2 Defensive Organization

During defensive organization, we intend that the team follows the principle of zone "pressing" defence with the purpose of reducing opponents' space and time, thus inducing error and regaining possession. So that this principle can be contemplated, there are some sub-principles that should also be considered, such as: (i) compressing the team, both in width and length, creating a block; (ii) driving the opponent towards pressure zones and (iii) pressing to induce error and regain possession.

DRILL 1

DESCRIPTION AND ORGANIZATION OF THE DRILL

1X1 drill + two floaters. The player in possession of the ball attempts to beat the defender and score in one of the two goals that the opponent has to protect and is supported by two side floaters to maintain possession. The defender presses the attacker, reducing space and time to decide and execute, thus blocking his/her progression.

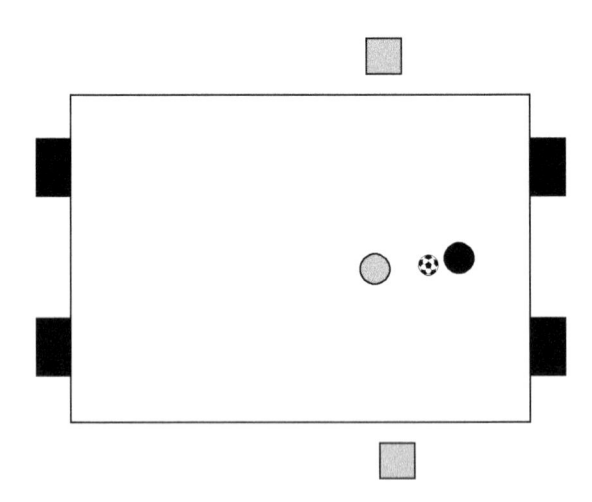

PRINCIPLES AND SUB-PRINCIPLES INVOLVED

Scale: individual

- Drive the opponent towards zones that are far from the goal.
- Individual pressing to reduce space and time so as to induce error and gain possession.

DRILL 2

DESCRIPTION AND ORGANIZATION OF THE DRILL

4X4 drill + two floaters. The team in possession attempts to score in the two goals the opponent has to protect. The defending team coordinates their actions so as to block spaces and press the opponent with the purpose of gaining possession.

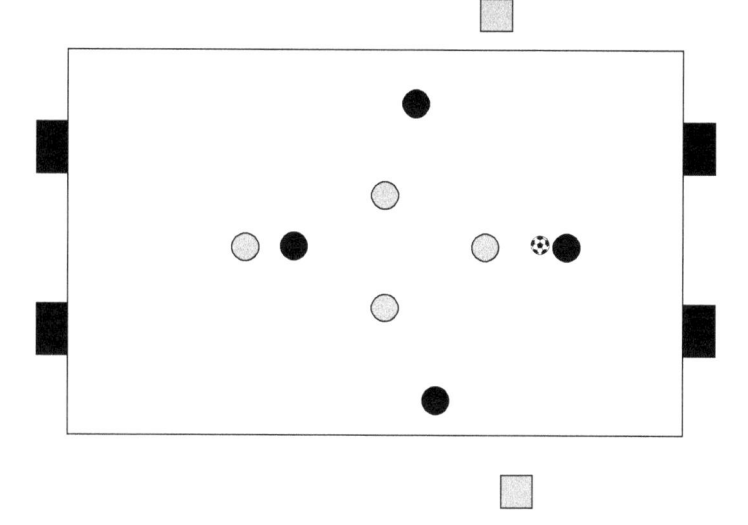

PRINCIPLES AND SUB-PRINCIPLES INVOLVED

Scale: group or sectorial

- Compressing the team both in width and length.
- Driving the opponent towards zones that are far from the goal.
- Group pressing to reduce space and time so as to induce error and gain possession.

DRILL 3

Description and Organization of the Drill

6X6 drill. The team in possession attempts to score in one of the two opposite goals. The defending team coordinates their actions so as to block spaces and press the opponent with the purpose of gaining possession.

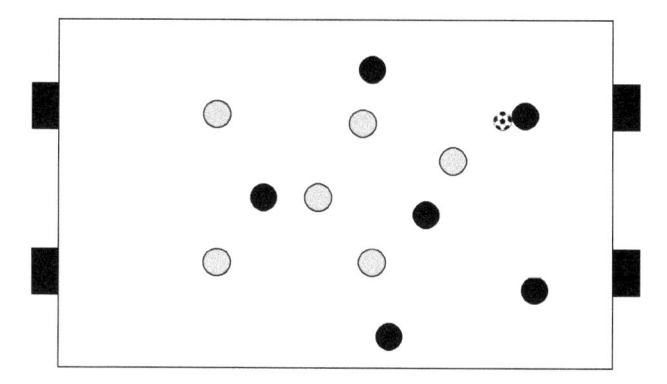

PRINCIPLES AND SUB-PRINCIPLES INVOLVED

Scale: sectorial

- Compressing the team both in width and length.
- Driving the opponent towards zones that are far from the goals.
- Sectorial pressing to reduce space and time so as to induce error and gain possession.

DRILL 4

DESCRIPTION AND ORGANIZATION OF THE DRILL

(GK+7) versus (8+GK) drill. The team with eight players is made up of one goalkeeper, four defenders and three forwards. The team with nine players includes one goalkeeper, two defenders, three midfielders and three forwards. The field is divided into two different playing areas: area one, in which are located the four defenders and a goalkeeper from the team with eight players, as well as the three midfielders and three forwards from the team with nine players; and area two, where the three forwards from the first team and the two defenders from the second area. As it is a drill that intends to encourage defensive organization within the defensive area, the game starts in area one and with the midfielders—from the team with nine players—in possession of the ball. The purpose of the team in possession is to coordinate their actions so as to create spaces to score. In turn, the purpose of the four defenders from the defensive area is to organize their actions so as to prevent opponents to shoot, and, whenever they regain possession, they should pass the ball to area two, in which the three forwards attempt to score. After the ball is passed to area two, one of the side backs can move up to this area with the purpose of supporting the forwards. Likewise, one of the midfielders from the opposite team can move down to help the two defenders. Whenever there is a shot or the defenders gain possession, the midfielder can stay in that area to support defenders passing the ball to area one, whereas the side back from the opposite team must necessarily move down to area one.

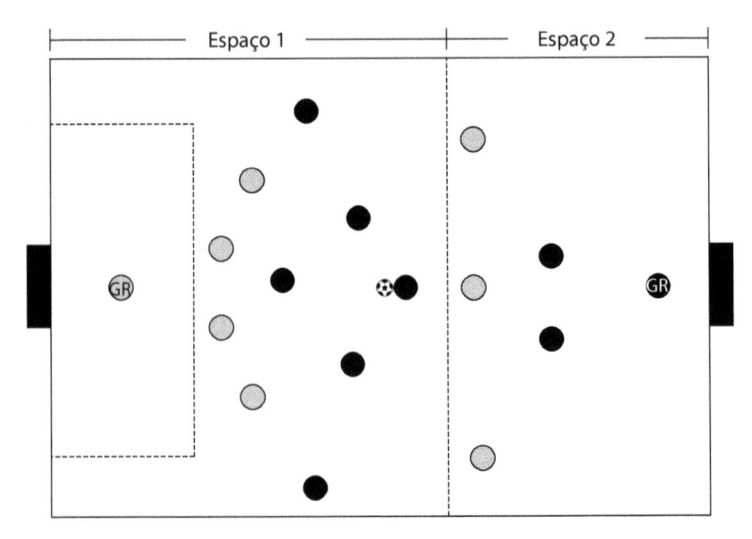

PRINCIPLES AND SUB-PRINCIPLES INVOLVED

Scale: sectorial (defence)

- Coordination of actions of pressing and coverage.
- Compression of the defensive block in width.
- Coordination of up and down movements of the defensive block.
- Individual and sectorial pressing to reduce space and time so as to induce error and gain possession.

DRILL 5

DESCRIPTION AND ORGANIZATION OF THE DRILL

(GK+7) versus (7+GK) drill. The team in possession is allowed to score in the goal protected by the opposite goalkeeper or in the three goals positioned at the centre of the field, by going inside them with the ball under control or by passing it through them to a teammate who must maintain possession towards the attack, rather than towards the defence. It is not allowed to score two consecutive goals in the same goal. Whenever a player scores in a goal positioned at the centre of the field, the game resumes as usual. The intention of placing the goals at the centre of the field is to force the defending team to move up the field as an intermediate or high block. For this game, the offside rule must apply.

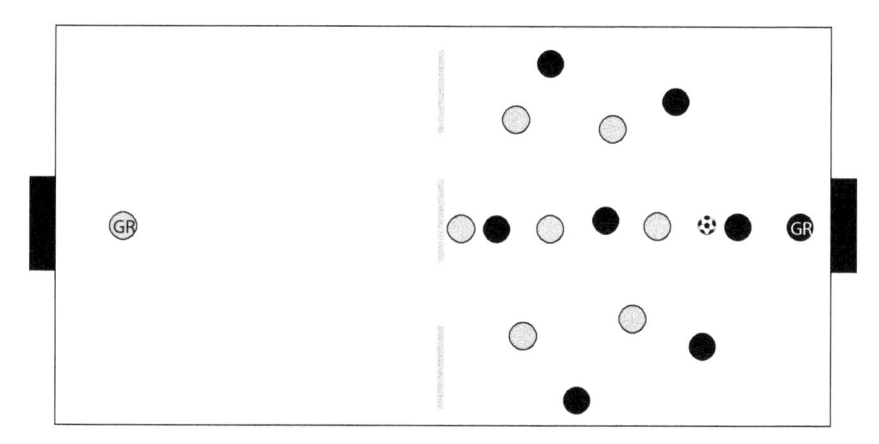

PRINCIPLES AND SUB-PRINCIPLES INVOLVED

Scale: intersectorial (midfield X attack or defence X midfield)

- Compressing the team both in width and length.
- Driving the opponent towards zones that are far from the goal, as an intermediate or high block.
- Intersectorial pressing to reduce space and time so as to induce error and gain possession.

DRILL 6

DESCRIPTION AND ORGANIZATION OF THE DRILL

(GK+8) versus (8+GK) drill. Teams are made up of one goalkeeper, four defenders, three midfielders and one forward. The players form the team in possession should be positioned in width and depth, coordinating their actions with the purpose of scoring. The defending team coordinates their actions so as to reduce spaces, in width and length, in order to induce opponents' error and gain possession. In this game, the offside rule must apply.

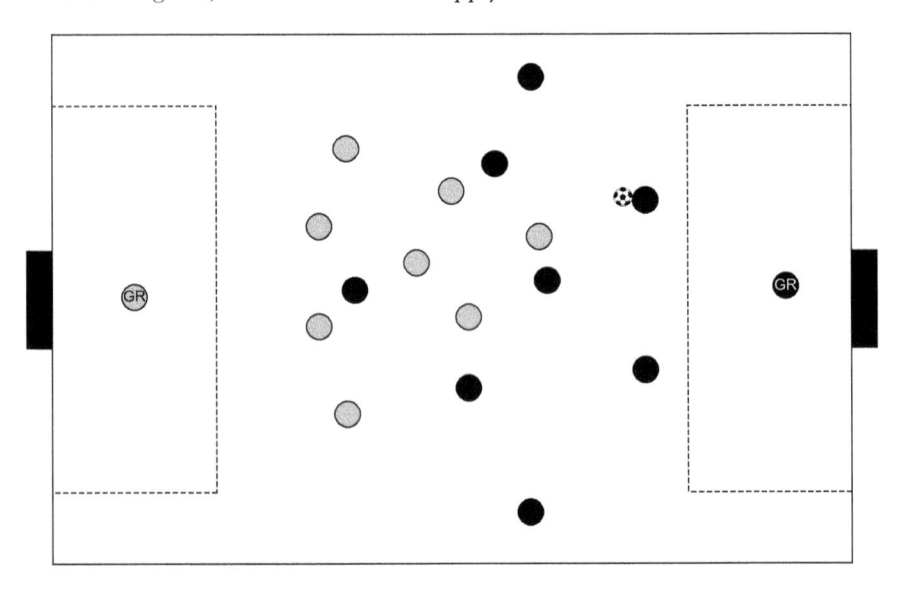

PRINCIPLES AND SUB-PRINCIPLES INVOLVED

Scale: intersectorial (defence X midfield)

- Compressing the team both in width and length.
- Driving the opponent towards the side corridors.
- Intersectorial pressing to reduce space and time so as to induce error and gain possession.

DRILL 7

DESCRIPTION AND ORGANIZATION OF THE DRILL

(GK+8) versus (8+GK) drill. The light team, which intends to develop the defensive coordination between defensive and midfield areas, is made up of one goalkeeper, four defenders, three midfielders and one forward. The dark team, which intends to develop the defensive coordination between midfield and offensive areas, is made up of one goalkeeper, two defenders, three midfielders and three forwards. When one of the teams is in possession, players should be positioned both in width and length, coordinating their actions with the purpose of scoring. The defending team should coordinate its actions to reduce space, in width and length, so as to induce error and gain possession.

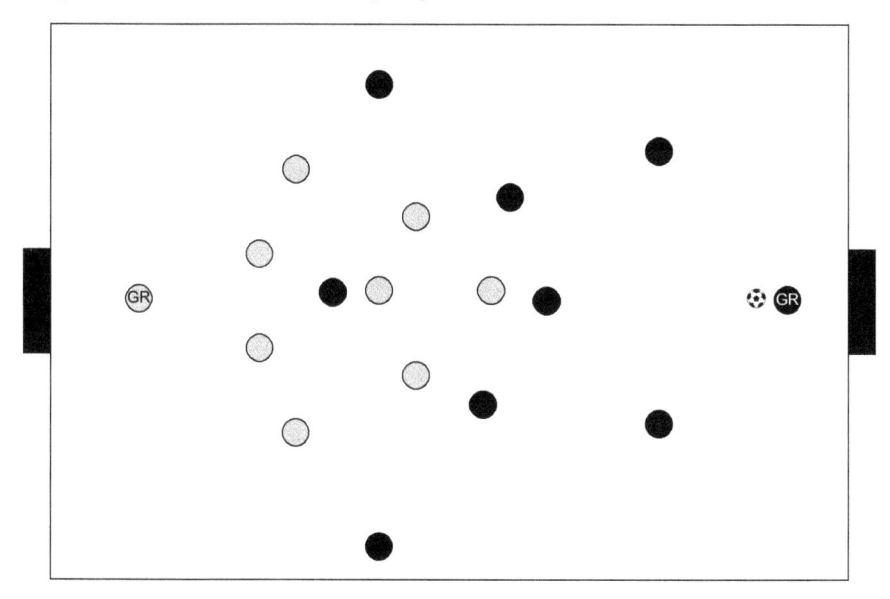

PRINCIPLES AND SUB-PRINCIPLES INVOLVED

Scale: intersectorial (light team: defence X midfield; dark team: midfield X attack)

- Compressing the team both in width and length.
- Driving the opponent towards the side corridors.
- Intersectorial pressing to reduce space and time so as to induce error and gain possession.

DRILL 8

DESCRIPTION AND ORGANIZATION OF THE DRILL

(GK+10) versus (10+GK) drill. Teams are made up of one goalkeeper, four defenders, three midfielders and three forwards. The team in possession should have their players positioned in width and depth, coordinating their actions with the purpose of crossing the opponents' defensive half line (one goal) and score. The defending team coordinates its actions so as to reduce space in width and length to prevent opponents from crossing a line positioned in their half and thus scoring goals. The line positioned in the defensive half of each team may have varied depth and its purpose is to force the team to defend further ahead or further back, according to the coach's intentions. For this game, the offside rule must apply.

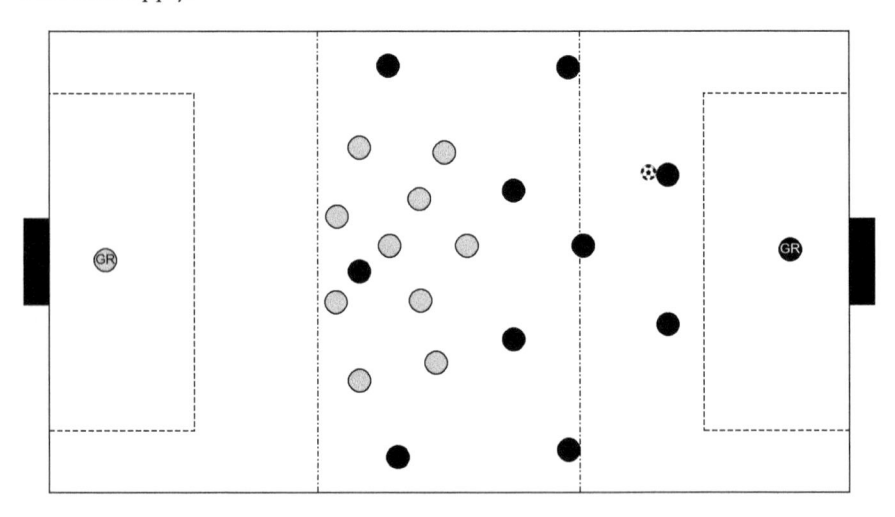

PRINCIPLES AND SUB-PRINCIPLES INVOLVED

Collective work

- Compressing the team both in width and length.
- Driving the opponent towards the side corridors.
- Collective pressure to reduce space so as to induce error and gain possession.

DRILL 9

DESCRIPTION AND ORGANIZATION OF THE DRILL

(GK+10) versus (10+GK) drill. Teams are made up of one goalkeeper, four defenders, three midfielders and three forwards. The team in possession should have their players positioned in width and depth, coordinating their actions with the purpose of scoring in the goal protected by the opponent's goalkeeper or in the six goals placed within the field, crossing between them with the ball under control or passing through these goals as a teammate maintains possession towards the attack, rather than towards the defence. It is not allowed to score two consecutive times in the same goal. Whenever one scores a goal within the field, the game resumes as usual. The purpose of placing the goals inside the field is to force the defending team to move up the field as an intermediate or high block. In this drill the offside rule must apply.

PRINCIPLES AND SUB-PRINCIPLES INVOLVED

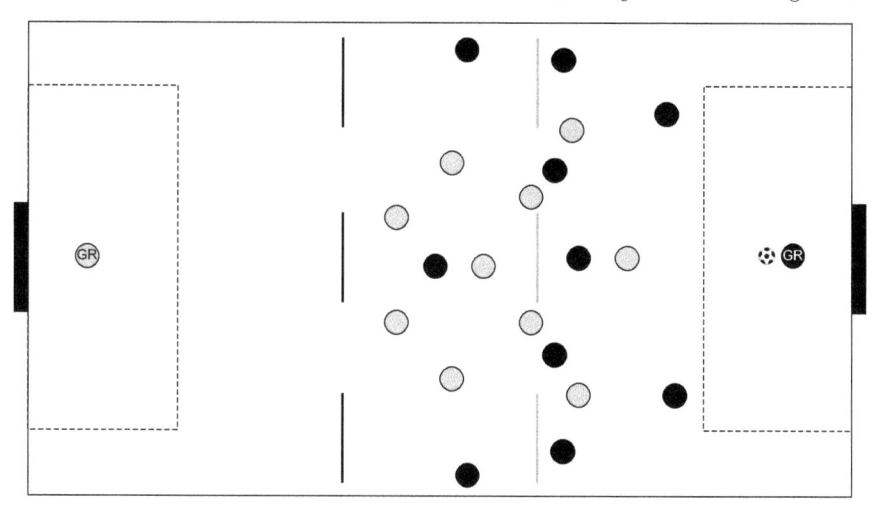

Collective work

- Compressing the team both in width and length.
- Driving the opponent towards the side corridors.
- Collective pressure to reduce space so as to induce error and gain possession.

4.5.3 Defence/Attack and Attack/Defence Transition

With respect to the defence/attack and attack/defence transitions, we will present drills in which both are being practised simultaneously, yet, by different teams or players.

Considering the behaviors linked to attack/defence transition the intention is, after lost of possession, to immediately press the player with the ball and the surrounding area (pressure zone) in order to: (a) gain possession or (b) buy time to get defensively organized, compressing the team both in width and length. So that this principle is contemplated, there are some sub-principles that should also be considered, such as: (i) change from a defensive to an offensive attitude; (ii) create a pressure zone to gain possession or prevent the opponent to counter attack; (iii) compress the team both in width and depth to start defensive organization and (iv) defend in numerical inferiority.

During defence/attack transition, the intention is that the team—after gaining possession—take the ball away from the pressure zone, so as to not be pressed and prevent the player and the team from losing it again, so as to: (a) give depth and start counter attack, taking advantage of the opponents' defensive disorganization or (b) start the offensive process if the opponent is defensively disorganized. So that this principle can be contemplated, there are some sub-principles that should also be considered, such as: (i) change from a defensive to an offensive attitude; (ii) take the ball away from the pressure zone to an area in which the opponents have no possibility of holding pressure; (iii) position players both in width and length and (iv) take advantage of open spaces to start counter attack.

DRILL 1

DESCRIPTION AND ORGANIZATION OF THE DRILL

1X1 situations.

The drill starts with player A from one of the teams progressing with the ball and, after crossing the midfield, shooting. Whenever this player A shoots, player (1), from the opposite team, who is positioned beside one of his/her goalkeeper's post, runs quickly with the purpose of shooting at the opponent's goal after crossing the midfield. Player A who shot at goal tries to prevent player (1) from shooting. When player (1) shoots or loses possession, then player B tries to progress and shoot and, in its turn, player (1) tries to prevent him/her from doing so. The sequence of the drill follows this logic until the coach's interruption.

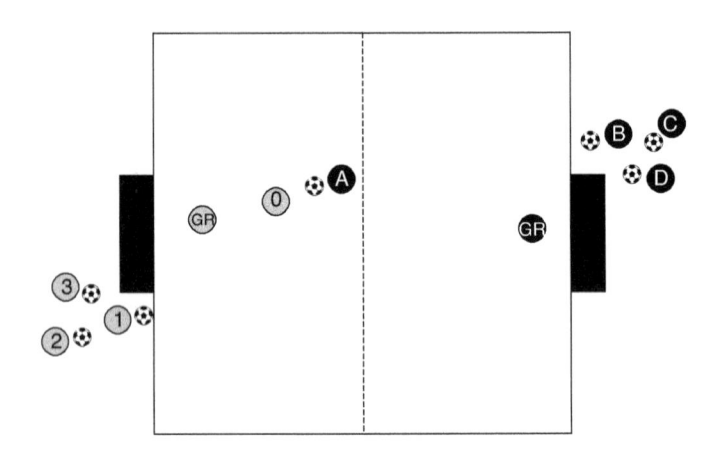

PRINCIPLES AND SUB-PRINCIPLES INVOLVED

Scale: individual

Attack/defence transition:

- Change from offensive to defensive attitude.

Defence/attack transition:

- Attempt to take advantage of spaces to attack in depth and shot.

DRILL 2

DESCRIPTION AND ORGANIZATION OF THE DRILL

6 versus (3+3) drill. Each team of six players is made up of two groups: A and B. Each team has their playing area. The light team is placed to the left and the dark one to the right.

The drill starts with one of the teams (light) in possession of the ball. The opposite (dark) team, through one of the groups (e.g. group A), attempts to gain possession and, whenever they do so, they have to pass the ball to their area. They can do it directly or through two teammates positioned outside the opponent's area. If one of those teammates gets the ball, they should immediately pass it to their own area. All dark players should quickly go into their area and try to maintain possession, while the players from the light team initially try to prevent the former team from passing the ball to their area and, if they do not succeed, they should move one of the groups to the dark team's area so as to gain possession and pass the ball to their own area.

The drill unfolds through this sequence, in which in one turn group A tries to gain the ball from the opponent and, in another turn, group B tries the same.

Whenever the team in possession of the ball in their own area loses it and tries to prevent the opponent from passing it to the respective area, they perform attack/defence transition. In its turn, the team that gains possession in the opponent's area and tries to pass the ball to their area, performs defence/attack transition.

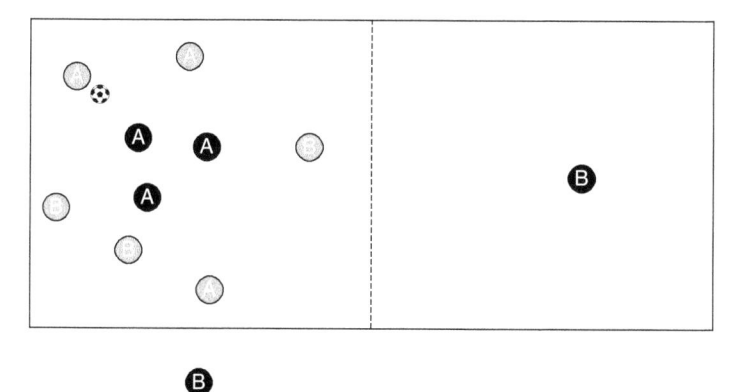

PRINCIPLES AND SUB-PRINCIPLES INVOLVED

Scale: group or sectorial

Attack/defence transition:
- Change from offensive to defensive attitude.
- Create a pressure zone to gain possession.

Defence/attack transition:

- Change from defensive to offensive attitude.
- Take the ball away from the pressure zone.
- Team open wide across the field.

DRILL 3

DESCRIPTION AND ORGANIZATION OF THE DRILL

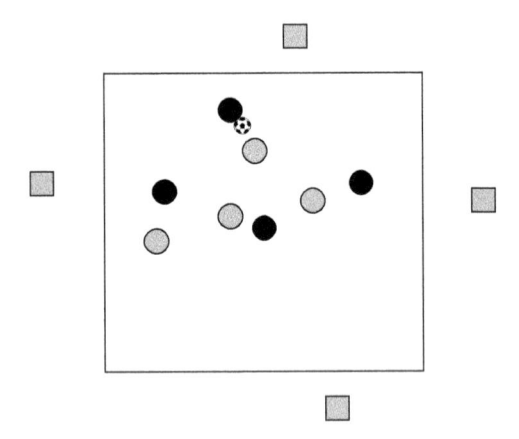

4X4 drill + four floaters.

The drill starts with one of the teams in possession, for example the dark team. The purpose of the dark team includes maintaining possession as long as possible through their four players, and they are not allowed to play with the outside floaters.

Whenever the defending team, for example the light team, gains possession, they must pass the ball to one of the floaters. When this floater passes the ball back to one of players from the light team, the team should try to maintain possession without resorting to the floaters. After the dark team recovers possession, they should follow the same procedures, that is pass the ball to one of the floaters and then maintain possession through their players.

The game must preserve this dynamics and the main purpose is to encourage the habit of the team who gains possession, of immediately taking the ball away from the pressure zone, while the team who loses possession should, immediately, press player in possession of the ball so that they cannot take the ball away from the pressure zone.

PRINCIPLES AND SUB-PRINCIPLES INVOLVED

Scale: group or sectorial

Attack/defence transition:

- Change from offensive to defensive attitude.
- Create a pressure zone to gain possession.

Defence attack/defence

- Change from defensive to offensive attitude.
- Take the ball away from the pressure zone.
- Team open wide across the field.

DRILL 4

DESCRIPTION AND ORGANIZATION OF THE DRILL

4X4 drill between three teams organized in waves.

Team A (dark) attacks team B (light) with the purpose of scoring a goal. In turn, team B tries to prevent this situation and, whenever they gain possession, they have two purposes: The first is to cross the midfield line with the ball under control, and the second is to overtake the two defenders from team C and score, within a maximum of 5 seconds. After the shot or the 5 seconds are over, the two players from team C who were outside get into the field and restart the drill as team B attacks team C and, on the other end of the field, two players from team A await for team's C counter attack.

The purpose of this drill is for the team who starts the attack (team A) after losing possession, fulfils the principles of attack/defence transition. On the other hand, the defending team (B), whenever they gain possession, should fulfil the principles of defence/attack transition and start counter attacking the team positioned on the other end of the field in numerical inferiority (C).

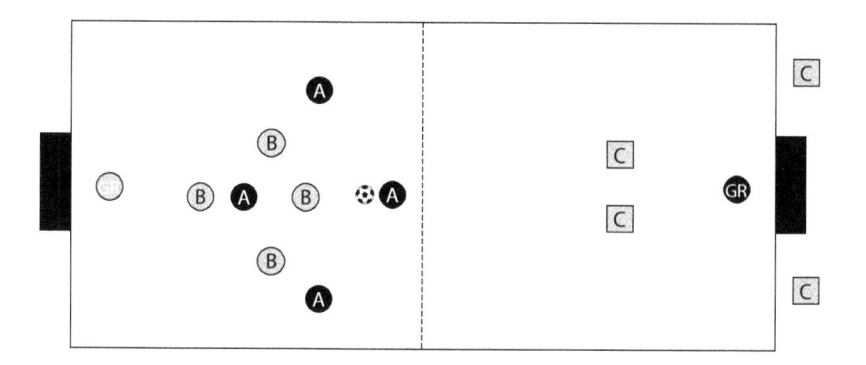

PRINCIPLES AND SUB-PRINCIPLES INVOLVED

Scale: sectorial

Attack/defence transition:

- Change from offensive to defensive attitude.
- Create a pressure zone to gain possession.
- Compress the team both in width and length, to start defensive organization.

128 *Improving Quality Play*

Defence/attack transition

- Change from defensive to offensive attitude.
- Take the ball away from the pressure zone.
- Take advantage of spaces in order to start counter attack.

DRILL 5

DESCRIPTION AND ORGANIZATION OF THE DRILL

(GK+5) versus (5+GK) drill + two floaters. Each team is made up of one goalkeeper, one defender, three midfielders and one forward. The playing area of each team is divided into three parts: defensive, intermediate and offensive areas. In the defensive area a goalkeeper and a defender are positioned; in the intermediate area, the three midfielders; and in the offensive area, the forward. The floaters are positioned on the sides of the playing area.

The drill starts in the intermediate area and the purpose of the team in possession is to pass the ball, without the support of the two floaters, to the offensive area where the two midfielders can go into and move down one of the midfielders from the defending team, thus turning the game into a 3 versus (2+GK) situation. However, whenever the defending team gains possession, in the intermediate or defensive areas, they can quickly start counter attacking, being allowed to resort to the two side floaters. Whenever they go into the offensive area, they can attack with the forward and the two midfielders who can get into the offensive area, while who defends can move down one of the midfielders.

The purpose of this drill is to practice defence-attack transition of the team who starts the game in defence, and the attack-defence transition of the team who starts the drill in possession and then loses the ball.

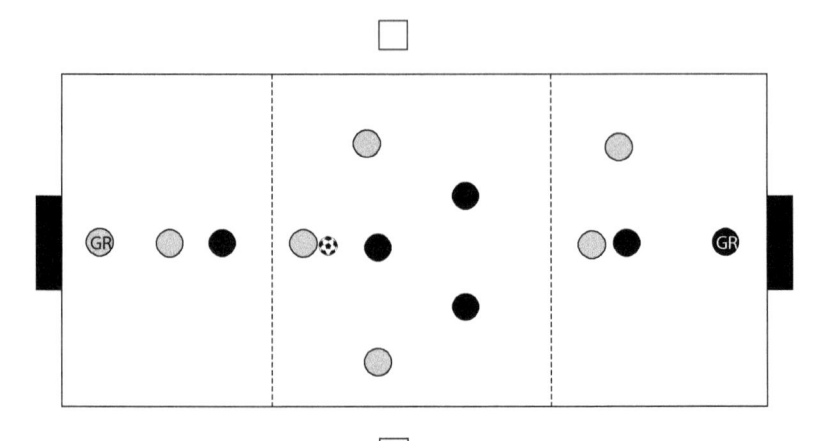

PRINCIPLES AND SUB-PRINCIPLES INVOLVED

Scale: sectorial

Attack/defence transition:

- Change from offensive to defensive attitude.
- Create a pressure zone to gain possession.
- Compress the team both in width and length, to start defensive organization.

Defence/attack transition:

- Change from defensive to offensive attitude.
- Take the ball away from the pressure zone.
- Take advantage of resorting to the side floaters to start counter attacking.

DRILL 6

DESCRIPTION AND ORGANIZATION OF THE DRILL

6X6 drill + two floaters between three teams organized in waves.

Team A (dark) attacks team B (light) with the purpose of scoring, resorting to the support of two players from team C. Team B tries to prevent this situation and when they gain possession, they try pass through with support of the two floaters, to cross the midfield line with the ball under control. If they succeed, they start attacking team C which will temporarily have four players. However, the players who were floaters take back their positions as two players from team A start playing that role.

The purpose of this drill is that the team which starts the attacking move (A), after losing possession, fulfils the principles of attack/defence transition. By its turn, the team which was defending (B), whenever it gains possession, should fulfil the principles of defence/attack transition and start counter-attacking the team positioned on the other end of the field, temporarily in numerical inferiority (C).

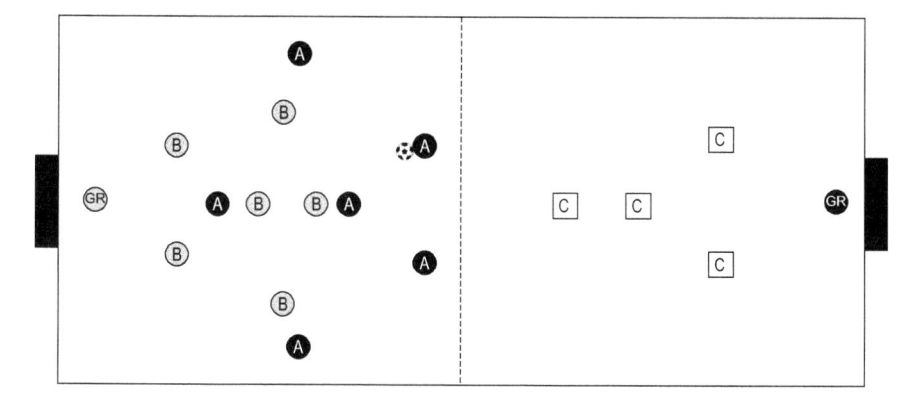

PRINCIPLES AND SUB-PRINCIPLES INVOLVED

Scale: intersectorial

Attack/defence transition:
- Change from offensive to defensive attitude.
- Create a pressure zone to gain possession.
- Compress the team both in width and length, to start defensive organization.

Defence/attack transition:
- Change from defensive to offensive attitude.
- Take the ball away from the pressure zone.
- Take advantage of spaces in order to start counter attack.

DRILL 7

DESCRIPTION AND ORGANIZATION OF THE DRILL

(GK+9) versus (9+GK) drill. Each team is made up of one goalkeeper, three defenders, three midfielders and three forwards.

The playing area of each team is divided into three parts: defensive, intermediate and offensive areas. In the defensive area a goalkeeper and three defenders are positioned; in the intermediate area, the three midfielders; and in the offensive area, three forwards.

The drill starts in the intermediate area and from this moment the game is played in the intermediate and offensive areas of the team in possession (e.g. light team). The purpose of the team in possession is to coordinate their actions with the intention of scoring. Whenever the defending team gains possession, they can quickly start counter attack, being allowed to resort to the 3 forwards who can move down to the intermediate area in order to receive the ball. When they pass the ball to the offensive area, only the defenders may be within this space, as the forwards may be supported by two midfielders who are allowed go into the offensive area.

The game restarts with the ball in the opponent's intermediate area.

The purpose of this drill is to practice the defence-attack transition of the team which starts the game in defence, and the attack-defence transition of the team which starts the game in possession, and then loses it.

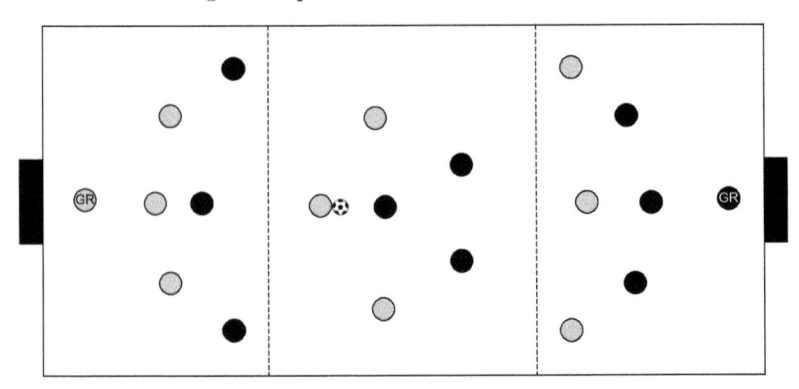

PRINCIPLES AND SUB-PRINCIPLES INVOLVED

Scale: intersectorial

Attack/defence transition:

- Change from offensive to defensive attitude.
- Create a pressure zone to gain possession.
- Compress the team both in width and length, to start defensive organization.

Defence/attack transition:

- Change from defensive to offensive attitude.
- Take the ball away from the pressure zone.
- Take advantage of spaces in order to start counter attack.

DRILL 8

DESCRIPTION AND ORGANIZATION OF THE DRILL

(GK+8) versus (8+GK) drill. Each team is made up of one goalkeeper, two defenders, three midfielders, two wingers and one forward.

The drill starts in a given central area, in which the three midfielders of each team confront each other. If the game starts with the dark team in possession, their purpose is to successfully pass the ball to the forward and, after having done so, both the team's midfielders and two wingers quickly run deep, taking advantage of their numerical superiority, since only the two defenders can perform defensive tasks, with the purpose of coordinating their actions in order to score, within a period of 5 seconds.

In case the light team gains possession, their purpose is to quickly start counter attack. In order to do so, they can play with the forward or any of the wingers from their team, positioned on the sides of the delimited area. To score, they have only 5 seconds and, such as in the previous situation, only the two defenders can perform defensive tasks.

The game restarts in the central area with one of the midfielders trios in possession of the ball.

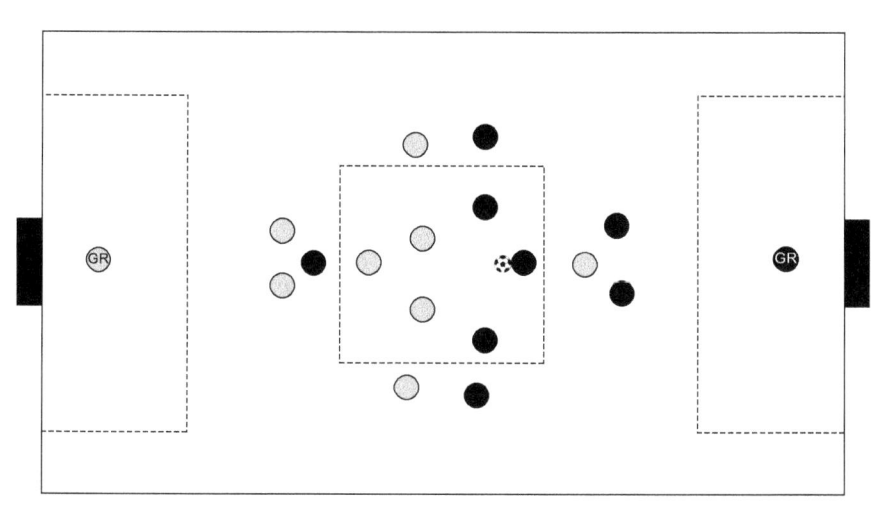

PRINCIPLES AND SUB-PRINCIPLES INVOLVED

Scale: intersectorial

Attack/defence transition:

- Change from offensive to defensive attitude.
- Create a pressure zone to gain possession.
- Defend in numerical inferiority.

Defence/attack transition:

- Change from defensive to offensive attitude.
- Take the ball away from the pressure zone.
- Team open wide across the field, in width and length.
- Take advantage of spaces in order to start counter attack.

DRILL 9

DESCRIPTION AND ORGANIZATION OF THE DRILL

11X11 drill. The drill we present next is configured in 11X11. However, it can be presented in any other functional structure, depending on whether one intends to practice collective, intersectorial or sectorial aspects.

The drill is presented in a conventional playing format, in which the coach (C), whenever deems relevant, puts a new ball into the field, so that the players drop the one that was being played with and adapt to the new ball.

The purpose of this drill is to enable the coach to control the kind of transitions he/she wants the team to practice (either defence/attack or attack/defence).

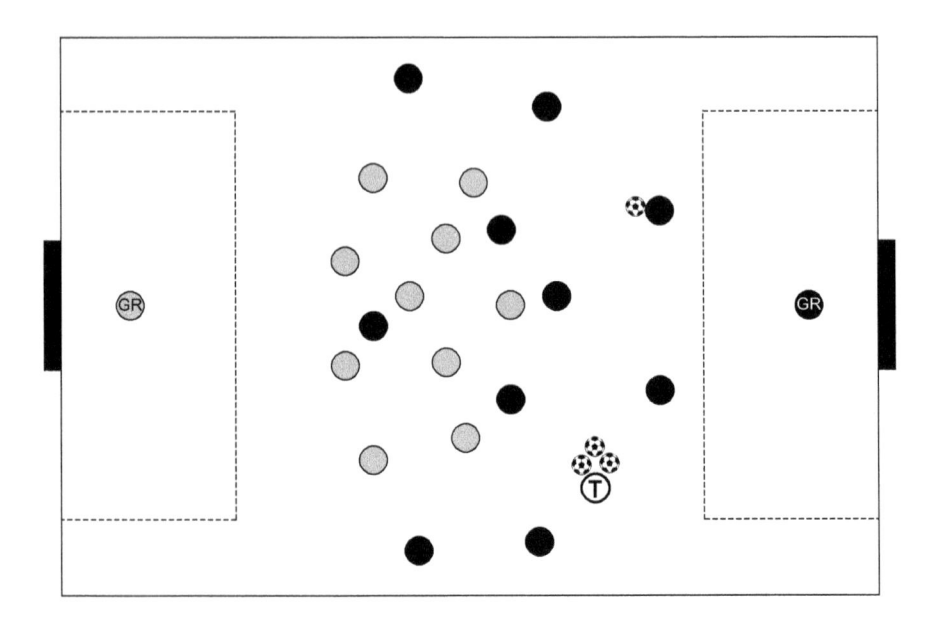

PRINCIPLES AND SUB-PRINCIPLES INVOLVED

Scale: collective

> Attack/defence transition:

- Change from offensive to defensive attitude.
- Create a pressure zone to gain possession or prevent the opponent to start counter attack.
- Compress the team both in width and length, to start defensive organization.
- Correct positioning in order to defend in numerical inferiority.

> Defence/attack transition:

- Change from defensive to offensive attitude.
- Take the ball away from the pressure zone.
- Team open wide across the field, in width and length.
- Start of offensive organization.
- Take advantage of spaces in order to start counter attack.

4.6 Training Context: The Desirable Synergy Between Coach and Players

The knowledge structure acquired through the experiences lived throughout the development period is very important to develop an intelligent and creative player for the game. In all these development contexts, the active participation of the coach/teacher, especially in training, is essential for the player to be able to act autonomously during games. The instructions coming from the coach must be sufficiently qualified and structured, so the players, especially the younger ones, don't create a "dependency" on the instructions coming from the sidelines on gameday.

In this sense, the player must be prepared to read the situation and make the best decision, based on the identity of play that was built for his/her team. In this context, and as previously discussed, the game principles become extremely important, once they allow that the player's actions in the game develop in a universe of possibilities. These possibilities will allow "new games" to be created inside the game itself and that players become increasingly capable of performing on the field the prime of their subjectivity without losing their identity with the team (Fonseca & Garganta, 2006).

In this context, it is also important that coaches develop their player's independency in training and let them act during games. Only allowing the initiative of game reading and acting will develop the essential processes of decision-making and quality in playing. In this perspective, players must be encouraged to develop flexible behaviour patterns that will have to attend to the invariable[2] and variable[3] aspects of the game. Thus, in order to acquire flexible patterns of movement that best adapt to new game situations it is necessary to provide a certain level of freedom in the choice of answers during the learning process and encourage players to explore their potential movements and tactical solutions. When this freedom is eliminated, making the learning process too directed, the emphasis is put only in the invariable aspect of playing skills, contributing to the development of patterns that are mechanized and of low adaptability.

In addition to these points, the strategies of discussion and talks with the group about the positioning of the team and/or the opponent can be very beneficial to the development of game awareness and improvement of tactical knowledge. Through this action, players will be able to understand that training is much more than just "replicating" the activities planned by the coaching staff. In this case, training involves an active and "thoughtful" participation in the activities, where the socialization of concepts, understandings and points of view between the players and coaching staff will contribute to the growth of everyone's knowledge.

Through this encouragement of active player participation, the coaching staff will be able to discover new possibilities of exercises, explore possibilities of change/creation according to the potentialities and difficulties presented by the players and, among other factors, work on the players' understanding about a particular training content. With this information, the coach will be able to choose training methodologies that provoke in the player the necessity of making creative and intelligent decisions. This way of conceiving training can take players to paths that not even the coach knows and, because of that, coaches might not even imagine how to get there and if the objective will not be changed in the course of the project. However, the most important thing is that the coach knows how to help the player to find ways that can be completely different from his/her in order to achieve the goals that were proposed for the team and for the player himself/herself.

In this context, the evaluations of the potentialities and limitations of the players become extremely important, once they will help to guide the training dynamics and organize the training methodologies and planning. Given this importance, we will address in the next chapter the main tools/tests used for the assessment of tactical behaviour, whether in field assessments or in a specific environment that allows obtaining objective information about essential aspects of athletic performance on the field.

Notes

1 Scales refer to the level of structural and functional interaction that the different players from a team may display. Therefore, there might be a collective scale, in which all team players interact; an intersectorial scale, regarding the interaction between the players from two different sectors/areas; a sectorial scale regarding the interaction of players from a given sector/area; a group scale regarding the interaction of a group of players who have very close relations during the game, but are not part of the previous scales; and, lastly, an individual scale that is manifested by the tasks that each player has to fulfill in relation to the interactions with other teammates (Guilherme, 2004).
2 The invariable aspects are associated with the fixed rules (order and consistency).
3 The variable aspects are related to the disorder and variability

5 Instruments for Assessment of Tactical Behaviour

TACTICAL ASSESSMENT IN SOCCER

> The assessment of human activities should be a routine, since only the awareness of their limitations and potentialities will support their development!
>
> The authors

The importance tactical component has gained in soccer within recent years has made coaches, particularly modern ones, interested in instruments for tactical assessment that assist in guiding the training based on players' characteristics and team's potentialities.

This interest in instruments for assessment of tactical behaviour is justified by the fact that they support characterizing the authenticity of practices experienced by players in training and matches. Scientific evidences confirm that such assessments have been beneficial in providing information that allow optimizing training methods and improving players' and teams' performances (Franks, Goodman, & Miller, 1983; Lee & Ward, 2009). In addition, tactical assessments have also supported the configuration of models of play, the refining of working strategies and predicting evolutionary trends of the game in certain contexts and competitions (Castellano Paulis, Perea Rodríguez, & Blanco-Villaseñor, 2009; Godik & Popov, 1993; Guilherme, 2004).

5.1 Characteristics and Instruments

In order to benefit from tactical assessment, some aspects must be taken into consideration, such as the characteristics and potentialities of tests and their frequency of application. In general, the tests that comprise tactical assessments are classified as field and laboratory tests. These tests provide more precise and assertive knowledge about the indicators associated with the loss of players' performance quality in training and competition, like tardiness in decision-making, difference in peripheral perception, lack of concentration when executing particular drills, lack of movement of the players without possession of the ball within the field,

DOI: 10.4324/9781003223375-7

reactivity instead of anticipation of playing response, loss of timing and movement coordination, among others.

The frequency of application of tactical assessments should be compatible with the work to be developed, whereas some tests may be administered weekly or monthly, others can be performed every six months or even annually. For this reason, it is recommended that tactical assessments are part of an integrated work of development of a particular playing model and, with respect to youth levels, of players' development. Furthermore, they should be in line with the objectives and periodization phases of training and competition, since their adjustment to training contents and to the reality of the team in the competition will boost the impact of their results on individual and collective performances (Gréhaigne & Godbout, 1998).

Regarding the frequency of the tactical assessments, field tests are usually carried out in a shorter period of time (weekly or monthly), depending on the team's needs, whilst laboratory tests, except for TacticUP®,[1] can be biannual or annual, due to the characteristics of the variables to be assessed and the outlay of human and financial resources. However, the demand for a laboratory evaluation may arise at any time within the group of players.

Frequently, this need arises from the coach's or staff's empirical observations in daily training sessions or competition. Within these environments, they spot with the naked eye the limitation(s) of the player(s) and the impact they have on the team's performance and also on the full development of the player(s). After this analysis, if further study on the limitation the player has presented is considered relevant, the technical staff suggests a more thorough assessment of the tactical component. Through the use of more advanced technology in laboratory, it is possible to identify, measure and quantify/qualify the variables that might be associated to the existing issue. In subsequent stages, from the results displayed it is possible to know the precise extent of the issue and, with this information, the proposed solutions for improving on field performance are planned along with the technical staff.

The results from these assessments might have a very positive impact on the training practices, suggesting modifications when detecting, for example, dissonances between the work being done, the full development of the player and the training scheme. Scientific evidences have already shown that the player's amount and quality of knowledge about the game are closely related with their skill level, and that the imbalance in the structuring and planning of training sessions might have an impact on player's tactical knowledge and decision-making in different playing situations (Blomqvist, Vänttinen, & Luhtanen, 2005). Blomqvist and others show that players' tactical knowledge and decision-making in situations with possession of the ball are higher than those of players in situations without ball possession, most likely because the training sessions have excessively focused on teaching of actions with the ball rather than of off-ball movements (Blomqvist, Luhtanen, Vänttinen, Norvapalo, & Hayrinen, 2002; Blomqvist et al., 2005).

In such cases, it is possible to amend the discrepancies of knowledge and performance between the players by changing the structures of some training drills or by qualifying the interventions of the technical staff during training sessions. It is important to highlight that the sooner the issue displayed in training or competition is detected, measured and defined, the faster the amends will be, reducing time loss and providing greater development of the team.

So that the variables that comprise the problem are properly detected, the person in charge for the tactical assessment should gather knowledge on the available tests and select the most suitable one, according to the current needs. If the current stage of tactical development of the player and the team is being assessed, the evaluator should be aware of the available instruments in order to, in accordance with the results, issue a more complete and accurate feedback.

The same is true for determining the physical component: the choice for a test will depend on the physical aspect to be evaluated (endurance, speed, strength, etc.) and only after all variables are assessed is that a complete feedback on the player's current level of physical fitness may be issued.

The first topic of this chapter aims at presenting the range and limitations of the instruments for assessment of tactical behaviour applied in soccer.

5.2 Range and Limitations of the Instruments for Assessment

A concise and assertive assessment of tactical performance requires that the main variables that are interrelated and directly influence the behaviour of the player within the field are taken into account. These variables are present in the way the player manages the space of play and in his/her cognitive processes. In regard to the management of the space of play, the available playing space, the position in the field of the player being assessed, the position of his/her teammates and opponents, and the position of the ball are the main information to be considered during the evaluation. Regarding cognition, it is possible to highlight the (central and peripheral) perception, the (short- and long-term) memory, the (declarative[2] and procedural)[3] knowledge, information processing and decision-making as the most important factors to be examined during the evaluation.

Due to the characteristics of all variables involving tactical performance and to their measurement and control features, the evaluations might be conducted within the field (*in vivo*) and in laboratory (*in vitro*).

Laboratory tests allow better standardization and control of the variables to be measured. Besides, the access to advanced technologies enables the assessment of variants that are rather hard to control and measure in match context,[4] that is decision-making, viewing direction and range, visual search pattern, among others. In addition, the development of technological tools has enabled the reproduction of match situations within the laboratory through simulators, something that has helped increase the perception of relevance of the test by the player being evaluated, thus influencing his/her effective participation and, consequently, qualifying even more the data collected and his/her performance.

Simulators have already been broadly explored and used in medicine (Colt, Crawford, & Galbraith, 2001), in aviation (Taylor et al., 2002), in car racing (Yan, Jingjing, Danmin, Xia, & Yebing, 2011) such as Formula 1 and, more recently, have also been employed in sports[5] and displaying relevant results for the performance of soccer players (Ward & Williams, 2003).

Scientific studies have confirmed that tennis players who underwent training in simulators, even those of short duration (15 minutes) and for relatively short period (8 sessions), improved their performances in match situations (Farrow, Chivers, Hardingham, & Sachse, 1998). In soccer, although there are no studies on this subject, there are some professionals who have been using this resource with injured players as a means to have them better prepared and to reduce the time of their return to competition.

Other soccer match simulation studies that have also employed the Eye-Tracking technology have shown that there are differences in players' visual search strategies (where they look), according to their experience/training level and different configurations of play. Results indicate that in 1X1 situations the more experienced and higher level players, called experts, employ their central vision to search for clues in the movement of the player in possession of the ball and try to predict what would happen next during the play. However, in the 11X11 situation, this visual search pattern is modified and begins to integrate information emerging from the ball, the space of play, the player in possession of the ball, the positioning of other opponents and teammates (Ward & Williams, 2003). Within this modification in the visual search pattern, it was also verified that the expert players have less fixation time in certain game information spots (opponents, ball, teammates, space of play), and as consequence they are able to observe more game events, reaching improved performance (Roca, Ford, McRobert, & Williams, 2011). Another interesting fact of these investigations is the realization of a sort of visual search strategy that expert players employ in certain game situations to obtain important information during a particular play. In such cases, they "play" with the central visual field, deceiving the opponent with two visual clues and trying to benefit from the peripheral vision to obtain crucial information about the playing sequence (Roca, Ford, McRobert, & Williams, 2013). Through this resource, opponents present the possibilities for finishing/playing on more clearly, thus allowing the expert to benefit, from anticipating opponents' actions (Ward, Williams, & Hancock, 2006).

Based on this information, it is possible to verify that the progress of technology has enabled, within recent years, the approximation between data collected through laboratory evaluations and their application in match context, reflecting in better performances in the field (Williams & Burwitz, 1993). Despite this evolution and the integration of benefits for soccer training and practice, these tests also possess some limitations for their large-scale, more assertive use.

According to some researchers, there is still room for improving technology and representativeness of simulators, so as they can project with higher reliability the behaviour the player displays when facing a similar situation in match or in training (Placek & Griffin, 2001; Vaeyens, Lenoir, Williams, Matthys, & Philippaerts, 2010). In soccer, the improvement of these simulators will support even more the player's assessment and decision-making skills according to actual match situations. Besides, the suitability of the test to the reality of the team and of the training routine will maximize the results of the evaluations.

In regard to the availability of the results, another limitation lies in the fact that some tests possess a high response time between its conduction and the feedback to the technical staff. Despite many of them deliver responses just after the end of the test, others, depending on the variables analysed, might take up to 24 hours to come up with a diagnosis to the technical staff or to the player. This limitation lies in the fact that some tests do not possess yet a specific software that is capable of automatically performing the analyses and grouping the information collected. This limitation, depending on the urgency, might be crucial for the use of some tests from the tactical performance assessment system.

Two other limitations of these tests are related to their high cost and to the fact that the information on their potentialities for training and performance have not yet arrived appropriately to many professionals who work at clubs. In relation to the costs, it does not mean that the equipment is expensive and difficult to acquire by the clubs, derailing the assembly of a Department of Tactical Assessment. Actually, it is possible for many soccer clubs to obtain the benefits of tactical assessment, gathering in their existing departments a division of tactical assessment or even developing partnerships with university that have the equipment and that deliver this service, as in Liverpool John Moores University and Universidade Federal de Viçosa, through the Football Exchange program and the Centre of Research and Studies in Soccer (NUPEF), respectively, which develop multiple partnership with soccer clubs from the UK—as well as from all over Europe—and from Brazil—and, likewise, from all over South America.

On the other hand, field tests, in which the assessments are performed in training situations, have opposing characteristics in relation to laboratory tests. They generally depend on fewer technological resources in comparison to *in vitro* tests, so they are financially more accessible and easier to implement within the club's daily life. In addition, they possess higher ecological validity,[6] since the variables are observed and collected during the performance of the tactical behaviours in match context (Godbout, 1990).

Despite these advantages, these tests have the limitation of being less standardized and display less operational control of the variable to be observed and measured. For this reason, specialists advise for the qualification of the professional who will conduct these tests, since in cases in which there is limited knowledge and experience of the evaluator there might be a debility of identifying and quantifying the tactical indicators that express performance in soccer (Garganta, 2009; Tenga, Kanstad, Ronglan, & Bahr, 2009).

Furthermore, if the professional who is responsible for conducting the tests lacks the criteria and theoretical models of framework and interpretation of the actions that represent the specificity of the game, it might result in a waste of the club's financial and human resources or even in an impairment of the work being done by other professionals within the technical staff (McGarry, Anderson, Wallace, Hughes, & Franks, 2002). In such cases, the saying "you get what you pay for" applies, since there is an investment of club's time and resources to perform the evaluation, but it turns out not to be adequate to the needs of players and the club.

Another aspect that should be taken into account when conducting field tests is the thorough selection of the test to be performed, since only some of them allow the establishment of a link between the content taught in the teaching-training process and the behaviours performed by the players in a match (Teoldo, 2010; Gréhaigne & Godbout, 1998). For this reason, the procedures of some tests that might be used for the assessment of tactical behaviour will be covered within the following topic of this chapter.

In order to select some of them, it is important to be aware of the players' tactical skills that one intends to identify, observe and quantify/qualify during the several stages within the training process (Memmert, 2002). The greater utility of a test is closely related to its possibilities of transcending the data to the reality of the team's play or to the club's needs. If such needs are related to players' development, the chosen test should be able to assess his/her progress through the formation levels, thus securely and assertively indicating its potentialities, needs and limitations. Therefore, the adequacy and utility of the results in practice and, consequently, in the successful development of such player are closely related to the selection of the appropriate test to the current needs of his/her soccer development.

Among the instruments that will be described, all of them have presented progresses in regard to the assessment of players' tactical behaviour, with respect to the playing interactions and the consideration of the movements of the players involved, with and without ball possession. The Game Performance Assessment Instrument (GPAI) (Oslin, Mitchell, & Griffin, 1998) is an instrument of easy manipulation that allows the identification of players' behaviours in the game, prioritarily including tactical indicators. The Team Sports Performance Assessment Procedure (TSAP) (Gréhaigne & Godbout, 1998) was developed to gather information on players' performance with respect to the behaviours performed during the offensive phase of play. The KORA (Konzept Orientertes Rating) tests battery or Game Test Situation (Memmert, 2002), b) focus its analyses in two tactical parameters—offering and orientating, and recognizing spaces of play—the assessment being conducted under the convergent and divergent perspectives that are related with playing smart and creative, taking into account the general tactical principles of the game. The Game Performance Evaluation Tool (GPET) (Garcia-Lopez, Gonzalez-Villora, Gutierrez, & Serra, 2013) was conceived with the aim of assessing the performance of soccer players in the offensive phase of play taking into account the tactical operational principles of play. Based on GPET's protocol the cognitive, decision-making and motor execution components are evaluated in every action performed by the players, with and without possession of the ball. In turn, the System of Tactical Assessment in Soccer—FUT-SAT and TacticUP—allows to assess the offensive and defensive tactical behaviours performed by the players (with and without possession) based on the ten core tactical principles of the game (Teoldo, Garganta, Greco, Mesquita, & Maia, 2011), through procedural and declarative approaches, respectively. From the information that comes from the field and video tests, these systems, which also consider the location where the tactical action was performed and its outcome to the sequence of play, calculate the player's and team's tactical performance indexes and assess the quality/efficiency of the tactical behaviours performed by the players.

The first two instruments (GPAI and TSAP) have resorted to compound variables in an attempt to ponder the actions performed according to the context and peculiarities of the game and to obtain a performance index. Due to the flexibility and range of the instrument of assessment, the GPAI is more suitable to be used in initial practice levels, since the coach can arrange and adjust the system of assessment according to the content being taught. As the game complexity increases, it is suggested that other instruments are used in an attempt to approximate the instrument of assessment to the reality of the soccer development context.

With respect to the other four instruments (KORA, GPET, FUT-SAT and TacticUP), they could be used so as to complement the assessment of players' tactical component during the process of sports development. The KORA tests battery evaluates tactical parameters that are closer to the general principles of soccer; the GPET is based upon the assessment of tactical behaviours related to the operational principles; and FUT-SAT and TacticUP® were developed to assess players' tactical behaviours according to the core tactical principles of the game.

Hence, according to the player's development phase, the evaluator might resort to the best among these four instruments to verify the tactical limitations and potentialities of his/her players. In initial development phases, in which the basic concepts of offering and orienting, and recognizing spaces of play are essential, the KORA tests battery is suggested for players' evaluation. Yet, in phases in which the operationalization of the game becomes more evident, the GPET is an instrument that will allow more reliable and concise results. Finally, in the phases of sports development in which the players begin to understand abstract concepts and perform more complex movements, usually at the age of 13, FUT-SAT and TacticUP® are the instruments suggested to represent the essentiality of soccer, and establish a link between test results and the content developed during the process of teaching and training process.

It is noteworthy that GPET, FUT-SAT and TacticUP® were developed according to the operational and core tactical principles of soccer[7] and, for being more recent, they tried to fill gaps and shorten some weaknesses displayed by previous instruments.[8] The presence of the principles within the central structure of GPET and FUT-SAT supports the comprehension of the tactical organization of the game, since the dynamics of its interactions and applications operationalizes and characterizes both the teams' models and levels of play. In addition, the utilization of modified spaces for the evaluation of tactical behaviour meets the needs of teaching and training, since many coaches resort to modifications in the structure of their training drills, whether to facilitate the flow of play or to encourage the occurrence of actions related to tactical skills (Holt, Strean, & Bengoechea, 2002).

Due to such characteristics, these instruments allow to move forward in objective measurements of the players' movements in the field, which has been highlighted by literature as a limitation for the design of reliable instruments of assessment of players' performance (Olsen & Larsen, 1997). The consideration of tactical principles as nuclear aspects of evaluation also presents advantages in contextualized and longitudinal assessment, since all tactical principles taught during the player's development process and the design of the team's model of play are considered (Gréhaigne & Godbout, 1998).

Another advantage regards the flexibility of use of its categories and variables according to the coach's or researcher's objectives. These systems also meet the need of assessing specific tactical aspects of the game, which had not been addressed by the existing instruments present in literature (Gréhaigne, Mahut, & Fernandez, 2001; Memmert, 2002; Oslin et al., 1998), and allow to infer the dynamics established by the players, with and without possession of the ball during the match, taking the presence and quality of opposition into account (Tenga et al., 2009).

As a strength of their conceptions it is possible to highlight the integrated assessment of the player to the context of play. This feature is important because it allows to simulate the reality of the game and assess players' tactical behaviour in situations closer to their maximum capacity, even considering the degree of opponents' interaction (Teoldo, Garganta, Greco, & Mesquita, 2011). According to some researchers, the assessment of the quality of opponent's interaction is another positive aspect of these instruments because it is an important indicator of player's performance, providing a more precise representation of his/her skills in game context (Anastasi, 1988). Associated with this characteristic, the possibility of an integrated evaluation as a training activity and in situations similar to those real playing conditions facilitates the effective participation of players and influences the quality of information, since the players being assessed are engaged in demonstrating their repertoire of skills (Blomqvist et al., 2005; Lee & Ward, 2009).

Another positive aspect regards the possibility of establishing a link between the results of the evaluations and the content taught in training sessions. According to researchers, this is one of the main characteristics that a test should have, since it allows its systematic use and the execution of longitudinal assessments that help increasing the control and awareness about the learning process and player's development (Richard, Godbout, & Griffin, 2002; Tenga et al., 2009). On the other hand, this control supports the gathering of information with respect to the methodological guidance of the processes of teaching and training, allowing (i) the planification and organization of training with higher specificity given the nature of the tasks; (ii) the regulation of learning of the technical-tactical behaviours according to the dynamics of the interactions of the tactical principles and the team's model of play and (iii) the interpretation of teams' organization and the actions that contribute to the quality of the game (Garganta, 2001).

Having these characteristics is an important factor for the assessment instruments, since the information they provide might contribute decisively to the sport development process. Research has shown that, according to the different playing arrangements (3X3, 4X4, 5X5 and 6X6), players display different behaviour patterns (Castelão, Garganta, Santos, & Teoldo, 2014; Silva, Garganta, Santos, &

Teoldo, 2014), and that players from different positional roles present behaviours that are specific to their tasks in the field. Besides, a study conducted by Teoldo, Garganta, Greco, and Mesquita (2010) involving the date of birth and tactical behaviour efficiency of soccer players between 11 and 17 years of age has verified a positive association between players' tactical performance and birth date, and the tactical behaviour efficiency. This study evidenced that players who were born within the first months of the year (January to March) displayed higher defensive tactical performance in comparison with their counterparts who were born in other months, whereas players who were born within the last quarter of the year (October to December) have shown superior offensive tactical behaviour when compared to those born in the other months.

Therefore, the evaluations stemming from more ecological instruments might assist players in developing their knowledge and tactical behaviour, increasing their abilities to recognize game situations and supporting the transfer of their learning to the contexts that demand decision-making and motor execution consistent with the typical and atypical problems that arise from the game (Teoldo et al., 2011).

5.3 Description of the Characteristics of the Tests and Respective Procedures

5.3.1 Field Tests

5.3.1.1 Team Sports Performance Assessment Procedure (TSAP)

In 1997, Gréhaigne, Godbout and Bouthier proposed an instrument of performance assessment in team sports named Team Sports Performance Assessment Procedure (TSAP). This instrument allows to obtain quantified information about the global offensive performance of an individual in sports such as soccer. The positive feature of this instrument lies in the fact that the evaluation considers the positional role and even the environment and space of play.

The player's performance assessment performed through TSAP comprises six parameters grouped into two categories: (i) the way the player has possession of the ball and (ii) the way the player disposes the ball. The first category comprises two parameters: (1) conquering the ball "CB"—the intercepted balls, the stolen balls and the balls regained after a shot at goal or poor passes; (2) balls received "BR"—balls received from teammates and that remain under control of the player. The second category comprises the other four parameters: (3) playing a neutral ball "NB"—a pass that does not result in a risk for the opposing team; (4) losing the ball "LB"—the ball is stolen by the opposition; (5) playing an offensive ball "OB"—passes that put the team in favourable conditions to shoot at goal and (6) executing a successful shot "SS"—shot followed by goal.

After proceeding with the observation and recording of these parameters, the assessment of players' performance is computed based on two scales: the volume of play and the efficiency index. The volume of play, which is represented by the first category, consists of the sum of the data obtained within the parameters *conquering the ball and balls received* [volume of play = CB + BR]. The calculation of the efficiency index is obtained through the result of sum of the conquered balls, offensive balls played and successful shots, divided by the sum of the number of lost balls plus ten [efficiency index scale = (CB+OB+SS)/(LB+10)].

From these results it is possible to obtain the performance level of the player through a nomogram comprised by three scales, in which, the left side scale represents the efficiency index and includes values ranging from 0 to 1.50; the right side scale represents the volume of play and presents values that range from 0 to 30; and the central scale represents the performance level and comprises values ranging from 0 to 30. The performance score of a certain player is determined by the point of intersect of the straight line between the values of the efficiency index and volume of play in the central scale, as in Figure 5.1:

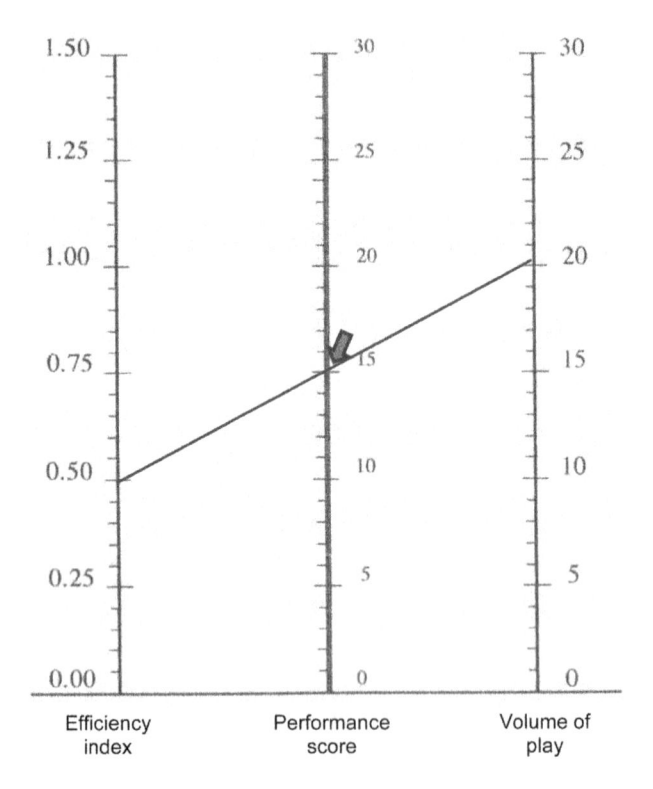

Figure 5.1 Nomogram for assessing performance in team sports
Source: Gréhaigne, Godbout, and Bouthier (1997)

After conceiving TSAP, Gréhaigne, Mahut, and Fernandez (2001) proposed another way of assessing players' performance, more specifically for the context of soccer, which considered the game as a whole, with its structures and configurations. This new proposal was designed in an attempt to obtain objective, reliable and valid performance indicators. For such, the authors used a method that combined the study of qualitative and quantitative variables of players' actions in the field. The qualitative observation tools were based on the effective play-space, the action zone and the configurations of play, whereas the quantitative assessment was supported by the nomogram utilized in TSAP (Gréhaigne et al., 1997).

To assess the effective play-space, the authors presented a division of the field in four areas (defensive, pre-defensive, pre-offensive and offensive) that consists of a static observational grid. Based on this, the effective play-space was defined as a polygonal area linking all the players involved in the action located in the periphery of play at a given moment. Subsequently, the authors defined five categories of effective play-space, taking into account the location of the ball in the offensive half, which were named B1 to B5 according to their variations among the central and lateral positions of the field. After this procedure, they reported to the teams' centre of gravity, obtained through an imaginary line linking the locations of the players within the two main defensive axes, so as to verify whether there were indications of the notion of "in block" or "in pursuit" for the defence.

In order to assess the players' action zone, the researchers divided the field in forty equal squares (A1, A2, ... H5) and recorded the location of the players every 30 seconds, thus providing a cloud of 180 points per player. Players' movements were represented through points within the respective movement spaces. Thus, the darker the space (more points), the higher the frequency of appearance of the players and, the lighter the space, the lower the frequency of appearance of the player within that given space, as in Figure 5.2.

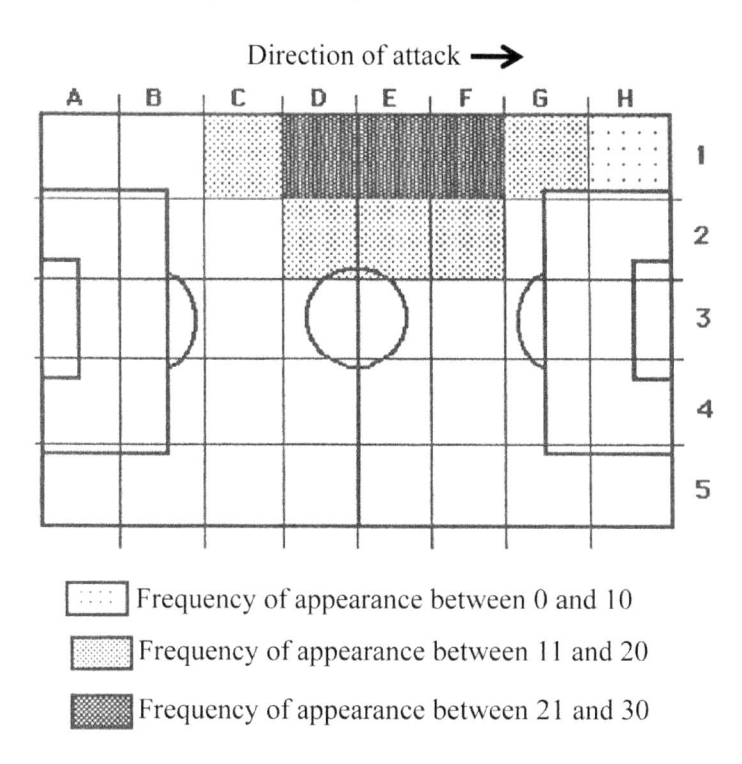

Figure 5.2 Example of assessment of a player's action zones
Source: Gréhaigne et al. (2001)

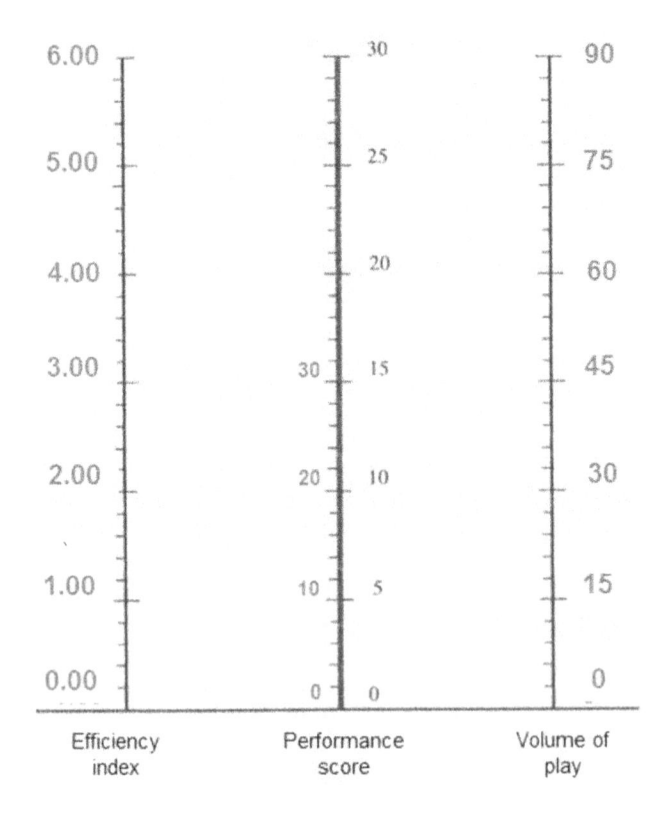

Figure 5.3 Nomogram with two performance scores
Source: Gréhaigne et al. (2001)

In order to assess the quantitative data, the authors referred to the nomogram used in TSAP; however, they have made some modifications in regard to the scales used in order to adjust the assessment of players' positioning in the field. The addition of this variable is important, since the position the player occupies in the field during a match might provide him/her with more or less opportunities to receive the ball, thus favouring his/her volume of play, efficiency and performance indexes. To nullify such effect, the authors proposed two performance score scales: one for a volume of play up to 45 minutes and another one for a volume of play higher than 45 minutes.

5.3.1.2 Game Performance Assessment Instrument (GPAI)

In 1998, Oslin Mitchel and Griffin proposed a sports performance assessment instrument named Game Performance Assessment Instrument (GPAI). It was conceived as a multidimensional, flexible observation instrument to be used in playing context or through video footage, in order to evaluate players' offensive and defensive playing tactical behaviour. Through this instrument, it is possible to assess the skills displayed by the players so as to solve tactical problems of the game by means of three components: making decisions, moving appropriately and executing skills.

The instrument includes seven game components: (1) base: appropriate return of performer to a "home" or "recovery" position between skill attempts; (2) adjust: movement of performer, either offensively or defensively, as required by the flow of the game; (3) decision-making: making appropriate choices about what to do with the ball during the game: (4) skill execution: Efficient performance of selected skills; (5) support: off-the-ball movement to a position to receive a pass; (6) cover: defensive support for player making a play on-the-ball, or moving to the ball; and (7) guard/mark: defending an opponent who may or may not have the ball. From these components, only "base" is not important for soccer performance, due to its specificity.

GPAI might be employed to measure individual performance components and game involvement. For this, some performance indexes were proposed:

Game involvement = total appropriate responses + number of efficient skill executions + number of inefficient skill executions + number of inappropriate decisions made

Decisions Made Index (DMI) = (number of appropriate decisions made)/(number of inappropriate decisions made)

Skill Execution Index (SEI) = (number of efficient skill executions)/(number of inefficient skill executions)

Support Index (SI) = (number of appropriate supporting movements)/(number of inappropriate supporting movements)

Game performance = (DM1 + SEI + SI)/3

Particularly conceived to be used in early sports development stages, GPAI may also meet the coach's needs in terms of performance assessment within the context of competition, not being absolutely necessary to consider all of its components, but only those that are more specific for the evaluation context (Mesquita, 2006; Memmert & Harvey, 2008).

5.3.1.3 KORA Tests Battery

In another proposal, German researchers suggested the KORA tests battery to assess tactical performance. These tests comprise assessment procedures through experts' rate that allows to evaluate two parameters regarding tactical skills: offering and orienting (O.O) and recognizing spaces (R.S). Within the group of activities and games that are employed to provide tactical tasks, the first skill refers to the player's awareness in obtaining optimal position at the right moments, whereas the second regards the player's ability to recognize chances to reach the goal (Kröger & Roth, 2002).

The aim of the assessment is to determine the level of game intelligence and tactical creativity, since both parameters are assessed through the perspectives of

148 *Improving Quality Play*

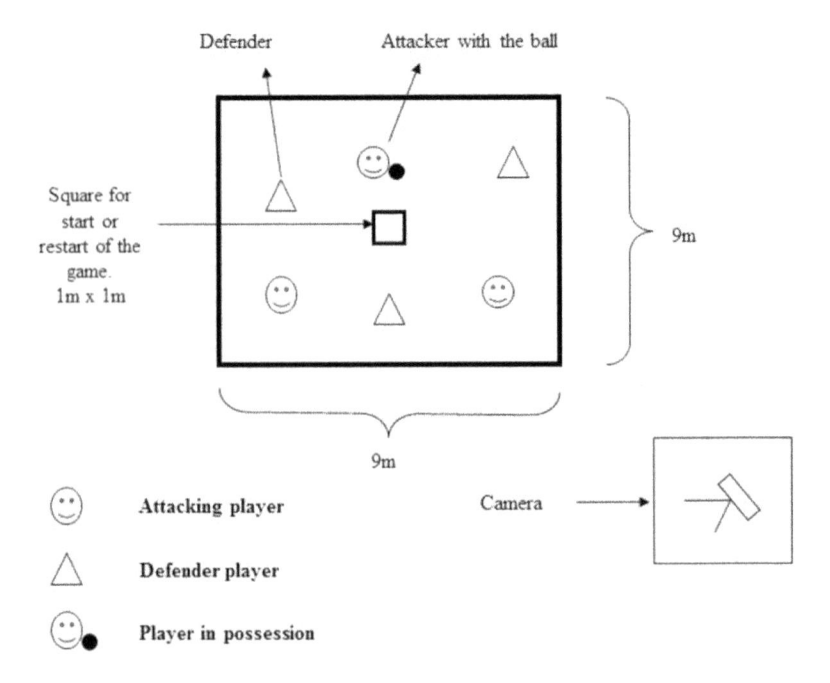

Figure 5.4 Structure and organization of the KORA:O.O test
Source: Greco et al. (2004)

convergent and divergent thinking and their relations with tactical intelligence and creativity, respectively (Greco, Roth, & Schörer, 2004).

In the KORA (O.O) test, the participants are grouped in threes, with vests numbered 1 to 6. Each group has a set of vests of different colours, numbered 1 to 3, for one colour, and 4 to 6, for the other colour, with the aim of facilitating player's identification by the experts. The test consists of video recording participants' actions that play a game with tactical arrangement in the three versus three system, in a space of 81 m^2, playing with their feet, with the aim of retaining ball possession, with free movement allowed inside the delimited area (as in Figure 5.4).

The tactical actions are video recorded for 3 minutes for each group in the possession of the ball, with an exchange of attack-defence tasks between the groups after the end of the protocol's stipulated time. According to the protocol, every time the ball is touched by the team whose task is to intercept the opponent's pass, the game should be stopped and restarted in the centre of the delimited area.

In contrast, in the KORA (R.E) test, seven players are allocated in three groups: (Group 1)—two players; (Group 2)—three players; (Group 3)—two players. Inside a total area of 7 m by 8 m, two players of each of the groups one and three are placed in a delimited area of 3 m by 8 m. The three players from group two are positioned in an area of 1 m by 8 m, located between the areas of groups one and three. The players from groups one and three should, during the 2 minutes of assessment, exchange passes between them, with their feet. Players from group two should try to intercept such passes with any part of their bodies, except their hands, respecting the area delimited for each group. Players from groups one and three cannot carry the ball, being allowed only to shift freely and/or pass the ball to a group mate until the moment of passing the ball to the other area of the test arises. In the test protocol, a maximum height of 1.5 metres is also established in which the ball may exceed the defensive space. Every time the ball exceeds this height, the tactical action is invalid. Whenever there is an interception of the pass between groups one and three by the players from group two, the ball should return to the group which originated the intercepted pass. The tactical actions performed by the players during the game are video recorded for 2 minutes.

The process of evaluation of both tests is performed by three raters and is based on the criteria established by Memmert (2002), which present an ordinal scoring scale, ranging from 0 to 10 points. The assessment of the participants' performance is conducted through the acknowledgement of the patterns formulated by the experts, with a scale of the scores awarded being established for the parameters "offering and orienting" and "recognizing spaces", thus analysing the underlying forms of divergent and convergent thinking within the performed actions.

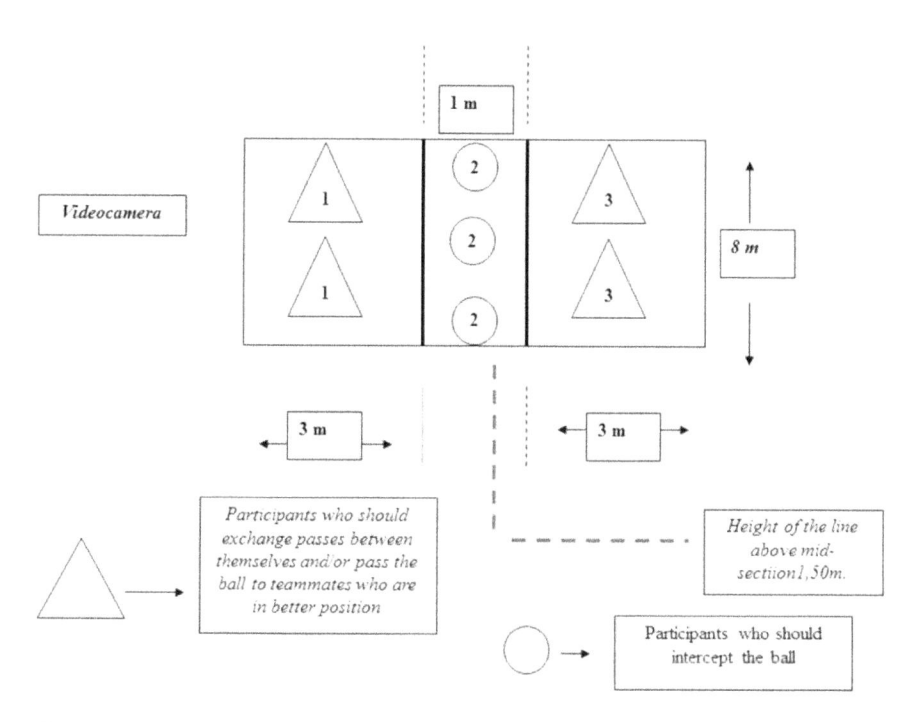

Figure 5.5 Structure and organization of the KORA:R.E test
Source: Greco et al. (2004)

5.3.1.4 Game Performance Evaluation Tool (GPET)

The Game Performance Evaluation Tool (GPET) is a proposal by a group of professors from Universidad de Castilla—La Mancha, Spain, which aims to assess players' movements with and without ball possession based on the offensive operational tactical principles of soccer (Garcia-Lopez et al., 2013).

GPET evaluates players' movements in two levels: decision-making and motor execution. With respect to decision-making, the parameters that are taken into account are the movements of the players with and without ball possession throughout the (offensive and defensive) playing field, the offensive operational tactical principles of soccer and the ball, teammates and opponents' positions. In regard to the motor execution, the assessment parameters are based on ball control, passing, dribbling and shooting on goal.

Based on this information, the evaluators register in an *ad hoc* spreadsheet all actions performed by the players, and classify them with 0 (zero) and 1 (one) values, whereas 0 (zero) refers to negative actions or results, and 1 (one) to positive actions or results.

The field test designed in GPET's protocol takes into account a game of 8 minutes with the following setup: two versus two (2X2) up to five versus five (5X5) with no goalkeepers, and six versus six (1+6X6+1) and seven versus seven (1+7X7+1) with goalkeepers. The test field should have dimensions ranging from seven to 15 metres wide by 20–40 metres long. The video footage of the tests is recorded and subsequently evaluated by trained observers.

Although currently it is not possible to assess players' defensive actions in the game with GPET's protocol, the information provided are enough to support the development process of young soccer players. It is also noteworthy that this group of researchers has been working to propose the assessment of defensive actions through GPET, and this purpose should be available soon.

5.3.1.5 System of Tactical Assessment in Soccer—FUT-SAT

5.3.1.5.1 FUT-SAT's Purpose and Structure

FUT-SAT was built with the aim to provide coaches, teachers and researchers with a means to access specifically, and objectively the information that reflect tactical behaviours performed by players in game situations. Its conceptual structure is based on the core tactical principles of soccer, being for the offensive phase: penetration, offensive coverage, depth mobility, width, length and offensive unity; and for the defensive phase: delay, defensive coverage, balance, concentration and defensive unity.[9] These principles were chosen for representing the core aspects of the process of teaching and training of the tactical capability, and because the main structure is present in all coaches' models of play. Besides, this set of principles has objective measures of the players' motion according to the management of game space performed by them.

Assessment of Tactical Behaviour 151

FUT-SAT comprises two macro-categories, seven categories and 76 variables that are organized according to the type of information dealt with by the system (see Figure 5.6). The Macro-Category Observation comprises three categories and 24 variables. In it, the Tactical Principles category features ten variables. The category Place of Action in the Game Field features four variables, and the category Action Outcomes features ten variables. The Macro-Category Outcome features four categories and 52 variables. In this Macro-Category, all four categories Tactical Performance Index (TPI), Tactical Actions, Error Percentage and Place of Action Related to the Principles (PARP) feature the same 13 variables. The Macro-Category Outcome has this designation due to its variables being dependent on the information coming from the variables that compose the Macro-Category Observation.

Observational Macro-Category

Tactical Principles

Offensive
- Penetration
- Offensive Cover
- Width and Length
- Depth Mobility
- Offensive Unity

Defensive
- Delay
- Defensive Cover
- Balance
- Concentration
- Defensive Unity

Place of Action

Offensive Midfield
- Offensive Actions
- Defensive Actions

Defensive Midfield
- Offensive Actions
- Defensive Actions

Action Outcomes

Offensive
- Shot at goal
- Keep possession of the ball
- Earn a foul, win a corner or throw-in
- Commit a foul, give away a corner or throw-in
- Loss of ball possession

Defensive
- Regain the ball possession
- Earn a foul, win a corner or throw-in
- Commit a foul, give away a corner or throw-in
- Ball possession of the opponent
- Shot at goal of the opponent

Produce Macro-Category

| Tactical Performance Indexes (IPT) | Tactical Actions | Percentage of Error | Location of the action in relation to tactical principles (LARP) |

Offensive
- Penetration
- Offensive Cover
- Width and Length
- Depth Mobility
- Offensive Unity

Defensive
- Delay
- Defensive Cover
- Balance
- Concentration
- Defensive Unity

Game Phases
- Offensive Phase
- Defensive Phase

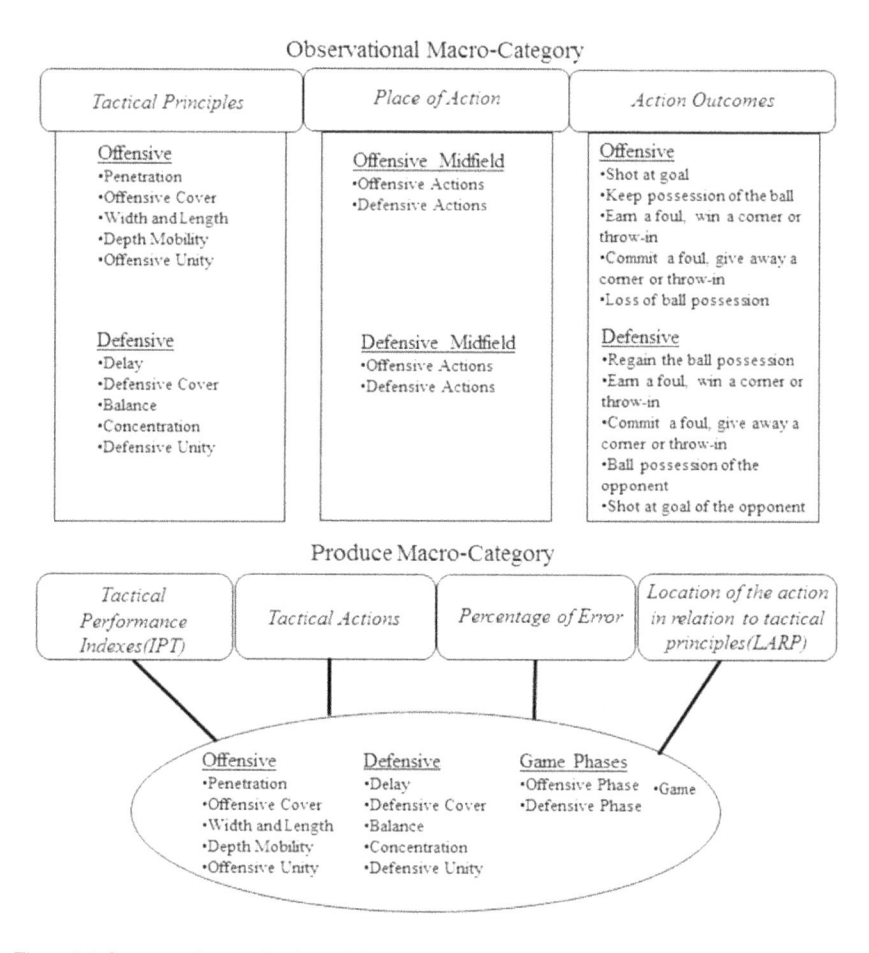

• Game

Figure 5.6 Structural organization of FUT-SAT's variables
Source: Teoldo, Garganta, Greco, Mesquita, and Maia (2011)

5.3.1.5.2 FUT-SAT's Observation Instrument

The observation instrument integrated in this systemic conception of assessment enables the analysis, assessment and classification of the tactical actions, offensive and defensive, performed by the players with and without the ball, according to the variables within the categories Tactical Principles, Place of Action in the Game Field and Action Outcomes, that comprise the Macro-Category Observation. Chart 5.1 shows the categories, sub-categories, variables and definitions used in the observation instrument.

The tactical actions that represent each principle were identified having as criterion the possibility to observe them during the game through players' motion (James, Mellalieu, & Hollely, 2002). Through this procedure it was possible to reference tactical actions, establish spatial references and identify the performance indicators during the performance of each of the principles. This information is displayed on the following chart.

Chart 5.1 Categories, sub-categories, variables and definitions of FUT-SAT's Observation Instrument

Categories	Sub-Categories	Variables	Definitions
Tactical Principles	Offensive	Penetration	Movement of player with the ball towards the goal line.
		Offensive Coverage	Offensive supports to the player with the ball.
		Depth Mobility	Movement of players between the last defender and goal line.
		Width and Length	Movement of players to extend and use the effective play-space.
		Offensive Unity	Movement of the last line of defenders towards the offensive midfield, in order to support offensive actions of the teammates.
	Defensive	Delay	Actions to slow down the opponent's attempt to move forward with the ball.
		Defensive Coverage	Positioning of off-ball defenders behind the "delay" player, providing defensive support.
		Balance	Positioning of off-ball defenders in reaction to movements of attackers, trying to achieve the numerical stability or superiority in the opposition relationship.
		Concentration	Positioning of off-ball defenders to occupy vital spaces and protect the scoring area.
		Defensive Unity	Positioning of off-ball defenders to reduce the effective play-space of the opponents.

Chart 5.1 (Continued)

Categories	Sub-Categories	Variables	Definitions
Place of Action	Offensive Midfield	Offensive Actions	Offensive actions performed in the offensive midfield.
		Defensive Actions	Defensive actions performed in the offensive midfield.
	Defensive Midfield	Offensive Actions	Offensive actions performed in the defensive midfield.
		Defensive Actions	Defensive actions performed in the defensive midfield.
Action Outcomes	Offensive	Shoot at goal	When a player shoots at goal, and (a) scores a goal, (b) the goalkeeper makes a save, (c) the ball touches one of the goalposts or the crossbar.
		Keep possession of the ball	When team players execute passes to each other and keep up with the ball.
		Earn a foul, win a corner or throw-in	When the match is stopped due to a foul, corner or throw-in, the team that was attacking KEEPS possession of the ball.
		Commit a foul, give away a corner or throw in	When the match is stopped due to a foul, corner or throw-in, the possession of the ball CHANGES to the team that was in defence.
		Loss of ball possession	When the attacking team loses the ball possession.
	Defensive	Regain the ball possession	When the defensive players regain the ball possession.
		Earn a foul, win a corner or throw-in	When the match is stopped due to a foul, corner or throw-in and the possession of the ball CHANGES to the team that was in defence.
		Commit a foul, give away a corner or throw in	When the match is stopped due to a foul, corner or throw-in, the team that was attacking KEEPS possession of the ball.
		Ball possession of the opponent	When the defensive players do not regain the ball possession.
		Take a shot at own goal	When the defensive team takes a shot at their own goal, and (a) takes a goal, (b) the goalkeeper makes a save, (c) the ball touches one of the goalposts or the crossbar.

Source: Teoldo, Garganta, Greco, Mesquita, and Maia (2011)

Chart 5.2 Spatial references, tactical actions and performance indicators of the core tactical principles assessed through FUT-SAT

PENETRATION
Spatial References
Opponent's goal (convergent); or opponent's goal line (divergent).
Tactical Actions
Carrying the ball through the available space (with or without defenders ahead).
Perform dribbles searching for numerical advantage in attacking situations or that enable the sequence of the play towards the opponent's bottom line or goal.
Carry the ball towards the opponent's bottom line or goal.
Perform dribbles towards the opponent's bottom line or goal searching for favourable conditions for a pass/assistance to a teammate to resume the play.
Performance Indicators
Successful (+)
a. Enables shooting, passing or dribbling.
Unsuccessful (−)
a. Allows opponent's tackle/b-Force the play to an occupied space.
Description of Performance Indicators
Successful (+)
a. When the movement of the player in possession of the ball enables (offensive) shooting, passing or dribbling.
Unsuccessful (−)
a. When the movement of the player in possession of the ball allows the opponent to recover possession.
b. When the player in possession of the ball goes towards a space that is already occupied by other players, thus hindering his/her team's offensive action.
OFFENSIVE COVERAGE
Spatial References
Centre of play; or less offensive half and the playing corridor
Tactical Actions
Offer constant passing lines/zones to the player in possession of the ball.
Closer support to the player in possession of the ball that allows to keep possession.
Perform 1–2 and/or triangular combinations with the player in possession of the ball.
Closer support to the player in possession of the ball that allows to keep possession.

Chart 5.2 (Continued)

Performance Indicators
Successful (+)
a. Ensures passing lines/zones.   b. Decreases the pressure on the player in possession of the ball.   c. Allows shooting possibilities.
Unsuccessful (−)
a. Does not ensure passing lines/zones.   b. Does not decrease the pressure on the player in possession of the ball.   c. Does not allow shooting possibilities.
Description of Performance Indicators
Successful (+)
a. When players' movement ensures passing lines/zones to the player in possession of the ball.   b. When players' movement enables the decrease of the number of players around the player in possession of the ball.   c. When players' movement allows shooting possibilities.
Unsuccessful (−)
a. When players' movement does not ensure passing lines/zones to the player in possession of the ball.   b. When players' movement does not enable the decrease of the number of players around the player in possession of the ball.   c. When players' movement does not allow shooting possibilities.
DEPTH MOBILITY
Spatial References
Line of the last defender and opponent's goal; or line of the last defender and opponent's goal line
Tactical Actions
In-depth or wide moves "behind the back" of the last defender towards the opponent's bottom line or goal.
In-depth or wide moves "behind the back" of the last defender aimed to the gain of offensive space.
In-depth or wide moves "behind the back" of the last defender that favour ball reception.
In-depth or wide moves "behind the back" of the last defender aimed at creating opportunities to the offensive sequence of the play.

(Continued)

Chart 5.2 (Continued)

Performance Indicators
Successful (+)
a. Enables a deep pass to a teammate. b. Enlarges the EP-S "behind the back" of the defence.
Unsuccessful (–)
a. Does not enable a deep pass to a teammate. b. Player is "offside".
Description of Performance Indicators
Successful (+)
a. When players' movement provides the player in possession of the ball with the possibility of performing a deep pass to a teammate in an action of disruption in relation to the opponent's defence. b. When players' movement allows the enlargement of the team's effective play-space "behind the back" of the last defensive line.
Unsuccessful (–)
a. When players' movement does not provide the player in possession of the ball with the possibility of performing a deep pass to a teammate in an action of disruption in relation to the opponent's defence. b. When players' movement puts him/her into an "offside" situation.
WIDTH AND LENGTH
Spatial References
Line of the ball and line of the last defender; or line of the ball, side line and team's goal.
Tactical Actions
Search for spaces not occupied by opponents within the field.
Movements of enlargement of the space of play that allow numerical advantage in attack.
Dribbling backwards/sideways that allow to decrease opponent's pressure on the ball.
Movements that allow to (re)start the offensive process in zones further from that where the recovery of possession occurred.
Performance Indicators
Successful (+)
a. Enlarges EP-S in width. b. Enlarges EP-S in depth. c. Creates spaces for teammates' movements. d. Goes to safer zones. e. Decreases pressure (sideways or behind the CP)/f-Keeps ball possession.

Chart 5.2 (Continued)

Unsuccessful (−)
a. Does not enlarge EP-S in width.   b. Does not enlarge EP-S in length.   c. Does not create spaces for teammates' movements.   d. Does not go to safer zones.   e. Does not decrease pressure (sideways or behind the CP)/f-Allows opponent to recover possession.
Description of Performance Indicators
Successful (+)
a. When players' movement enables his/her team to enlarge the space of play in width, that is, enlarges the transverse limit of the effective play-space.
b. When players' movement enables the enlargement of the space of play in depth, until the last defender's line, that is, enlarges the longitudinal limit of the effective play-space.
c. When players' movement (even towards a zone of higher pressure) enables the creation of spaces for teammates' movements or a successful pass.
d. When players' movement allows him/her to be positioned in zones with lower opponent's pressure (inside the effective play-space).
e. When players' movement (sideways or backward displacements) enables the decrease of pressure on the ball and ensures the conditions to resume the offensive play.
f. When players' movement (sideways or backward displacements) enables the team to keep possession.
Unsuccessful (−)
a. When players' movement does not enable his/her team to enlarge the space of play in width, that is, does not enlarge the transverse limit of the effective play-space.
b. When players' movement does not enable the enlargement of the space of play in depth, until the last defender's line, that is, does not enlarge the longitudinal limit of the effective play-space.
c. When players' movement (even towards a zone of higher pressure) does not enable the creation of spaces for teammates' movements or a successful pass.
d. When players' movement does not allow him/her to be positioned in zones with lower opponent's pressure (inside the effective play-space).
e. When players' movement (sideways or backward displacements) does not enable the decrease of pressure on the ball and does not ensure the conditions to resume the offensive play.
f. When players' movement (sideways or backward displacements) does not enable the team to keep possession.

(Continued)

Chart 5.2 (Continued)

OFFENSIVE UNITY
Spatial References
Less offensive half of the centre of play and the team's goal; or less offensive half of the centre of play and the side line; or less offensive half of the centre of ply and the playing corridor.
Tactical Actions
• Progression of the last defensive line, allowing the team to play as a block.
• When the last defensive line moves away from the defensive zones and approach the midfield line.
• Progression of the defensive players allowing more players to take part in the actions within the centre of play.
• Movements of player(s) that contribute(s) to the execution of collective offensive actions behind the ball line.
Performance Indicators
Successful (+)
a. Approximates the team to the CP.
b. Takes part in the subsequent action.
c. Contributes to offensive actions behind the ball line/d-Helps the team to progress towards the PO area.
Unsuccessful (−)
a. Does not approximate the team to the CP.
b. Does not take part in the subsequent action.
c. Does not contribute to offensive actions behind the ball line.
d. Does not help the team to progress towards the PO area.
Description of Performance Indicators
Successful (+)
a. When players' movement allows other teammates to take part in the team's actions or to approach the centre of play.
b. When players' movement enables him/her to take part in a subsequent offensive/defensive action.
c. When players' movement contributes to the execution of team's offensive actions behind the ball line.
d. When players' movement helps the team to progress towards the offensive half.
Unsuccessful (−)
a. When players' movement does not allow other teammates to take part in the team's actions or to approach the centre of play.
b. When players' movement does not enable him/her to take part in a subsequent offensive/defensive action.

Chart 5.2 (Continued)

c. When players' movement does not contribute to the execution of team's offensive actions behind the ball line.
d. When players' movement does not help the team to progress towards the offensive half.
DELAY
Spatial References
Defending goal and the more offensive half of the centre of play.
Tactical Actions
• Marking the player in possession of the ball, preventing the action of penetration. • Action of "protecting the ball" that prevents the opponent to reach it. • "Double mark" the player in possession of the ball. • Perform technical fouls to hold the opposite progression, when the defensive system is disorganized.
Performance Indicators
Successful (+)
a. Prevents shooting. b. Prevents progression. c. Delays opponent's action. d. Forces the player in possession of the ball to go safer zones.
Unsuccessful (−)
a. Does not prevent shooting. b. Does not prevent progression. c. Does not delay opponent's action. d. Does not force the player in possession of the ball to go safer zones.
Description of Performance Indicators
Successful (+)
a. When players' movement/opposition prevents the player in possession of the ball to shoot at goal.
b. When players' movement prevents the player in possession of the ball to progress towards the goal.
c. When players' movement delays the opponent's offensive action, allowing his/her team to be defensively organized.
d. When players' movement forces the player in possession of the ball to go to safer zones.

(Continued)

160   *Improving Quality Play*

Chart 5.2 (Continued)

Unsuccessful (–)
a. When players' movement /opposition does not prevent the player in possession of the ball to shoot at goal.
b. When players' movement does not prevent the player in possession of the ball to progress towards the goal.
c. When players' movement does not delay the opponent's offensive action, and does not allow his/her team to be defensively organized.
d. When players' movement does not force the player in possession of the ball to go to safer zones.
DEFENSIVE COVERAGE
a. **Spatial References**
b. Player in delay, defending goal and more offensive half of the centre of play.
c. **Tactical Actions**
d. Actions of coverage to the player in delay.
e. Positioning that allows the obstruction of potential passing lines/zones to opposite players.
f. Marking opponent(s) who may receive the ball in advantageous attacking situations.
g. Adequate positioning that allows to mark the player in possession of the ball whenever the player in delay is beaten.
h. **Performance Indicators**
Successful (+)
a. Is positioned between the player in delay and the goal/b-Enables 2nd delay action/c-Obstructs passing lines/zones.
Unsuccessful (–)
a. Is not positioned between the player in delay and the goal/b-Does not enable 2nd delay action/c-Does not obstruct passing lines/zones.
Description of Performance Indicators
Successful (+)
a. When players' movement allows positioning between the player in delay and the goal, within the more offensive half of the centre of play.
b. When players' movement allows him/her to be a new obstacle to the player in possession of the ball, in case the player in delay is beaten.
c. When players' movement enables the obstruction or interception of passing lines/zones from the player in possession of the ball to other opponents.
Unsuccessful (–)
a. When players' movement does not allow positioning between the player in delay and the goal, within the more offensive half of the centre of play.

Chart 5.2 (Continued)

b. When players' movement does not allow him/her to be a new obstacle to the player in possession of the ball, in case the player in delay is beaten.
c. When players' movement does not enable the obstruction or interception of passing lines/zones from the player in possession of the ball to other opponents.
BALANCE
Spatial References
More offensive half of the centre of play, zones and areas of play; or less offensive half of the centre of play.
Tactical Actions
Movements that ensure defensive stability.
Movements of defensive recovery performed behind the ball line.
Positioning that enables the obstruction of potential passing lines/zones.
Marking opposite players who support offensive actions of the player in possession of the ball.
Performance Indicators
Successful (+)
a. Stabilizes lateral zones of the CP.   b. Obstructs passing lines/zones.   c. Stabilizes CPO zone.   d. Pressurizes the player in possession of the ball within the CPO zone/e-Obstructs passing lines/zones.
Unsuccessful (−)
a. Does not stabilize lateral zones of the CP.   b. Does not obstruct passing lines/zones.   c. Does not stabilize CPO zone.   d. Does not pressure the player in possession of the ball within the CPO zone.   e. Does not obstruct passing lines/zones.
Description of Performance Indicators
Successful (+)
a. When players' movement allows to create defensive stability in the relations of opposition within the lateral zones in relation to the centre of play (through marking opponents who may receive the ball or obstructing passing lines/zones), preventing the opponent's offensive progression.
b. When players' movement allows to obstruct or intercept passing lines/zones of the player in possession of the ball to another opponent positioned in the lateral zones in relation to the centre of play.

(Continued)

Chart 5.2 (Continued)

c. When players' movement allows to create defensive stability in the relations of opposition within the less offensive half of the centre of play, by marking opponents who may receive the ball or by obstructing passing lines/zones.
d. When player's defensive recovery movement (less offensive half of the centre of play) interferes in the action of the player in possession of the ball thus generating difficulties to the opponent's offensive sequence or facilitating ball recovery by his/her team.
e. When players' movement allows to obstruct or intercept passing lines/zones of the player in possession of the ball to other opponents within the less offensive half of the centre of play.
Unsuccessul (−)
a. When players' movement does not allow to create defensive stability in the relations of opposition within the lateral zones in relation to the centre of play (through marking opponents who may receive the ball or obstructing passing lines/zones), and does not prevent the opponent's offensive progression.
b. When players' movement does not allow to obstruct or intercept passing lines/zones of the player in possession of the ball to another opponent positioned in the lateral zones in relation to the centre of play.
c. When players' movement does not allow to create defensive stability in the relations of opposition within the less offensive half of the centre of play, by marking opponents who may receive the ball or by obstructing passing lines/zones.
d. When player's defensive recovery movement (less offensive half of the centre of play) does not interfere in the action of the player in possession of the ball thus generating difficulties to the opponent's offensive sequence or facilitating ball recovery by his/her team.
e. When players' movement does not allow to obstruct or intercept passing lines/zones of the player in possession of the ball to other opponents within the less offensive half of the centre of play
CONCENTRATION
Spatial References
More offensive half of the centre of play and zones of the playing field.
Tactical Actions
• Movements that enable defensive support within the zone of lower risk to the team.
• Marking opposite players who search for the enlargement of the offensive play-space.
• Movements that enable an increased number of players between the ball and the goal.
• Movements that force the opponent's attacking actions towards the sides of the field.

Chart 5.2 (Continued)

Performance Indicators
Successful (+)
a. Reduce opponent's depth.
b. Force opponent's play towards safer zones.
Unsuccessful (−)
a. Does not reduce opponent's depth.
b. Does not force opponent's play towards safer zones.
Description of Performance Indicators
Successful (+)
a. When players' movements help the team reducing the opponent's offensive amplitude (or effective play-space) in its depth.
b. When players' movements help the team forcing the opponent's play towards safer zones.
Unsuccessful (−)
a. When players' movements do not help the team reducing the opponent's offensive amplitude (or effective play-space) in its depth.
b. When players' movements do not help the team forcing the opponent's play towards safer zones.
DEFENSIVE UNITY
Spatial References
The line of the ball and the opponent's goal line; or the next area(s) in relation to the zone where the more offensive half of the centre of play is; or the wing opposite to where the ball is, delimited by the line of the ball and the border of the next area of the game.
Tactical Actions
Organization of defensive positioning after losing possession, with the purpose of recreating the defensive lines.
Players' movements, particularly full-backs and wingers, towards the central corridor when playing actions are developed in the opposite side.
Defensive packing within the zone of the field that represents higher risk to goal.
Movements of players who make up the last defensive line so as to reduce opponent's play-space (through the "offside" rule).
Performance Indicators
Successful (+)
a. Reduces opponent's amplitude/b-(Re)balances defensive organization/c-Contributes to defensive actions behind the ball line/d-Approximates the team to the CP/e-Takes part in subsequent action.

(Continued)

Chart 5.2 (Continued)

Unsuccessful (−)
a. Does not reduce opponent's amplitude.
b. Does not (re)balance defensive organization.
c. Does not contribute to defensive actions behind the ball line.
d. Does not approximate the team to the CP.
e. Does not take part in subsequent action.
Description of Performance Indicators
Successful (+)
a. When players' movement allows the reduction of opponent's offensive amplitude in width and/or depth.
b. When players' movement allows to constantly balance or rebalance the distribution of forces of the defensive organization according to the momentary game situations (subsequent area in relation to the more offensive half of the centre of play).
c. When players' movement contributes to the execution of defensive actions behind the ball line (by marking opposite players who may receive the ball or by obstructing passing lines/zones).
d. When players' movement allows other defensive player to take part in the actions within the centre of play.
e. When players' movement allows him/her to take part in a defensive/offensive subsequent action.
Unsuccessful (−)
a. When players' movement does not allow the reduction of opponent's offensive amplitude in width and/or depth.
b. When players' movement does not allow to constantly balance or rebalance the distribution of forces of the defensive organization according to the momentary game situations (subsequent area in relation to the more offensive half of the centre of play).
c. When players' movement does not contribute to the execution of defensive actions behind the ball line (by marking opposite players who may receive the ball or by obstructing passing lines/zones).
d. When players' movement does not allow other defensive player to take part in the actions within the centre of play.
e. When players' movement does not allow him/her to take part in a defensive/offensive subsequent action.

Source: Teoldo, Garganta, Greco, and Mesquita (2009)

5.3.1.5.3 Characterization of FUT-SAT's Field Test

The field test within this system is named "GK+3X3+GK" test, which is performed during 4 minutes in a field of 36 metres long by 27 metres wide. The dimensions of this test were calculated based on the measures of a soccer field permitted by the International Football Association Board and on the ratio calculation of the use of game space by outfield players. The amount of time was established through a pilot study, in which it was found that four minutes, comparatively with the time length of up to eight minutes, would suffice for all players to perform the actions related with all of the tactical principles assessed by FUT-SAT's observation instrument. The next chart displays information regarding other arrangements of FUT-SAT's field test.

Chart 5.3 References of values for the arrangements of FUT-SAT's field test

Arrangement	Length	Width	Radius Centre of Play	Duration	Goal Size	Goalkeeper Area
GK+3X3+GK	27 m	13.5 m	5 m	4 min	5–6 m × 2–2.2 m	5 m
GK+3X3+GK	30 m	19.5 m	5 m	4 min	5–6 m × 2–2.2 m	5 m
GK+3X3+GK	36 m	27 m	5 m	4 min	5–6 m × 2–2.2 m	5 m
GK+4X4+GK	36 m	18 m	6 m	4 min	5–6 m × 2–2.2 m	5 m
GK+4X4+GK	40 m	26 m	6 m	4 min	5–6 m × 2–2.2 m	5 m
GK+4X4+GK	48 m	36 m	6 m	4 min	5–6 m × 2–2.2 m	5 m
GK+5X5+GK	45 m	22.5 m	6 m	4 min	5–6 m × 2–2.2 m	5 m or 8 m
GK+5X5+GK	50 m	32.5 m	6 m	4 min	5–6 m × 2–2.2 m	5 m or 8 m
GK+5X5+GK	60 m	45 m	6 m	4 min	5–6 m × 2–2.2 m	5 m or 8 m
GK+6X6+GK	54 m	27 m	7 m	4 min	5–6 m × 2–2.2 m or 7.32 m × 2.44 m	5 m or 8 m
GK+6X6+GK	60 m	39 m	7 m	4 min	5–6 m × 2–2.2 m or 7.32 m × 2.44 m	5 m or 8 m
GK+6X6+GK	72 m	54 m	7 m	4 min	5–6 m × 2–2.2 m or 7.32 m × 2.44 m	5 m or 8 m
GK+7X7+GK	63 m	31.5 m	8 m	6 min	5–6 m × 2–2.2 m or 7.32 m × 2.44 m	8 m or 11 m
GK+7X7+GK	70 m	45.5 m	8 m	6 min	5–6 m × 2–2.2 m or 7.32 m × 2.44 m	8 m or 11 m
GK+7X7+GK	84 m	63 m	8 m	6 min	5–6 m × 2–2.2 m or 7.32 m × 2.44 m	8 m or 11 m
GK+8X8+GK	72 m	36 m	8 m	6 min	5–6 m × 2–2.2 m or 7.32 m × 2.44 m	11 m or 16.5 m
GK+8X8+GK	80 m	52 m	8 m	6 min	5–6 m × 2–2.2 m or 7.32 m × 2.44 m	11m or 16.5 m

(Continued)

Chart 5.3 (Continued)

Arrangement	Length	Width	Radius Centre of Play	Duration	Goal Size	Goalkeeper Area
GK+8X8+GK	96 m	72 m	8 m	6 min	5–6 m × 2–2.2 m or 7.32 m × 2.44 m	11 m or 16.5 m
GK+9X9+GK	81 m	40.5 m	9 m	8 min	7.32 m × 2.44 m	11 m or 16.5 m
GK+9X9+GK	90 m	58.5 m	9 m	8 min	7.32 m × 2.44 m	11 m or 16.5 m
GK+9X9+GK	108 m	81 m	9 m	8 min	7.32 m × 2.44 m	11 m or 16.5 m
GK+10X10+GK	90 m	45 m	9.15 m	8 min	7.32 m × 2.44 m	16.5 m
GK+10X10+GK	100 m	65 m	9.15 m	8 min	7.32 m × 2.44 m	16.5 m
GK+10X10+GK	120 m	90 m	9.15 m	8 min	7.32 m × 2.44 m	16.5 m

Source: The authors

Resorting to the Goalkeeper+3 versus 3+Goalkeeper structure for the field test is explained through the comprehension that this structure ensures the occurrence of all tactical principles inherent in the formal game. This arrangement allows, in offensive terms, to go from a binary choice to a multiple choice and preserves the notion of playing without the ball, since it gathers the player in possession of the ball and two potential receivers. From the defensive perspective, it gathers a direct opponent to the player in possession of the ball (1st defender) to perform the delay and two defenders (second and third), relatively further away from the player in possession of the ball, to perform eventual covers, double marking and compensations, thus respecting the remaining defensive tactical principles.

To conduct the test, the participants are randomly allocated in two teams of three players each, and numbered from one to three for one team and four to six6 for another, aiming at facilitating the identification of players in the video. During the application, the players are asked to play according to the official laws of the game, except by the offside rule. The images are recorded by a video camera placed diagonally in relation to the goal line and the sideline (see Figure 5.7)

5.3.1.5.4 FUT-SAT's Protocol

FUT-SAT's protocol comprises three procedures, which can be performed in a simple way (by only one individual) or favouring dual-input data. The first consists in analysing the actions performed by the players during the match, with the ball possession being the analysis unit. This is considered when a player meets at least one of the following assumptions: (a) performs at least three consecutive contacts with the ball; (b) performs a correct pass (enables the team to keep ball possession) or (c) shoots at goal (Garganta, 1997).

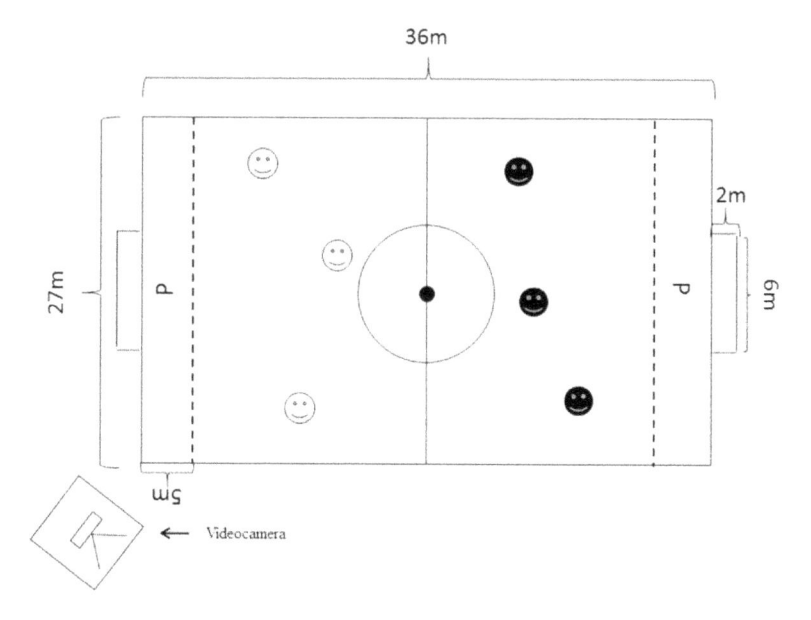

Figure 5.7 Representation of the physical structure of FUT-SAT's field test
Source: Teoldo, Garganta, Greco, Mesquita, and Maia (2011)

The second procedure refers to the assessment, classification and recording of the tactical actions. To accomplish these three actions, the observer relies on the observation instrument and has the support of the software Soccer View®, which was specially designed for FUT-SAT and enables the insertion of the test's spatial references within the video and enables the rigorous assessment of players' positioning and movement within the playing field.

The third procedure is performed automatically by the software Soccer View® and allows you to quickly view the results of individual tactical behaviour and its impact in the team's collective performance (see Figure 5.8).

Figure 5.8 shows the results of the evaluation of two different players. The graphs contain the results of the efficiency of the players' movements in each of the core tactical principles (orange line) and also show the impact of these movements on the team's collective performance (green line). Among the results shown in these graphs, let's analyse the penetration principle and the impact of these progression movements with the ball in the team's collective performance. When analysing these graphs, we find that player 1 is effective in his/her movements of progression with the ball (orange line); however these actions have little impact on the team's collective performance (green line). This is due to the fact that these actions, despite allowing the player and the team to keep possession of the ball, have a reduced impact on the individual and collective tactical behaviour of the opposing team. In this case, the head coach and coaching staff must verify the

168 *Improving Quality Play*

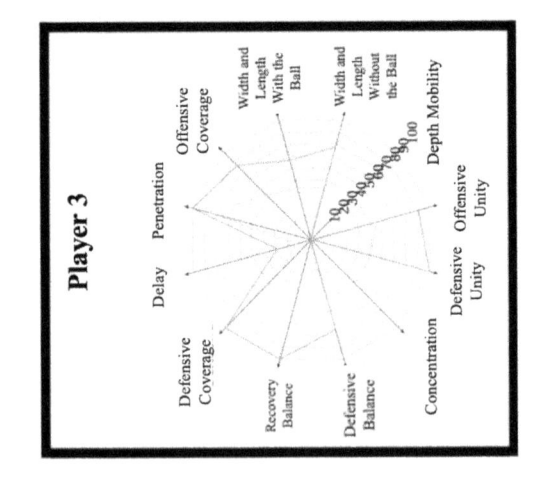

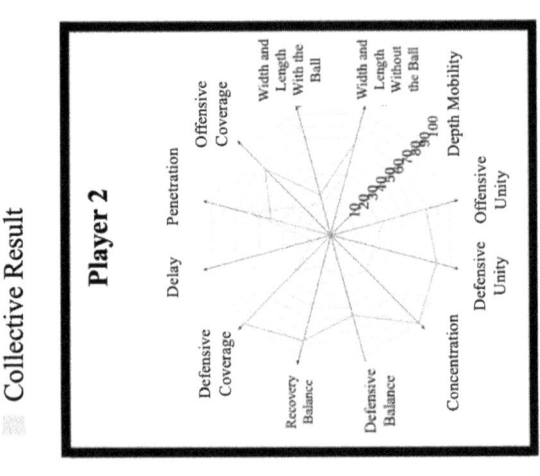

Figure 5.8 Graphical information generated by FUT-SAT through software *Soccer View*®

Source: The authors

reasons why the movements of the teammates of the player with the ball (player 1) are not allowing the team to put the opposition under difficult situations.

Player 2, on the other hand, presents a different pattern, as he/she has low efficiency in movements of progression with the ball (orange line), but even so the collective results for his/her team are positive (green line). In this case, it is clear that the collective offensive support helped minimize this individual difficulty of the player. This same type of analysis can be done to the other results in the graphs, allowing a deeper understanding of the individual characteristics of the player's game space management and the collective impact they exert for the team. Understanding all the limitations and potentialities of the players regarding offensive and defensive movements, near and far from the ball will help to optimize the training process so the players are better able to make quick, intelligent and creative decisions during games.

5.3.2 Laboratory Tests

5.3.2.1 TacticUP®

TacticUP® is an online (www.tacticup.com.br) assessment platform that allows one to know objectively and assertively both game reading and decision-making skills. Based on real match situations and resorting to artificial intelligence, the player is assessed with respect to the time he/she takes to read a play and make a decision for different situations within the game, which take place near or far from the ball.

TacticUP® has four versions for exhaustively assessing the player, taking into account all the theoretical and scientific assumptions (previously described) employed for the development of FUT-SAT. With respect to the initial versions, the game concepts that underpin the reading of a play and/or movements within the field are easier to identify. In the last two versions, these concepts "touch" each other and may generate confusion in reading and interpreting the play, enabling a more rigorous and accurate assessment of the player's knowledge about the game, in order to make a decision. This information is evident both in performance (score) and time spent to read the situation and make a decision.

In TacticUP® all the possible movements the player performs in the field are assessed through videos. Thus, the player is presented with scenes and, at the end, the scene is paused for a few seconds and the player is asked what the player indicated should do.

Next, the screen shows four pictures of the last video image, with four possible solutions for the play (see Figure 5.9). These four pictures comprise four different solutions for conclusion of the play, with arrows that indicate the displacements by the players and the ball. Every picture contains the description of the possible solution to be selected by the player in possession. After analysing each of the four solutions, the participant has to choose the best one and write it down on a registration form.

170　*Improving Quality Play*

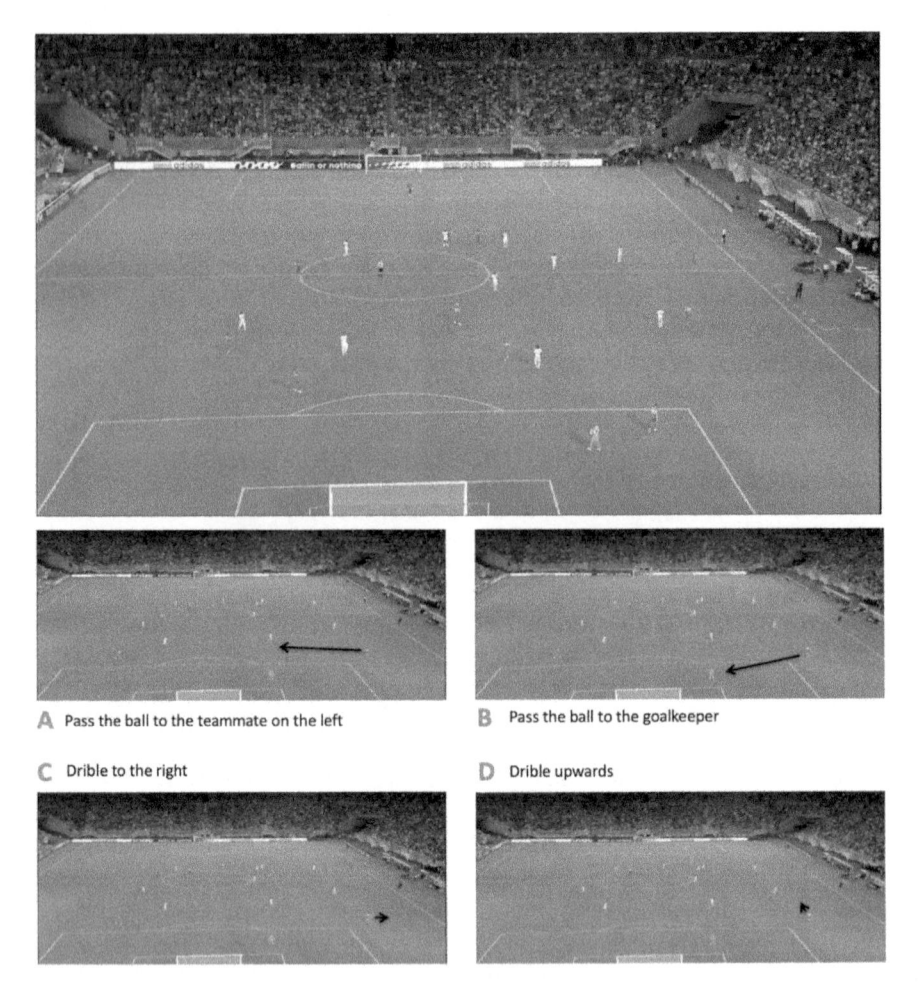

Figure 5.9 Representative image of the moment when the participant has to make the decision for the sequence of play, according to TacticUP®

Source: TacticUP®

5.3.2.1.1 Interpreting Results

HOW TO READ THE INFORMATION?

The results from TacticUP® are displayed graphically, allowing the visualization of the player's complete profile with respect to his/her game reading and decision-making skills. Information are organized so as to enable the visual and quick extraction of information regarding the player's offensive and defensive actions near or far from the ball (see Figure 5.10).

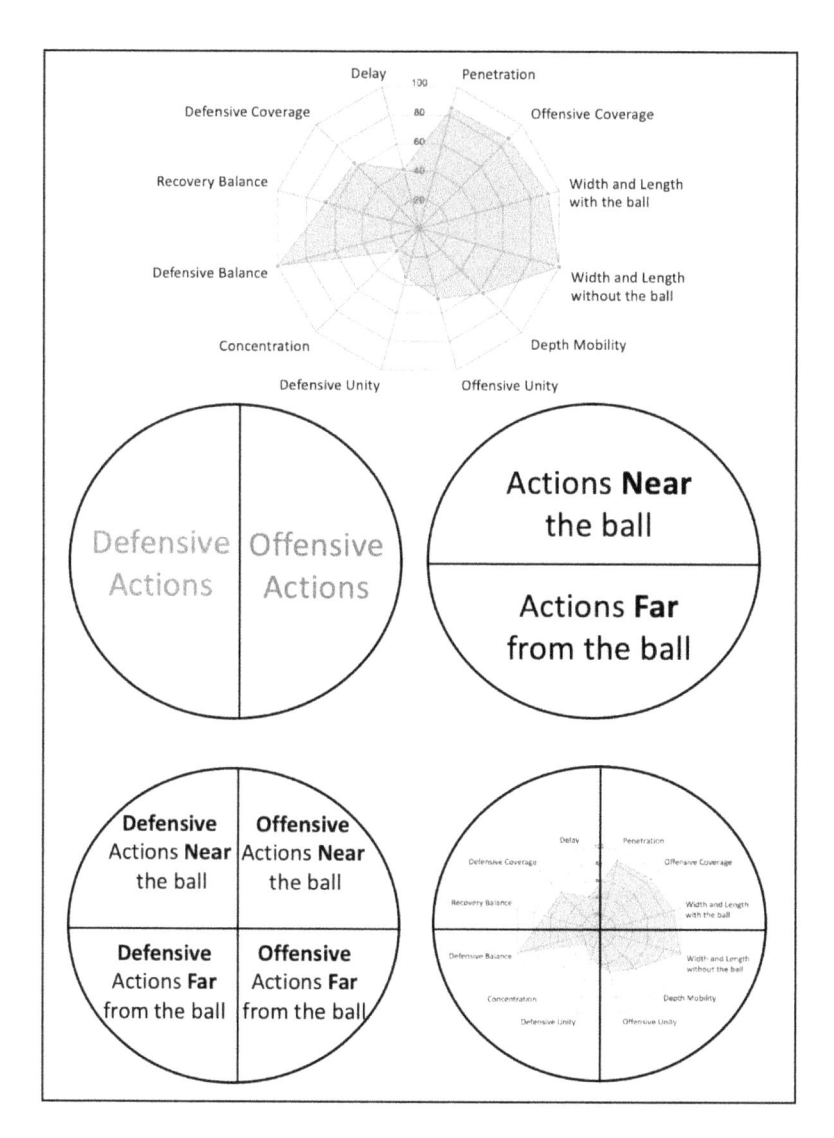

Figure 5.10 Graphic information scheme
Source: TacticUP®

The graphic is organized as follows: (i) the left side displays the results regarding the defensive actions; (ii) the right side displays the results regarding the offensive actions; (iii) the upper side displays the results regarding the actions performed near the ball and (iv) the bottom part displays the results of actions performed far from the ball.

Therefore, it is possible to interpret the graphical information through a subdivision in "quadrants": (i) the upper left quadrant displays the results of the defensive actions near the ball; (ii) the upper right quadrant displays the results of offensive actions near the ball; (iii) the left bottom quadrant displays the results of the defensive actions far from the ball and (iv) the bottom right quadrant displays the results of the offensive actions far from the ball.

5.3.2.1.2 Individual Assessments

ANALYSIS OF ATHLETES' PERFORMANCE

Considering the results of the player in Figure 5.10, it is possible to observe that, overall, he/she displays better game reading and decision-making skills in the offensive actions than in the defensive ones. Also, he/she also exhibits greater ease in actions near the ball, when compared to those far from the ball. In a more detailed interpretation of the results, it is possible to observe that this player has difficulties in offensive actions far from the ball, such as actions of movements behind the last line of defence (Mobility) and also in actions regarding the organization of the attacking lines behind the ball line, thus allowing the team to play in a cohesive and balanced fashion, across their longitudinal and transversal lines (Defensive Unity). On the other hand, he/she displays fair game reading and decision-making skills in the offensive actions in which the player gets closer to the player in possession, thus generating offensive options through passing lanes or space in the opponents' defence for the player in possession to progress (Defensive Coverage).

GRAPHICAL COMPARISON OF ATHLETES' RESPONSE TIME

Figure 5.11 displays the results of response time, grouped according to each tactical principle, in addition to the general (Offensive, Defensive and Overall) indexes of a player. The results are organized according to the proximity of the actions of these principles, whereas those nearer the ball are located in the left side, and those more distant, in the right side. Also, the offensive principles are represented by the blue bars, while the defensive, by the red ones. Therefore, from the visualization of these data, it is possible to observe that, generally, such a player has the ability to respond more quickly in defensive, rather than offensive, actions. An example of offensive difficulty may be observed more clearly in the offensive actions in which the player assessed performs actions with the ball, be it progressing with the ball towards the goal or goal line (Penetration) or even temporization (Length and Width with the ball). These difficulties result in limitations in the performance of these offensive actions within the field, since the speed of play is higher in situations nearer the ball. Thus, it is recommended that training for this player should take into account the situations in which he/she has time pressure to perform actions related to this principle, so as to be able to perform these actions with lower response time.

Assessment of Tactical Behaviour 173

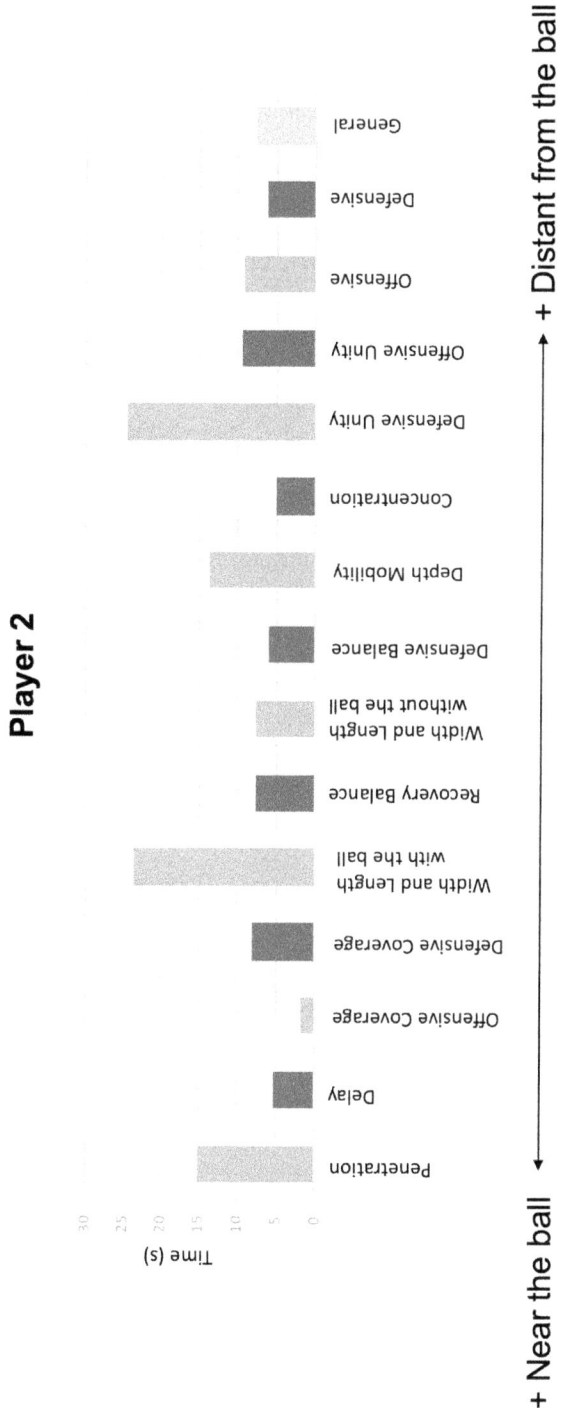

Player 2

Figure 5.11 Result of the individual response time
Source: TacticUP®

5.3.2.1.3 Collective Assessments

COMPARATIVE ANALYSIS OF ATHLETES' PERFORMANCE

TacticUP® collective results allow to examine the differences and similarities between athletes. Figure 5.12 displays results regarding game reading and decision-making skills of four athletes from the same team, which play as defensive midfielders. Through these results it is possible to verify, despite playing in the same position, these players display rather distinct profiles, which will certainly influence their functions, and individual and collective performances in the field.

Among these four athletes, we observe that players 1 and 3 display a more offensive profile, especially in situations near the ball, when compared to players 2 and 4. Hence, armed with this information, we have an indication that players 1 and 3 may be better at performing the role of defensive midfielders who participate more qualitatively at the offensive phase.

On the other hand, players 2 and 4 display a more defensive profile, whereas both are able to perform rather well their defensive actions near the ball. Player 4 may be particularly pointed out due to his/her high performance in defensive actions far from the ball. Given these results, the coaching staff can control the functions these players will perform in training and matches, based on their potentialities and limitations. Also, this information will help the coach develop more assertively his/her players' potentialities during the training sessions, and for the games, select those who are better adapted to his model of play and that, consequently, have better performance within the field.

COMPARATIVE ANALYSIS OF ATHLETES' PERFORMANCE AND DECISION-MAKING TIME ACCORDING TO THE TACTICAL PRINCIPLE

Another way to visualize collective results is by displaying athletes' decision-making time and performance according to the tactical principle. Displaying information in such a way enables a more global idea on how the team is fairing with respect to a collection of movements within the field, as well as obtaining more detailed information on how a given player is playing in comparison to his/her teammates.

In Figure 5.13 it is possible to observe that the athletes within this team display, in general, better performance in the principle of Offensive Coverage (variation between 51 and 87 points) in comparison to the defensive principle of Defensive Coverage (variation from 19 and 74 points). This indicates that they display greater ease in actions of offensive support near the player in possession, by generating passing lanes or space within the opponents' defence for the player in possession to progress (Offensive Coverage), rather than in actions of defensive support "behind the back" of the first defender (Defensive Coverage). This information allows obtaining an objective indication of the

Assessment of Tactical Behaviour 175

Figure 5.12 Results from different defensive midfielders

Source: TacticUP®

176 *Improving Quality Play*

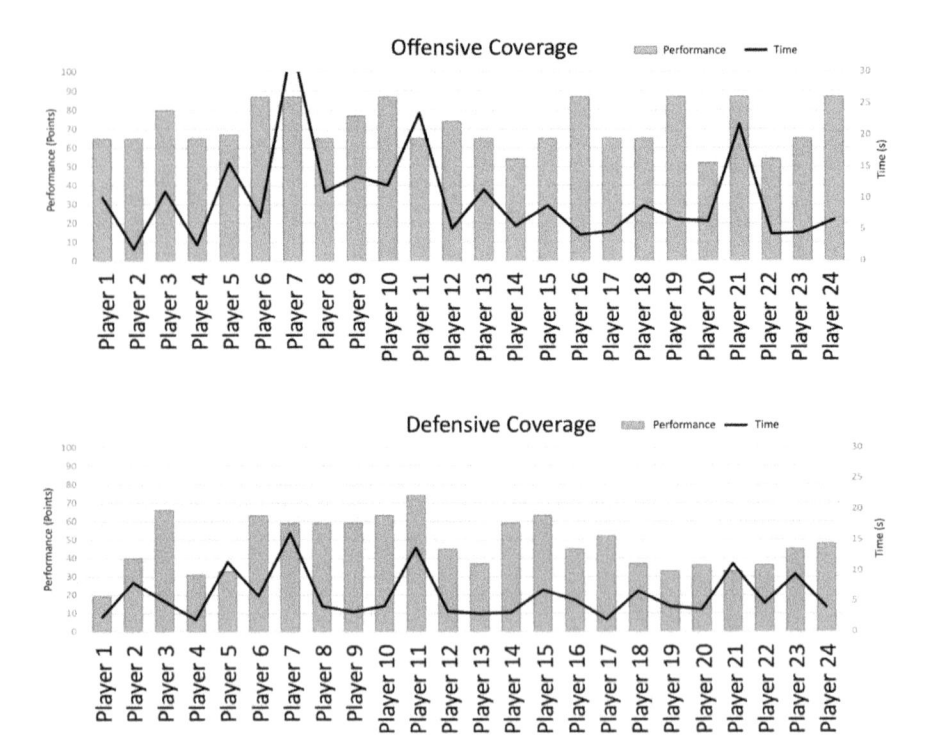

Figure 5.13 Athletes' performance and response time for the principles of offensive and defensive coverage

Source: TacticUP®

characteristics already developed by the athletes, thus backing the coaching staff to plan their work in training for aspects that need to be developed, individually or collectively.

Also, it is possible to obtain more detailed information of each athlete when compared to their teammates. Through Figure 5.13 it is possible to verify, for instance, that players 6 and 7 display similar performance values for the principle of Offensive Coverage. However, with respect to response time, we observe that player 6 responds much faster to these game situations when compared to player 7. This information indicates that, although player 7 is able to make correct decisions in these situations, he needs more time to read a situation and appropriately respond to it. Armed with this information, the coaching staff may control more specifically and assertively the training tasks for the learning and development needs of the player/team. For example, changes in training that encourage strong and pressurizing marking over player 7 will allow to stimulate more assertively the behaviours he/she needs to develop/learn.

PERIODIC ASSESSMENTS

Periodic assessments with TacticUP® allow to keep track of the development of players' game reading and decision-making. Figure 5.14 displays the assessments of two players in three distinct moments over the year. Through these results it is possible to verify that player 1 has two offensive skills already consolidated (indicated by the blue circle), as they maintained or slightly varied their performance over time. Also, it was possible to verify an evolution on the ability to provide offensive support to the player in possession by generating passing lanes or movements near the ball (Offensive Coverage); as well as in movements behind the back of the last line of defence (Mobility), generating more space to team's movement and/or moving towards a more appropriate space to score the goal. As for player 2, it was also possible to observe two consolidated defensive skills (indicated by the blue circle) that are related to the player's capacity to balance his/her team's defensive sector (Defensive Balance) and increase protection of the goal (Concentration). In addition, a decrease was observed in his/her capacity to provide offensive support to the player in possession, be it through the creation of passing lanes or through movements near the ball (Offensive Coverage). Armed with these results it is possible to conclude that training has been effective for maintaining/consolidating performances related to some movements in the field and, on the other hand, may be used to foster activities and feedbacks that seek to improve the understanding of some movements in the field that still display instability of game comprehension (see the example of player 2) and, consequently, of performance within the field.

COACH'S OPINION ABOUT THE PLAYER

From the assessments made through TacticUP® it is possible to ask the coach/coaching staff to also perform an assessment of the athlete's ability to read the game and make decisions (see Figure 5.15). By comparing these results, it is possible to verify the congruence between the coach's point of view and the athlete's real capacity. For instance, Figure 5.15 displays on the left side a graphic that represents the player's current profile, and on the right side the coach's perception of this athlete regarding these same capacities. By analysing these two graphics one notes a divergence between the coach's vision and the athlete's game reading and decision-making skills with respect to some movements within the field, such as situation of direct opposition from the defender on the player in possession (Delay). In this case the coach judged that his/her athlete has difficulties in reading these situations of the game and making assertive decisions. However, the player possesses high capacity to read these situations and respond assertively. With this information, the coach can acknowledge the athlete's real potential to perform movements of this kind in the field and, therefore, adjust his/her needs/guidance aiming to improve this player's performance, as his/her demands were below/underestimating the player's real capacities.

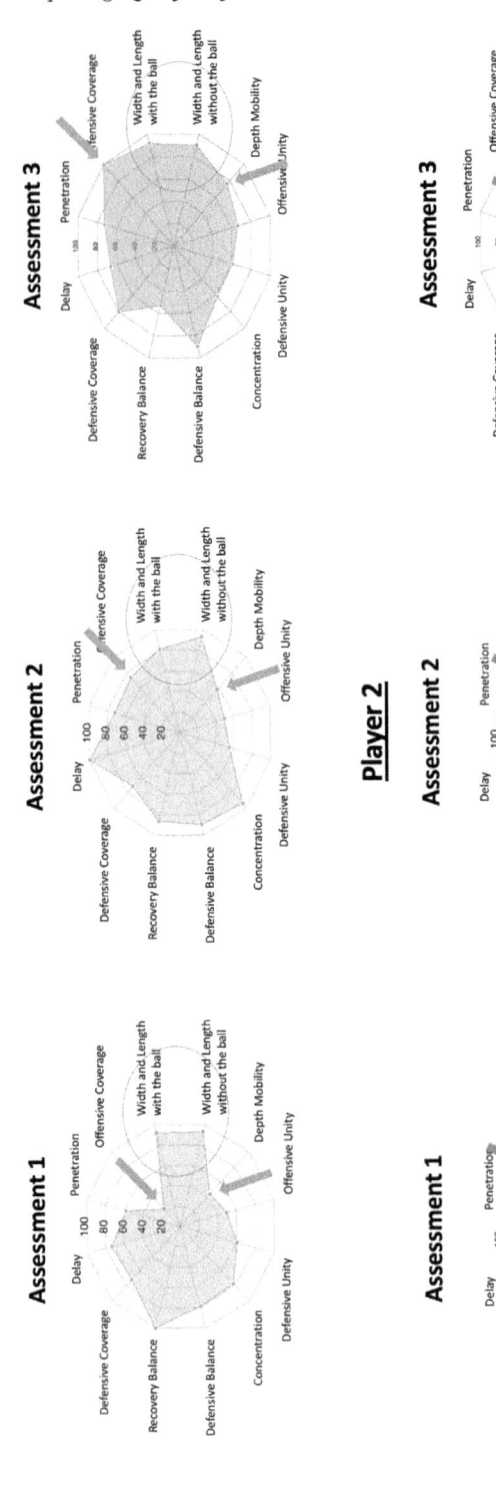

Figure 5.14 Assessment of two players in three different moments over the year

Source: TacticUP®

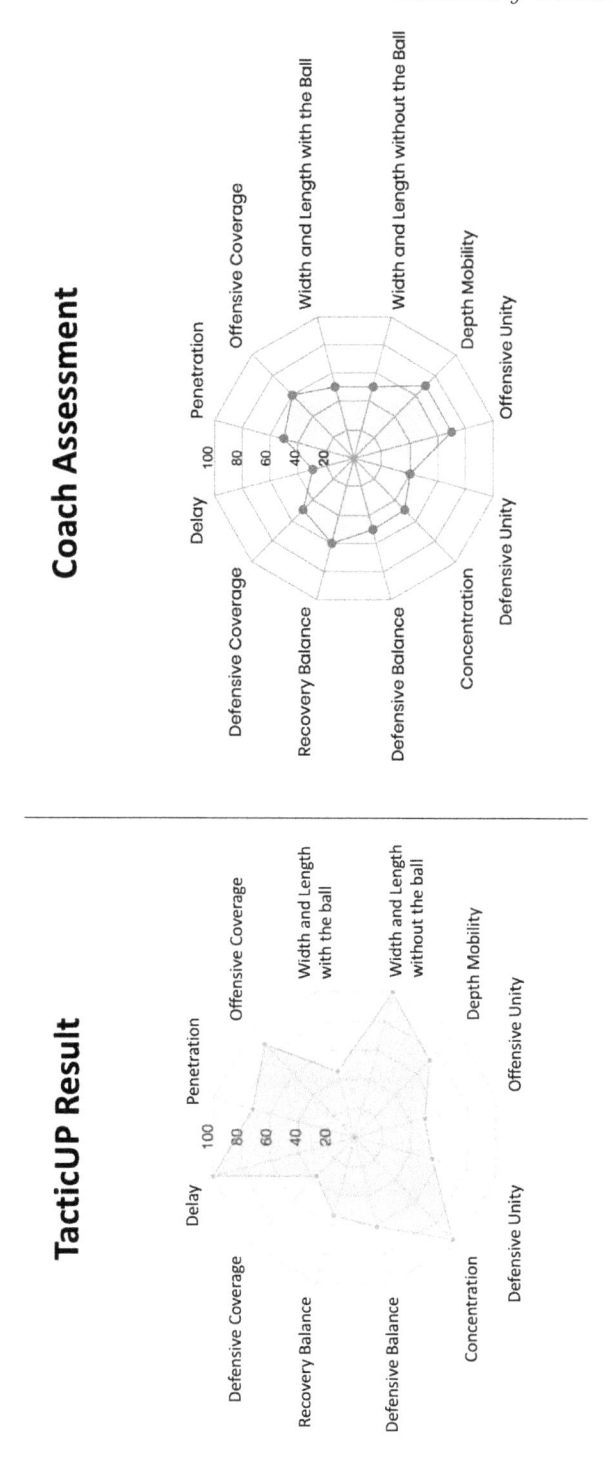

Figure 5.15 Comparison between assessments performed by TacticUP® and by the coach
Source: TacticUP®

5.3.2.1.4 Benefits of TacticUP

FOR COACHES

From the data obtained through TacticUP, coaches are able to learn his/her squad's real needs, with respect to their ability of reading the game and making decisions, and may, therefore, manage their training activities and interventions in a more individualized fashion, allowing time optimization and facilitating performance/knowledge improvement of his/her players in the field.

Hence, coaches may resort to this information to better organize the activities and increase specific knowledge important for the player's development and performance, both in training and matches. During the activities, the coach can organize the dynamics of interactions between the players so that they oppose or cooperate according to their needs of improving movements in the field.

The regular utilization of TacticUP® is also useful for coaches to show their supervisors (manager, director and others) the effectiveness of their work, that is how they were able to improve the player's understanding and reading of the game, which consequently helped improving decision-making.

FOR MANAGEMENT STAFF

TacticUP® can be useful to management staff as well, to assess the degree of players' understanding and reading of the game in their squad (from all age groups) and to check how training sessions are supporting a significant improvement with respect to players' tactical evolution.

Also, the results generated are highly useful for the club, with respect to the education of their employee, as it allows to evaluate whether the coaching staff have better capacity to develop activities and provide feedbacks for certain types of tactical behaviours in the game. If such aspects are detected, management staff can indorse internal employee training, so as to obtain broader benefits from TacticUP.

Furthermore, if the tests are performed regularly, in a short period of time the management staff may have access to game reading and decision-making profiles from all the players within their squad, what would help the work of the club's scouts, as well as the decision to select or release a player.

FOR SOCCER SCHOOLS

As for soccer schools, TacticUP® allows generating and printing players' individual reports, as a means to provide objective information about the development of players' game reading and decision-making skills. Armed with this information, the coaching staff is able to support the qualification of the work under development, so as to control the activities and interventions during the sessions in a more individualized and assertive fashion, to meet the real needs of their players with respect to their education and development. Besides, TacticUP® reports will be useful to show parents and guardians how effective the work being developed at the school has been, which makes it stand out from other schools.

FOR PERFORMANCE ANALYSTS

From the perspective of performance analysis, TacticUP® provides easy and quick generation of (individual and collective) players' performance reports. Also, by acknowledging the limitations and possibilities with respect to players' game reading and decision-making, analysts can design videos and provide information with greater emphasis on the aspects the players need to improve, thus enabling higher effectiveness in their actions.

FOR PLAYERS

Through the information generated by TacticUP, players are able to better acknowledge their potential, in addition to understanding the aspects they need to improve. Therefore, they are encouraged to understand their game reading and decision-making skills, as well as to compare their performance with the main players at national and international levels. In addition, they will have the opportunity to send their test results to that team he always dreamed to play for.

5.3.2.2 Other Video-Based Tests

Video-based tests have been used to assess players' knowledge and skills. Among the most common in literature are the tests of tactical knowledge and decision-making skills, playing patterns recognition, anticipation and situational probabilities.

Before TacticUP, the assessment of the tactical knowledge of soccer players used to be conducted through protocols proposed by Mangas (1999) for the offensive phase, and by Roca (2011) for the defensive phase. Both of these protocols are applied in laboratory and resort to video projection equipment. Through their verbal and written report protocols, it is possible to assess the level of tactical knowledge of the players for both of the phases of play.

The assessment performed with the protocol described by Mangas (1999) resorts to the presentation of 11 offensive soccer scenes, taken from the main European Leagues (Spain, England, Italy and Germany), with duration of 8 to 12 seconds. Through a protocol similar to TacticUP's, each of the scenes is presented to the participants and, at the end of the offensive sequence, the scene is paused for two seconds when the player in possession of the ball is about to decide "what to do" (see Figure 5.16). Subsequently, four pictures of the last scene appear on the screen, with four possible solutions to the play (see Figure 5.17). The limitation of this test refers to the fact that it only assesses a single concept, compared to the 12 concepts assessed by TacticUP®, in addition to only taking into account the actions performed by the player in possession. In these four pictures, there are

182 *Improving Quality Play*

Figure 5.16 Representative picture of the moment the player in possession of the ball should make the decision for the sequence of the play
Source: Mangas (1999)

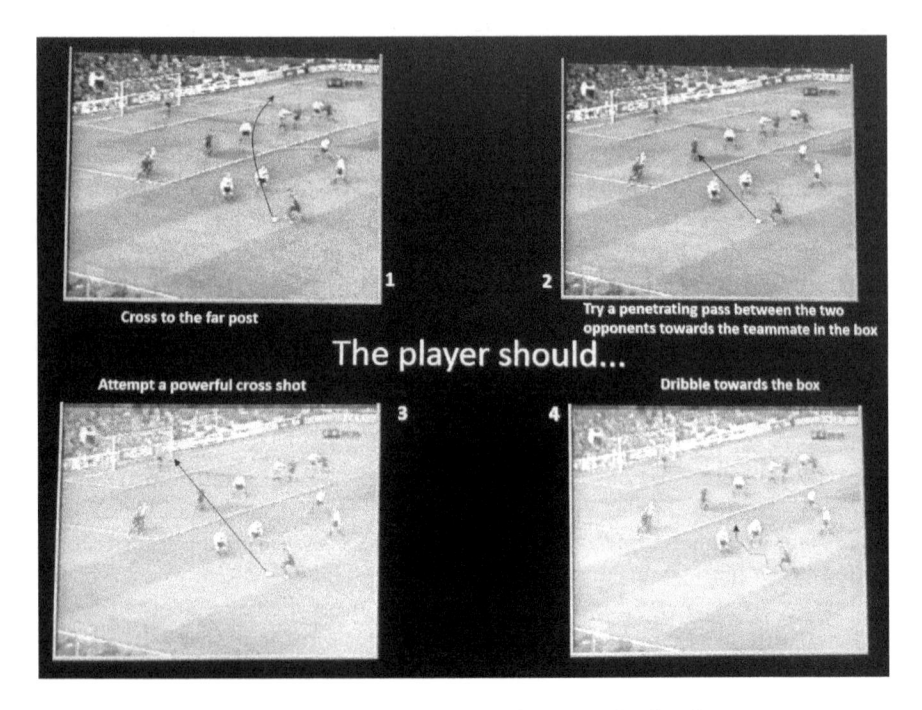

Figure 5.17 Representative picture of the options of solution for the play
Source: Mangas (1999)

four different solutions for the completion of the play, with arrows indicating the player's and the ball's displacements. Beside each picture, the possible decision to be taken by the player in possession of the ball is transcribed. After analysing each of the four solutions, the participant should decide for the best option and write it down on a registration form.

The assessment of declarative tactical knowledge for the defensive phase, performed through the protocol proposed by Roca et al. (2011) resorts to actual size projection (life-size video) of 20 defensive scenes of an 11X11 game, recorded from the perspective of the sweeper (see Figure 5.18). At the start of each scene, a red dot appears on the screen to facilitate the identification of the ball location. Such procedure allows the participant to be aware of the location of the field in which the ball will be at the start of the video clip, thus "freeing" him/her to focus his/her attention on the crucial points of the play, especially within the first moments (frames) of the video. At the start of each scene, there is also a picture of the first frame of the sequence of play, thus allowing the participant to identify his/her teammates and opponents through the playing field. Each scene presented to the participant lasts approximately six seconds, and is terminated immediately

Figure 5.18 Representative picture of the life-size video of the declarative knowledge test for tactical actions in the defensive phase

Source: Roca et al. (2011)

after (120 milliseconds) the player in possession of the ball performs an offensive pass, a shot at goal or a dribble in progression. Then, an answer from the participant with respect to the projected play is required, in which his/her decision-making and the solution for the play are assessed.

For assessing decision-making skills, pattern recognition, anticipation and situational probabilities, four tests developed by Prof. Mark Williams—College of Health of University of Utah—and by Prof. Paul Larkin from the University of Sidney have been widely used within the context of soccer (Ward & Williams, 2003; Larkin, Mesagno, Berry, & Spittle, 2014).

The decision-making and anticipation tests comprise 20 video scenes of a 11X11 soccer match, with duration between 5 and 10 seconds for each scene. These scenes are projected on a large screen and, for the decision-making test, participants are required to decide what to do if they were the player in possession of the ball, after the end of the sequence of play presented and the occlusion of the video. For the anticipation test, the participant should anticipate what he/she thinks will happen in the play right after the occlusion of the video. The options are: passing (P), carrying the ball (C), dribbling (D) or shooting (S). The participants should indicate their decisions by drawing a straight line and an initial (P, C, D, S) on the answer sheet (see Figure 5.19) and, in case of anticipation, should also indicate the players involved in the action, as, for example, in a pass: the player who performs the pass and the receiver. The classification is obtained through the direction and length of the arrow drawn and the indication of the

Figure 5.19 Representative picture of a participant's answer, according to the protocol of the decision-making test

Source: The authors

action. The answers given by the participants are compared and checked with the answer guide.

For the test of situational probability 20 other video scenes of a 11X11 soccer match are used. In this test, the participant should circulate the well-placed players who possibly could receive the pass in the sequence of the videos, and number them in order of importance, from one to three, based on the risk level of the play (see Figure 5.20). For the classification of the test, each player correctly identified will be awarded scores between the values 6 and 1. For instance, 6 points are awarded when player 1 is correctly identified; 3 points for player 2; and 1 point for player 3. If the participant correctly identifies the players, he/she will be awarded the total points. In case there is difference in the order the players were identified, the test protocol states that the number used to assess the player is subtracted from the value obtained on the scoring sheet. If, by chance, the participant identifies a player who is not in accordance with the answer guide, such will not be considered. The interval of values fixed by the test protocol is from 0 (zero) to 10 (ten), that is zero would be the minimum score, and ten, the maximum.

For its part, the pattern recognition test uses 10 scenes that were already presented in the three previous tests (decision-making, anticipation and situational probability) and other 10 new scenes are added to the group of 20 scenes that comprise this protocol. Therefore, as half of the scenes of this test has already been shown at a given moment in the previous tests, the participant should only indicate on the answer sheet whether he/she recognizes, or not, each presented scene.

Figure 5.20 Representative picture of a participant's answer, according to the protocol of the situational probability test

Source: The authors

5.3.2.3 Assessment of Tactical Knowledge Through Questionnaire

The instrument named Tactical Skills Inventory for Sports (TACSIS), proposed by Elferink-Gemser, Visscher, Richart and Lemmink (2004), has been used to assess the declarative and procedural tactical knowledge of soccer players. The pillars of this instrument are supported by the structure developed by McPherson (1994), with two continuums: one that moves between the selection of the answer until the motor execution and another, between the knowledge of "what to do" until the proper action within the game. From this theoretical basis and considering the essential components of high performance, the authors formulated questions taking into account the concepts of anticipation of play, positioning, individual defence, zonal defence, interception and change of attitude between regaining and losing possession of the ball and vice versa.

The final version of the instrument of assessment comprises 23 questions that are categorized into four dimensions: Positioning and Deciding (nine items), Knowing about Ball Actions (5 items), Knowing about Others (five items) and Acting in Changing Situations (four items). After the questions are answered, the participants should choose from a scale with six possible answers, ranging from 1 to 6, whereas 1 = very poor, 6 = excellent, 1 = almost never and 6 = always.

The items that comprise the "Positioning and Deciding" and "Acting in Changing Situations" dimensions are related to the procedural tactical knowledge, whereas the items that comprise the "Knowing about Ball Actions" and "Knowing about Others" are related to the declarative tactical knowledge (Kannekens, Elferink-Gemser, Post, & Visscher, 2009).

5.3.2.4 Cognitive Assessment

5.3.2.4.1 Vienna Test System

Vienna Test System (VTS) integrates computer-assisted tools with field setups for assessing and training mental skills that are important for high-level athletes (Hackfort, Kilgallen, & Hao, 2009). VTS evaluates cognitive skills and performance through the verbal, non-verbal and sensorimotor test protocols. The major advantages of this system lie on its objectivity, efficiency, safety and time-saving test application. Besides, the possibility of obtaining instantaneous results of the tests and, consequently, faster decisions in evaluation processes can be made.

Its latest version of VTS is comprised by 78 tests, whereas 25 of them are destined to measure cognitive skills related to athletes' sports development. Among the tests specific for soccer, we can highlight the Peripheral Perception test, which allows to evaluate players' peripheral vision amplitude, and might even correlate results of this test with the tactical performance obtained in a match and, in addition, compare the performance of players from different playing positions.

Also, it is possible to highlight some other tests that may be used within the context of Soccer, such as visual memory, sensorimotor coordination, time and

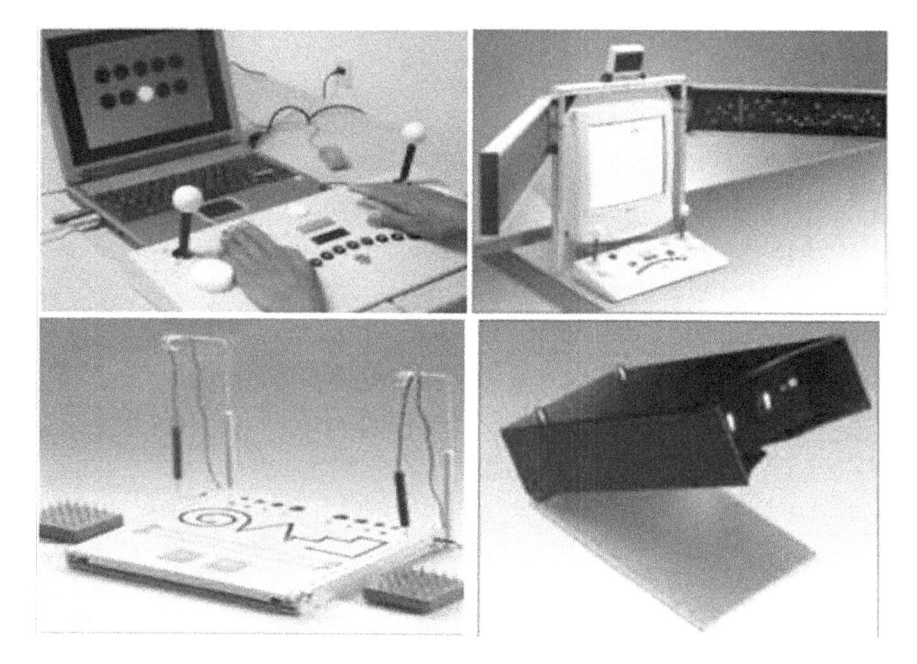

Figure 5.21 Hardware of Vienna Test System (VTS)
Source: The authors

movement anticipation, multiple and complete reactions, among others tests that enable to evaluate in detail and precisely the cognitive aspects that are more related to the player's performance within the field. Each one of the tests mentioned possess particularities that might be associated with the tactical component of the game, and the higher or lower impact of their results on players' performance in the field will depend on the ability to adjust and apply the data to context being assessed.

Conceptually, VTS is the combination of a system of assessment of mental skills and simulation of adapted training situations, based on the Action Theory[10] (Nitsch, 1985). Due to such multiplicity of potentialities, VTS has been used on the training of many soccer teams in Germany and Qatar, especially with the German National Soccer Team and also the seven times F1 world champion, Michael Schumacher, under the supervision of Prof. Dieter Hackfort.

The Academy for Sports Excellence, located in Doha, Qatar, known by its large investment in the development of young athletes of several sports, has been using this equipment for training and evaluating its athletes. With the support of VTS, coaches at this academy have witnessed increased performance of their athletes in competitions and have been having access to reliable and contextualized information about important cognitive skills for each sport.

5.3.2.4.2 Mobile Eye Tracking System—Eye Tracking System

The Mobile Eye Tracking System measures, through cameras mounted on a pair of glasses, the central vision of the participant during an action in game situation. The system acts detecting the pupillary and corneal reflection and projecting it over the image of the environment, thus allowing to show exactly the point(s) on which the participant has driven his/her attention, in order to obtain information from the environment. The most advanced systems provide the participant with freedom of movement inside the evaluation/simulation environment, so as not to restrain or prevent his/her natural behaviour in response to the game situation.

According to researches, the optical channel is responsible for more than 90% of the information withdrawn by a person from the environment (Biehl, Fischer, Häcker, Klebelsberg, & Seydel, 1975; Booher, 1978). For this reason, the video assessments performed in sports contexts (i.e. video simulation) and also the training performed through simulation (i.e. simulation training) have been utilizing the Eye Tracking System as an important resource to identify to which information the participant drives his/her attention within the environment. Through the results provided by this system it is possible to know and, if necessary, to correct, the player's visual search strategies, thus directing his/her visual search pattern to more crucial aspects of the game. Besides this, it is also possible to apply the results of the test to manage training information (feedback), focusing on aspects that might support the gain of performance in drills developed with the players and, consequently, improving performances in match contexts.

Laboratory tests that resort to this system commonly use life-size projection of the game situation, as a means to search for an approximation between the simulated and real game contexts. During the test, participant's movements are recorded, as well as his/her (verbal[11] and non-verbal) answers to the situations presented and the visual search pattern for information. From these results, the participant's performance in anticipation and decision-making is assessed.

In soccer, this ability to search for information available within the environment is essential for the successful action; once during the play, the player should quickly select, among all available stimuli, those whose importance and quick processing will allow to continue the play, in case this player belongs to the attacking team; or will allow the regain possession, in case the player belongs to the defending team.

Notes

1 TacticUP® will be described in details further ahead.
2 Declarative knowledge refers to the capacity of the practitioner of declaring, verbally or in written form, the most appropriate decision to be taken in a certain game situation and the reason why it was taken (Tenenbaum & Lidor, 2005).
3 Procedural knowledge is related to the player's ability of operationalizing appropriate answers to the problems arising from game situations, thus being closely linked to the motor execution within the correct timing of the play (Williams & Hodges, 2005).

4 The reference to the term "game context" is wide and takes into account game situations that occur during training and competition.
5 For results in other sports, the following studies are suggested:
Farrow, D., Chivers, P., Hardingham, C., & Sachse, S. (1998). The effect of video-based perceptual training on the tennis return of serve. *International Journal of Sport Psychology*, *29*(3), 231–242.
Williams, A. M., Ward, P., & Chapman, C. (2003). Training perceptual skill in field hockey: Is there transfer from the laboratory to the field? *Research Quarterly for Exercise & Sport*, *74*(1), 98–103.
6 Ecological validity refers to the adequacy of the test instrument to the reality of the evaluation.
7 More information can be obtained in the doctoral thesis of Costa, I. (2010). *Comportamento Tático no Futebol: Contributo para a Avaliação do Desempenho de Jogadores em situações de Jogo Reduzido*. [Tactical behaviour in soccer: Contribution for performance assessment in small-sided games]. Porto: Israel Teoldo. PhD Thesis, Faculty of Sport—University of Porto, Porto, Portugal.
8 More information about the process of development and validation of FUT-SAT can be obtained within the following study: Costa, I., Garganta, J., Greco, P., Mesquita, I., & Maia, J. (2011). System of tactical assessment in Soccer (FUT-SAT): Development and Preliminary Validation. *Revista Motricidade*, *7*(1), 69–84.
9 Further information about the tactical principles can be found in the study of Costa, I. T., Garganta, J., Greco, P. J., & Mesquita, I. (2009). Princípios Táticos do Jogo de Futebol: conceitos e aplicação. [Tactical principles of soccer: Concepts and application]. *Revista Motriz*, *15*(3), 657–668.
10 Information about the Action Theory in sports contexts may be obtained in the paper by Nitsch, J. R. (2009). Ecological approaches to Sport Activity: A Commentary from an action-theoretical point of view. *International Journal Sport Psychology*, *40*(1), 152–176.
11 More information about the protocols regarding the recording of verbal reports can be obtained in the following text: Ericsson, K. A. (2006). Protocol Analysis and Expert Thought: Concurrent verbalizations of thinking during Expert's Performance on representative tasks. In K. A. Ericsson, N. Charness, P. Feltovich, & R. R. Hoffman (Eds.), *The Cambridge handbook of expertise and expert performance* (pp. 243–262). Cambridge: Cambridge University Press.

6 Contributions for the Observation and Interpretation of the Soccer Game

6.1 Learning to See to Better Understand

Since the early days of sports practice the performance levels of athletes have been evolving constantly. Multiple conditions have contributed to this end, among which we highlight the improvement of sports equipment, the refinement of preparation and observation methodologies, the progress of the coach education process and the increasing knowledge about how the human body works in sports contexts (Smith, 2003; Garganta, 2008).

Although much is speculated about the multiple factors that contribute to success in soccer, we admit that the training process is the most important and most influential way to prepare players and teams for competition (Garganta, 2004).

In strategical and tactical activities, such as soccer, the training process consists of implementing a "culture of play", which results in a dynamic state of readiness regarding concepts and principles. This means that the style of play is built and that training means modelling behaviours and attitudes of players/teams through a project oriented towards the concept of game/competition.

One of the principles of sports training, the principle of specificity, advocates that behaviours are practised taking into account the constraints closely related to the nature of the game being generated (movement structure, kinds of efforts, nature of tasks, prevailing tasks, model and conception of play, etc.), in order to enable greater and better transference of the acquisitions operated in training for the specific context of the matches. On the other hand, the characterization of the structure of the activity and the content analysis of the soccer game have uncovered increasing importance and influence on the structuring and organization of training in this sport.

For this reason, the conviction that, in soccer, one should train according to the intended way of play has gained more and more enthusiasts, which suggests a relation of identity and reciprocity between the particularities of players and teams' preparation and the respective development in competitive environments. It is clear, therefore, that the behaviours displayed by soccer players during the game largely reflect the result of the adaptations caused by the training process and that, on the other hand, the direction of the training process stems from the information

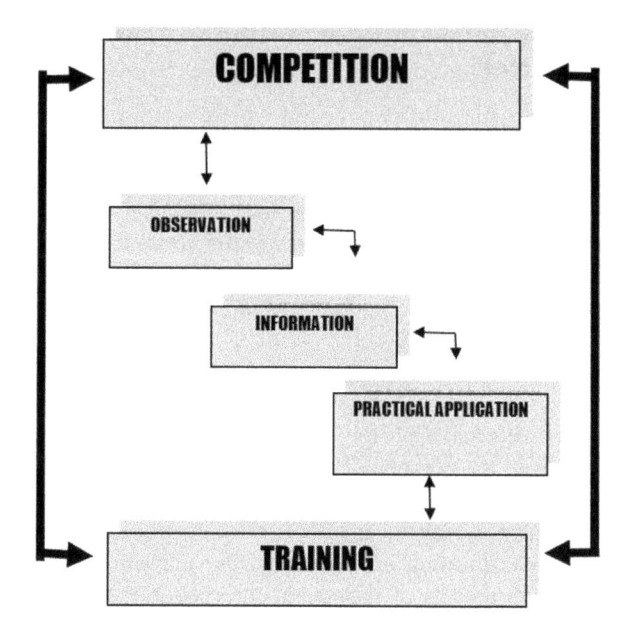

Figure 6.1 Reciprocity between training and competition
Source: Garganta (2008)

taken from the game (Rohde & Espersen, 1988). It is possible then to assume that training creates the game, which legitimises training (Figure 6.1).

By being able to resort to a wide range of means and methods that were improved over the years, coaches and researchers try to access information conveyed through performance analysis, and in it look for benefits to enhance knowledge about playing and training, therefore increasing the quality of players and teams' performances (Garganta, 2008).

Understanding the course of the game and the relation of forces between the opposing collectives is invariably related to the identification of behaviours that witness the efficiency and effectiveness of players and teams in different phases and moments of matches.

Since the purpose of the sports training process is to encourage performances that lead to success in competitions, such aim is mostly envisaged by the coach through the instructions given to the players within the different environments of the respective preparation.

Quite often, soccer is considered a "game of opinions", since the observers tend to have subjective opinions about the factors that are crucial to success, generating a great variety of conclusions about the same fact (Harris & Reilly, 1988). As mentioned by Bate (1988), although opinions may be valid, in order to outline effective strategies, it is necessary to go beyond them.

6.2 From the Analysis to the Overview of the Game, in Search for Relevant Information to Train Better and Play Better

The knowledge about the proficiency with which sports players perform their respective game tasks has proven essential for assessing the coherence of their performance with respect to the intended models of play and training. Therefore, it is assumed that the understanding of the logic of soccer, mainly the purposes that rule the game, has relevant implications to the areas of training and control of sports performance. In addition, such understanding influences the conception and selection of the appropriate methodological procedures in order to improve performance.

This perspective is based on the conviction that players and teams' behaviours, when observed several times and during confrontation with different opponents, are likely to exhibit traits that allow the identification of patterns of play (McGarry et al., 2002). However, the competencies to play are inscribed into a network of complex interactions operated in unstable conditions and contingents of collaboration and antagonism, which incorporates distinct organizational levels. Such characteristics, despite granting uniqueness to the plays and making the game more attractive, hinder the task of systematic observation and interpretation. Possibly due to this reason, the studies that resort to match observation and analysis in soccer are more descriptive than interpretative or explanatory.

As reported by Lames and McGarry (2007), the behaviour generated in a sport game is not the primary expression of participants' stable properties taken individually, as is the case of sports such as weightlifting or some disciplines in athletics. In sports games, the observable behaviour emerges from the dynamic interactions that occur between the individual and collective opposing parts.

Since it results from a network of relations whose conditions are constantly changing, the soccer game is a phenomenon of strong strategical and tactical implication. In fact, from the second half of the eighties onwards, the conscience that tactical constraints have a vital importance in soccer has caused the identification of tactical patterns, achieved based on the behaviours displayed by the players and teams, to start playing an important role in the researchers' agenda.

Currently, the search for models of tactical performance that work as regulators of players' activities and as important references for the coaches' interventions is a central matter that opens possibilities for fruitful investigation and reflection in the demand of sporting excellence.

Accordingly, it can be said that there is a prevailing investment in the tactical dimension, driven towards the model of play, seeking to identify behaviour patterns of players and teams in constant interaction, taking into account both the regularities and the variations (Barreira, Garganta, & Anguera, 2013).

One of the trends has to do with the study of game actions deemed representative, with the purpose of identifying the constraints that induce perturbation and positional imbalance between opponents. Given the variability inherent to game actions, observers have sought to detect and interpret the presence and/or absence of tactical performance markers held positive.

Another tendency has to do with the increase of the information regarding the performance, so as to facilitate decision-making and make it more effective on playing tactics and preparation models to operationalize them. Hence, the analysis of players and teams' behaviours extends, increasingly, to the training processes, in order to evaluate the effectiveness of programmes in regard to the respective correspondence to the ideas/concepts of play one intends to apply.

It means a greater incursion into what Goodwin (1994) calls "science of qualities" rather than a "science of quantities". This author states that while the latter seeks to understand the system for what it does, the former seeks to understand it by establishing an empathy with what it is.

6.3 Nature and Relevance of the Procedures Used in the Observation, Analysis and Interpretation of the Soccer Game

In soccer, players' skills are largely conditioned by the environments' impositions, that is by the successive configurations experienced by the game. Indeed, the web of behaviours that is forged as the game is played looms as a result of how teammates and opponents interact, according to the moment, ball position and area of the field in which actions occur. This spatial and temporal lability, associated to the impositions related to the skills that players are expected to use to solve the various game tasks, makes the observers' task more complex and delicate.

A soccer team has a mutable anatomy and physiognomy that shape each other up as the game is played, being traversed by forms and flows of energy and matter that evolve in space and time. According to this understanding, the importance of envisaging the game as a confrontation of dynamical complex systems has gained recognition (Garganta & Gréhaigne, 1999), which justifies the development of "reading frames", with sufficient refinement and robustness in order to access the "plot" of the game, rather than the amount of occurrences.

For some years we have been warning that understanding the tactical organization of the soccer game, based on the prevailing use of algorithmic methods rather than heuristic ones, is harmful to a better comprehension and development of the game (Garganta, 1997, 2000).

As it is known, the algorithmic procedures involve the identification of all states that are crucial for the selection of operations to be carried, with the purpose of embracing the entire class of possible initial states, whereas heuristics may be considered the art of discovery (Morin, 1973) or the science of finding solutions (Moles, 1995). To be effective, the algorithm related to the soccer game(s) should take into account all the possible alternatives, which collides with the randomness and unpredictability of numerous and various situations that take place during a game.

Instead, heuristic procedures, because they do not advocate such thoroughness, seem to be more appropriate to the not completely predictable nature of the game (Gréhaigne, 1992). Notwithstanding, as reported by Garganta (1997), experience has demonstrated that both procedures are important with respect to the

194 *Improving Quality Play*

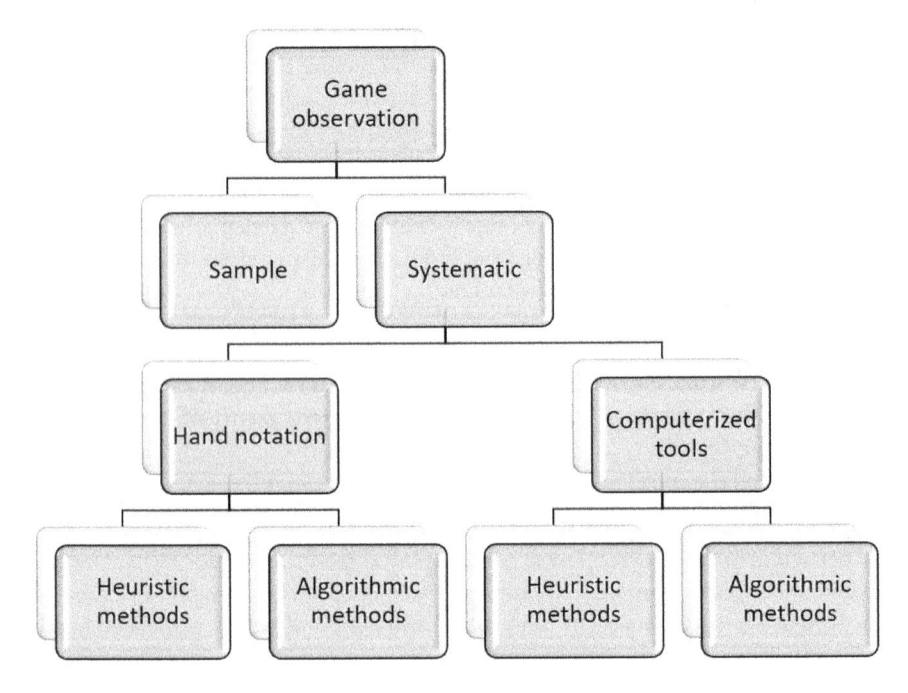

```
                    ┌──────────────────┐
                    │ Game observation │
                    └──────────────────┘
                             │
                ┌────────────┴────────────┐
           ┌─────────┐              ┌────────────┐
           │ Sample  │              │ Systematic │
           └─────────┘              └────────────┘
                             │
                ┌────────────┴────────────┐
         ┌──────────────┐          ┌──────────────┐
         │ Hand notation│          │ Computerized │
         │              │          │    tools     │
         └──────────────┘          └──────────────┘
           │       │                  │        │
       ┌───────┐ ┌──────────┐    ┌────────┐ ┌──────────┐
       │Heuris-│ │Algorith- │    │Heuris- │ │Algorith- │
       │tic    │ │mic       │    │tic     │ │mic       │
       │methods│ │methods   │    │methods │ │methods   │
       └───────┘ └──────────┘    └────────┘ └──────────┘
```

Figure 6.2 Means and methods used in the observation, analysis and interpretation of the soccer game

Source: Garganta (1997, 2000)

identification and interpretation of the numerous actions performed by players and team over the course of a game. The problem arises particularly at the level of its complementarity and compatibility (Figure 6.2).

The heuristic procedures, because they are related to the attributes of creative thinking and discovery, turn out to be particularly important for the qualification, adjustment and refinement phases of game actions descriptors (categories and indicators). The algorithmic procedures, because they entail the identification of the crucial states for the selection of operations, are useful in the systematization and planning of the descriptors, provided they do not cause a closing of the observation system (Garganta, 2001).

Nevertheless, the heuristic attitude is something that can never be left in the background; otherwise the history of game events might be submitted to the limitations of the observation system. To that extent, systems should possess sufficient opening to allow, whenever necessary, a redesign of categories and indicators, in order to ensure their continuous improvement and adequacy.

Thus, it is important to highlight that the work developed in the context of observation and interpretation of the soccer game should goes towards favouring the qualitative aspect, instead of the markedly quantitative records (Figure 6.3).

Quantitative Approach	Qualitative Approach
Analysis	Interpretation
Player	Team
Loose data	Tactical sequences
Technical skills	Phases/moments of play
Product/goals	Process/organization

Figure 6.3 Evolution of the processes of analysis and interpretation of the soccer game, during the transition from the quantitative to qualitative records
Source: Updated from Garganta (1997, 2000)

For coaches and researchers, the analyses that highlight teams and players' behaviours, through the identification of patterns of play, seem more fruitful than the knowledge about the number and result of de-contextualized individual actions. However, quite often, the observation systems favour the analysis of these actions, mainly the frequency and nature of those that result in goal.

Therefore, we have suggested (Garganta, 1997, 2000) the importance of designing observation systems that comply to the categories and indicators that allow obtaining information about:

- the organization of the game according to the characteristics of the team's sequences of actions (tactical units);
- the processes (sequences) that lead to certain outcomes (shots, goals);
- the situations that, either leading to goals or not, generate disruption or perturbation in the attack/defence balance;
- the quantities of the quality displayed in the various playing actions.

The process of match *observation* and *analysis* must allow the description of performance achieved in match context, through the codification of individual, group or collective actions, so as to synthesize relevant information with the purpose of positively changing the learning/training process. Usually, the information is presented in the form of feedback and it is used as preparation for future competitions (Carling, Williams, & Reilly, 2005).

Although the use of statistical procedures has increased considerably, and despite acknowledging that their contribution is relevant, we know that the problems related to game and training modelling go way beyond statistical issues (Garganta, 1997, 2008).

It has been observed, within the domain of game analysis and modelling, that quite often the observation and recording systems lose effectiveness due to the fact that the tail of data obtained consists of scattered and loose material. This means that, despite resorting to sophisticated methods, the proliferation of data bases does not automatically warrant the access to relevant information for coaches and researchers (Garganta, 2001). In order to address this problem, it is essential to give the gathered data some meaning by exploring it with the purpose of ensuring the access to information deemed essential (Garganta, 1997).

Balagué and Torrents (2005) confirm this interpretation as they suggest a change of perspective in the context of performance analysis (Chart 6.1).

Walter Dufour, one of the pioneers of match analysis in soccer, drew attention to the fact that the difficulties found in the definition of observation categories, as well as in the design of appropriate algorithms, are an obstacle to a better understanding of the game (Dufour, 1983). In 1989, the French researcher Jean-Francis Gréhaigne reinforced this understanding, as he reported that an important methodological impasse was generated at the level of comprehension of game organization, due to resorting to purely algorithmic procedures, instead of heuristic approaches.

Chart 6.1 Comparison between the elementary and complex perspectives used in the context of performance analysis

Elementary perspective	Complex perspective
Cause-effect relations	**Interactions**
Analysis	**Synthesis/Interpretation**
Quantitative	**Qualitative**
Descriptive	**Hermeneutical**
Evaluation of states	**Evaluation of processes**
Homogeneity	**Differentiation**
Generality	**Specificity**
Reductionism	**Holism**
Robustness	**Sensibility**
Determinism	**Uncertainty**
Errors X Successes	**Continuities X Variabilities**
Observer's neutrality	**Observer's commitment**

Source: Garganta (2008)

Observational Methodology has uncovered a fertile ground for research in the field of Sport Sciences, particularly in terms of understanding the conditions that contribute to success in sports games. However, it is important to move from a *passive observation*, without a defined problem, with low external control and lacking systematization, to an *active observation*, that is systematized, based on a problem and complying with external control (Anguera, Villaseñor, Losada López, & Hernández Mendo, 2000), which implies an increasingly accurate knowledge about the specific contents and the creation of instruments with higher sensitivity in order to address the typical problems of the game(s).

Pinto and Garganta, in 1989, warned about this need, as they indicated that the feasibility of adjusted match analysis and observation imposes, in addition to technological means, the clear definition of conceptual instruments (models) that address the development and application of methodologies consistent with the game to be produced.

For instance, the so-called Sequential Analysis (Anguera et al., 2000) is an important instrument, provided that it allows to acknowledge the probabilities that certain behaviours activate or inhibit others, considering the chain of game events. In this methodology, the probabilities of occurrence of different behaviours result in the retrospective and prospective assessments of the sequence of game events (Garganta, 2005).

In recent years, there has been an abundance of alternatives for the analysis of players' and teams' sports performances, confirming that authors have resorted to different strategies, such as the analyses named competition units (Álvaro et al., 1995), sequential analysis (Ardá, 1998; Anguera et al., 2000), analysis of tactical units/sequences of play (Garganta, 1997), analysis of polar coordinates (Gorospe, 1999) and the analysis of temporal patterns (BorrieJonsson, & Magnusson, 2002). For its part, Perl (2004) presents studies and proposals grounded on neural networks, based on the assumption that sports performance may be described from the identification of spatial and temporal patterns.

Despite the diversity of means and methods used, sports scientists agree with respect to the purpose of match analysis and observation: collecting and configuring data that translate information regarding the models of play and that allow to define predictive statements about the most effective tactics (McGarry & Franks, 1995).

The game is profiled as an event that emerges from teams' behaviour, which results from the way players interact under different sets of rules and various constraints. In this cascade process, teams co-evolve continuously, thus co-determining the respective adaptations. From this point of view, although the game is chaotic and locally unpredictable, it can be said that it possesses a stable global pattern (Garganta, 2013), that is it displays disorder within the order, for its systems tend to gravitate, not towards the chaotic behaviour, but rather towards an area of complexity between chaos and order (Phelan, 2001). However, as reported by Andrés Garcia (2001) and Drazin and Sandelands (1994), the emergent properties of complex systems are only distinguishable on the macro level of the system rather than on the micro level of analysis of the element, given that it concerns collective properties.

Modelling based on the interpretation of performance on the "macro" level is still a relatively unexplored territory, given that the "metrological" and biological perspectives have dominated the researchers' agenda within the last two decades.

Without disregarding such approaches, we understand that it is important to make room to another type of approach, of qualitative nature. The observation of behaviours assumes an approaching move in order to uncover what lies beyond the appearance of the measurable, of the "only seen" or "already known". This means moving away from the spontaneous to the specialized perception, thus discriminating relevant information in order to move from "see" to "know" (Garganta, 2008).

We can deceive ourselves when looking for something, but we should not be deceived with respect to what we are looking for. However, over the last few years of research, it is possible to observe that, when they start the adventure of unravelling the complexity of the game, quite often the "explorers" are equipped with an abundant number of variables and indicators, but poorly supplied with careful reflection about it, particularly with respect to the sensibility of observation systems to operate in the specific contexts they intend to prospect (Garganta, 2008).

In 2008, we claimed that, despite the acknowledged limitations of traditional models, the understanding of performance in sports games was still captive of an analytical reductionism, for what it urged to renounce to loose approaches, by favouring the hermeneutics of the game. We then advocated that the models for generating and managing interaction were the vital challenge in sports games and that, rather than focusing on game actions, it mattered that observers shifted their gaze to the interactions between players and their relation with the involvement (Garganta, 2008).

However, we do not deviate from this idea. Indeed, we acknowledge that each team has their own style, a "fingerprint" that translates their respective collective identity. Note that the term "superorganism" has been used to translate the idea of the "whole" that emerges from the way through which the elements of groups with shared interests interact among themselves, so as to take advantage of it (Garganta, 2013).

Authors like Hölldobler and Wilson (2009) and Gardner and Grafen (2009), among others, have developed reflections and studies in the field of sociobiology, particularly with respect to the mutualism and social semantics in insect societies. More recently, Duarte, Araújo, Correia, and Davids (2012) stated that sociobiological models may have important applications and implications also in the field of sports games, particularly regarding how to foresee teams' behaviour as groups which display unique patterns that arise from the interpersonal dynamics of their constituent players. In line with this, it is also important to mention the study of Vilar, Araújo, Davids, and Button (2012), as it highlights the advantages of the reasons through which an ecodynamic understanding may provide a coherent discourse with respect to the nature of performance in team sports.

Therefore, given the concern on how to move from data analysis to information and applicable knowledge regarding the behaviour of players and teams in soccer, we highlight the importance of "summary", which demands interpretation and condensation of relevant information, rather than the "analysis" that leads to the representation of data with little contextual relevance and meagre benefit (Garganta, 2013).

6.4 Suggestions for Observation and Recording of Tactical Events in Soccer Matches

Regarded as the most primitive way to acquire knowledge (D'Antola, 1976), the observation was and still is a privileged means to which humans have resorted in order to access knowledge, as well as an important guide for acting.

Such high importance given to observation, particularly the need to give it meaning and make it more effective, justifies the definition of reference frameworks that brighten its reach and its limits (Garganta, 1997). Therefore, it should be noted that the observation is not limited to the look, as a quintessential representative of all the sensitive knowledge (Marina, 1995). Through the look we collect and recognize data from reality. However, our look is not a harmless one. It is driven, in its glance, by our desires and projects and, to that extent, it is intentional and interpretative (Moles, 1995).

The support provided by match observers and analysts in the so-called soccer technical staff is related to the fact that, among other reasons, the coach is acknowledged, in his/her tasks of guidance and conduction of the team during competition, to be constrained, not only for his/her physical position at the level of the playing field (implicating in a limited visual involvement) but also for limitations arising from the characteristics of human memory (as he/she tends to remember only the critical, or the most recent moments of a match). Besides, it should be considered that, due to the effect of emotions, the coach is affected by stress and anger, which may lead to distortions of several match events.

Therefore, by intending to observe a soccer match in order to interpret it, it is important to take into account the respective levels of evidence, because they are the ones that allow to model the indicators and the criteria that enable the selection, identification and assessment of events. Such condition forces the observer to resort to different means, including the five senses, without however falling for a sample of impressionistic observation. It is then justified the option for a systematic observation, understood as a complex inquiry method that demands specialized training from the observers (Baker, 2006).

The understanding of the logics of performance demands ideas and concepts that allow to recognize how the behaviours are organized in the relation of cooperation among members of the same team, and of opposition, among the elements of the opposing teams. Therefore, the game is envisaged as a result of dynamics generated in order to deal with such constraints (Figure 6.4).

As we mentioned, performance in soccer is particularly difficult to analyse and assess, since it is about not only quantifying behaviours and actions but also, above

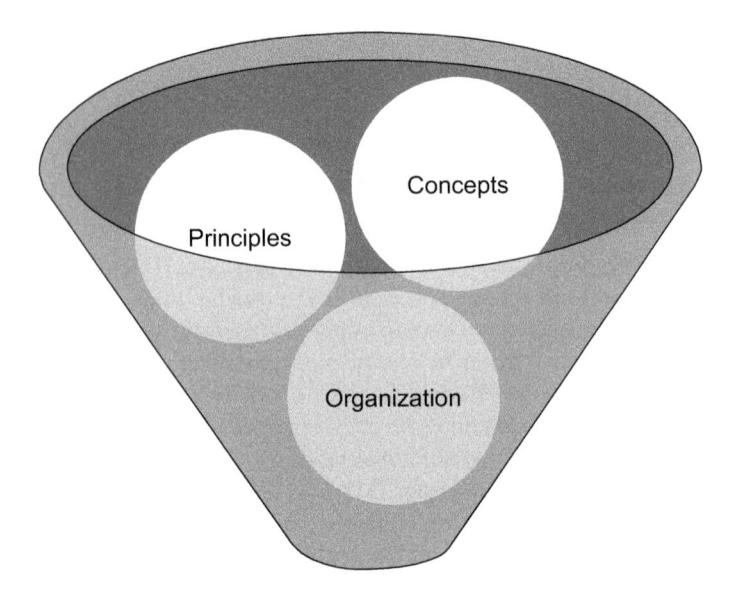

Figure 6.4 The soccer game as a consequence of the way(s) through which the organization of the different phases and moments is managed, with respect to the tactical concepts and principles

Source: The authors

all, qualifying them according to the purposes of the game, over the respective phases and moments it deals with.

The scenarios generated in a soccer match emerge from successive chains of events that result in the convergence of various polarities: the global polarity between opponents, the polarity between attack and defence, and the polarity between cooperation and opposition (Figure 6.5).

Therefore, it is not possible to know, from an initial state, what will be the final state of an action or sequence, which means that we are in the presence of open-ended dynamic system. Modelling such systems means mapping not only its input and output components and behaviours, but also, and above all, the variables that emerge from the performers' interactions.

According to Garganta and Cunha e Silva (2000), although players' behaviours are not entirely predictable, they are also not as imponderable as throwing dice. Soccer teams operate as dynamical systems that simultaneously face the predictable and the unpredictable, the established and the innovation. The course of play occurs in and through the interaction of the game rules, chance and the contingency of specific events with players' specific choices and strategies driven towards the utilization of the rules and chance to create new scenarios and new possibilities.

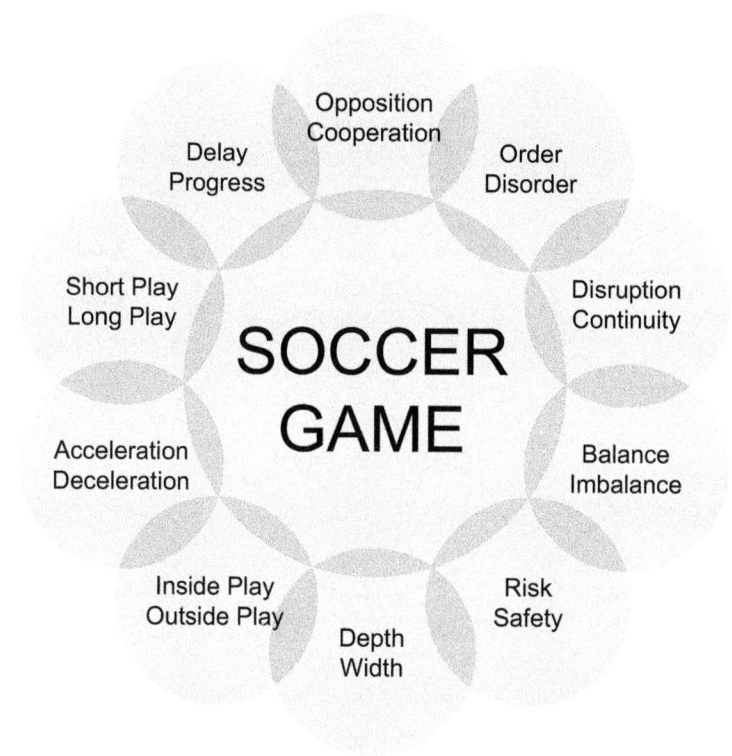

```
                    Opposition
                    Cooperation
        Delay                      Order
        Progress                   Disorder

    Short Play                          Disruption
    Long Play                           Continuity
                    SOCCER
                     GAME
    Acceleration                        Balance
    Deceleration                        Imbalance

        Inside Play            Risk
        Outside Play           Safety
                     Depth
                     Width
```

Figure 6.5 The soccer game as a phenomenon resulting from various polarities
Source: The authors

Indeed, it is precisely the complex nature of the interactions that occur within the active systems which provides some opacity to sports games, when envisaged as an object of scientific study. The robustness of some empirical designs that serve the current scientific model does not correspond to a sensibility likely to favour the systematic understanding of the nuances of the various logics of game organization. Therefore, an evolution is justified, not only at procedural level but also at conceptual level.

We have mentioned that the game responds to all that we know how to ask. This conviction gives meaning to the urgency of developing knowledge with respect to specific tactical behaviours acknowledged as negative and positive, that is regarding the events that "pollute" or "oxygenate" the game (Garganta, 2008).

In seeking the identification and interpretation of critical game behaviours, we highlight the usefulness of recording and interpretation, not so much of the quantities *per se*, but above all of the *quantities of quality*. Hence, we have emphasized the relevance of the study of the game story line, that is the respective flow of events, rather than occasional and loose players' behaviours. The storyline, as it is more focused on

Figure 6.6 Macrocategories that frame the tactical observation of the soccer game
Source: The authors

the process than on the product, comes to life from the interactions of behaviours, condensed in the dynamic of players and teams (Garganta, 2005).

Several questions can be addressed when one intends to observe and interpret the tactical behaviours of players and teams within the framework of a soccer match, when the observer's attention is driven towards either the opponent or his/her own team.

To illustrate, we will enunciate some of them, taking into account that the soccer game can be envisaged as a contingent sequence of two (offensive and defensive) phases[1] and two (attack-defence and defence-attack transitions) moments,[2] in addition to the so-called offensive and defensive set-plays (Figure 6.6).

Let us now move to a group of questions likely to frame the observation and interpretation of a soccer match and to help legitimate a roadmap for the elaboration of the match report.

Offensive Organization—Offensive Transition

Predominant Style of Play

- Indirect/direct?
- Speed of execution and ball circulation?
- Intensity and variations of game pace?

Methods of Play

- Positional attack, fast attack, counter-attack?
- Which players control the game pace?
- Are there tactical changes introduced according to the match status, that is when the team is winning, drawing or losing the match?

Initiation, Build-Up/Creation, Finishing

- Game pace: intense, moderate, alternate?
- Who (and how) takes on the game in the first moment of offensive transition?
- In positional attack, how do they start the play? Do they circulate the ball widely, through the full-backs? Do they wait for one of the midfielders to get free to receive the ball and resume the play?
- When midfielders are under pressure, which procedures do they follow? Do they play short or long passing?
- How do they coordinate the different lines (horizontally and vertically)?
- From which zones do they often generate more risk?
- Do they adopt fast transitions or opt for supported and more positional transition?
- Which circulation channels do they favour?
- Which are the typical tactical combinations?
- In which zones are they more predictable and more unpredictable?

Defensive Organization—Defensive Transition

- Game pace: intense, moderate, alternate?
- Reaction to loss of possession (strong/weak; high or low pressure)?
- Defensive consistency? More vulnerable zones?
- Density and depth of the block (in vertical, horizontal and diagonal fluctuations)?
- Zone pressing and defensive intensity?
- Defensive guidance (how do they constrain opponents' attack)?
- Where do they attempt to break opponents' play? When they do not succeed, how do they reorganize?

- How do the different (vertical and horizontal) lines behave?
- What is the defensive intensity within the different zones?
- Where and how is the block positioned (down, intermediate of high up the field)? High, low or moderate pressing?
- How many players are positioned behind the ball?
- Is it possible to identify the players who control the movement of the block?
- How does the team balance and/or unbalance in positional terms?

Offensive Set-Plays

- What are the players' starting positions and dynamics in offensive corner kicks and free kicks?
- How many players leave the rearmost zones of the field? What are their characteristics (slow, fast, strong, agile or fragile in 1X1 situations, etc.) and where are they positioned?
- Which players take corner kicks or free kicks, how do they take them and which zones do they favour to send the ball?
- How do they contact the ball and with which foot: internal or external rotation; left or right?
- Who are the target men in air play?
- How do they react to loss of possession when they face opponents' counter attack?

Defensive Set-Plays

- What are the players' starting positions and dynamics in defensive corner kicks and free kicks?
- Do they perform individual, zone or mixed defending?
- How many players leave the more advanced areas of the field? What are their characteristics (slow, fast, strong or fragile in 1X1 situations, etc.) and where are they positioned?
- Who are the target men in air play?
- How do they react to winning possession? Do they play straight and fast? Are they strong in counter attacking?

Roadmap for Functional Characterization According to Tactical Role

Goalkeeper

- Quality of behaviour under the posts, intercepting crosses and blocking opponents within the front area?
- Link-play with teammates (where, how does he/she play the ball? To whom, in order to start offensive organization?)
- How does he/she play with his/her feet?
- Verbal communication with teammates?
- Are teammates confident/secure about the goalkeeper?

Observation and Interpretation of Soccer 205

Defensive Third

- Where are they predominantly positioned (back, intermediate or offensive zones)?
- Fighting spirit? Quality? Safety? Strengths and weaknesses (defensive play, mobility and comfortable with the ball)?
- Which coordination between the centre-backs? Marking and coverage in which situations?
- Do they go forward in lateral free kicks and corner kicks?
- Do the full-backs take part in offensive actions (simultaneously or alternately)? Do they easily recover? Is defensive reorganization fast and effective?
- How does the goalkeeper coordinate with the intermediate third?

6.4.1 Intermediate Third

- Mobility and safety from players when in possession?
- Quality of reception and in the sequence of the play?
- Quality in building up/organizing the game?
- Management of game pace?
- How do the defensive and offensive thirds coordinate?
- How do they manage safety and risk when constrained?

Goalkeeper	Defensive third	Intermediate third	Offensive third
*Safe under and outside the posts. Displays problems when playing with his feet whenever he is under pressure	*Focus on individual references and neglect important zones, specially on full backs' back and between centre backs	*Balanced and acute with the ball. Intense in reacting to loss of possession, but exert excessive individual marking	*Strong, fast and coordinated in combinations between wingers, midfielders and forwards, often resorting to positional play

Sectorial characteristics

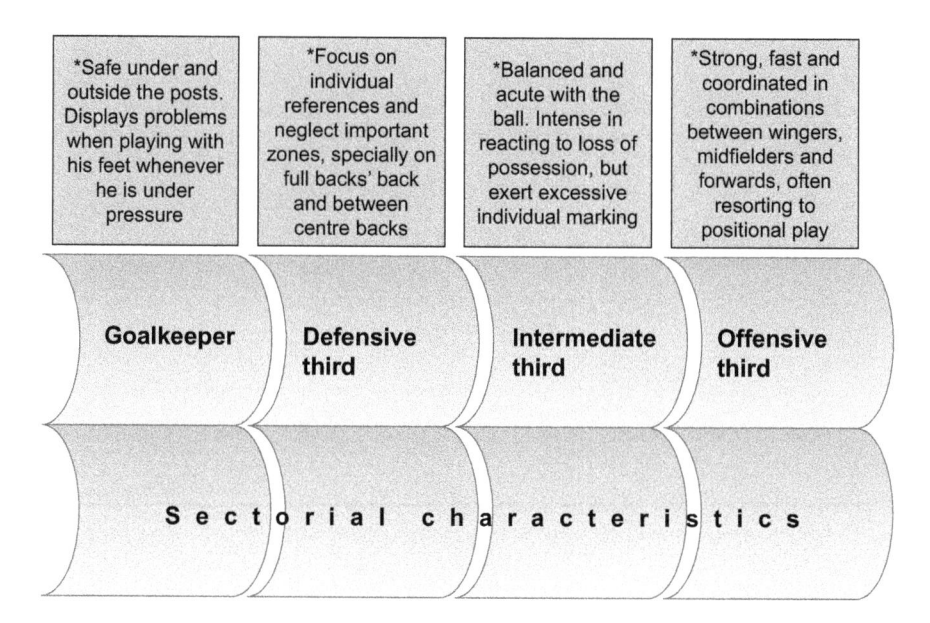

Figure 6.7 Summarized example of sectorial characteristics of a team
Source: The authors

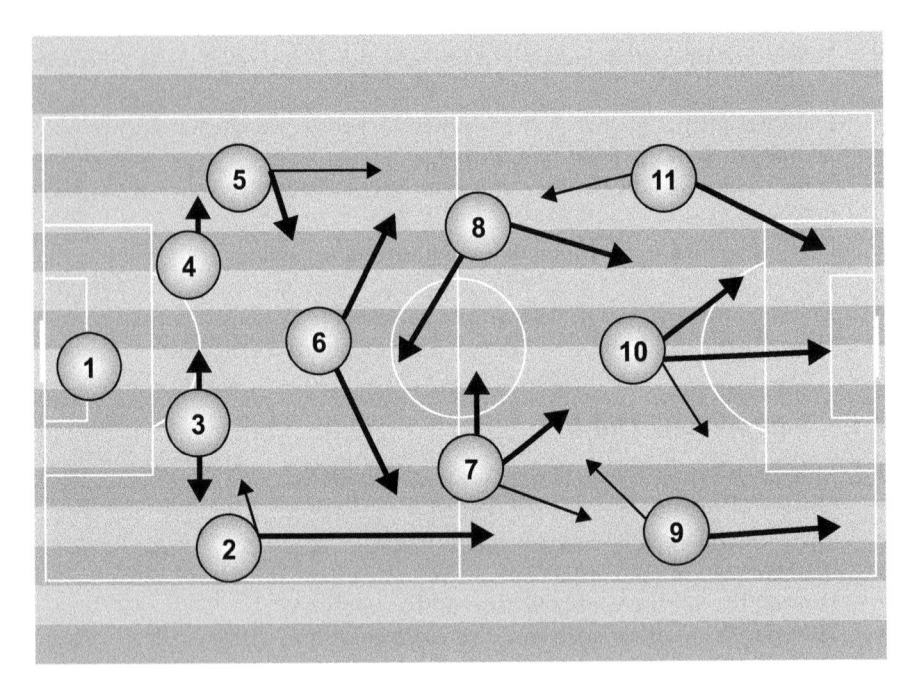

Figure 6.8 Example of basic positional arrangement and movement tendencies
Source: The authors

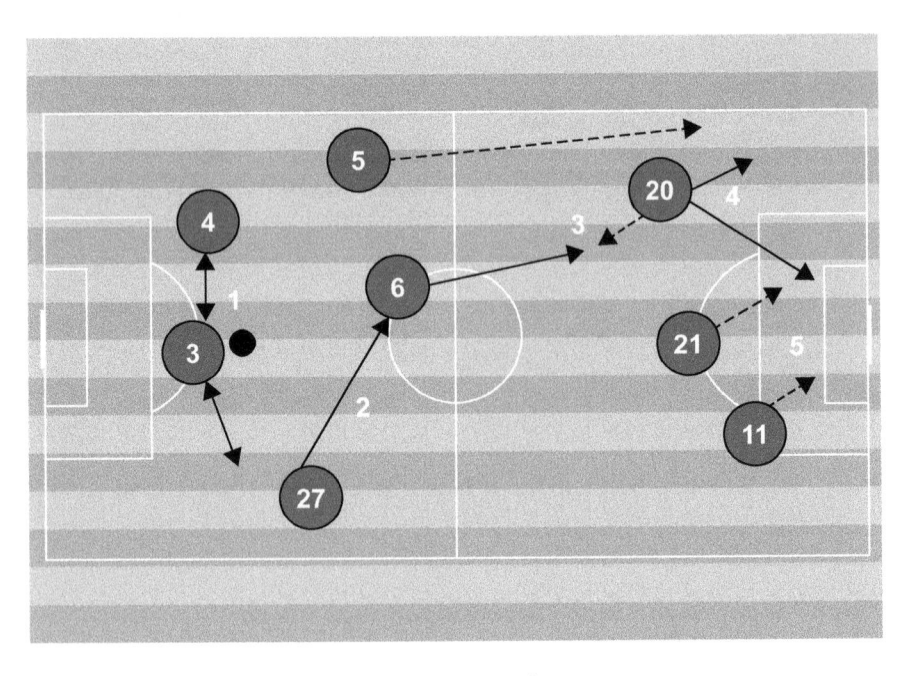

Figure 6.9 Example 1 of description of offensive routines
Source: The authors

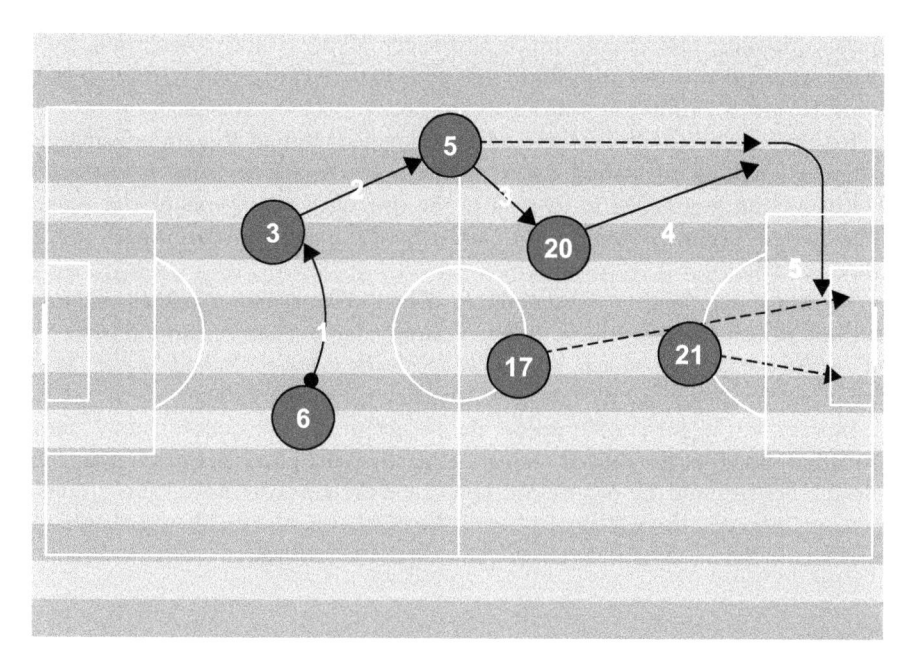

Figure 6.10 Example 2 of description of offensive routines
Source: The authors

Offensive Third

- How many forwards do they have?
- Target man-, mobility- or mixed-style centre-forward?
- What are the characteristics displayed by the centre-forward with respect to air play, availability for front support, horizontal, vertical and diagonal moves? How do wingers and midfielders coordinate?
- Strong in dribbling? Shooting? Assists?
- What is the wingers' behaviour with respect to inside versus outside play? Do they display tendencies to dribble towards the sideline or to come inside? How often do they show up to perform crosses? Are they strong in 1X1 situations (ability to destabilize)? Do they show up to support the player in possession of the ball (in which zones)?
- How do they coordinate with the intermediate third?

After regaining possession, they play positional attack with full-backs widely positioned. Player **6** goes down to receive the ball. One of the wingers, in this case, **20**, moves diagonally inside leaving the corridor free for full-back **5** going in. Acceleration is performed through the wing with crosses or the short diagonal to the inside, towards **21** or **11**.

Counter-attack: Player **6** gains possession, immediately switches the game towards **3**, who performs one-touch pass to the player on the closest wing. This player attempts one-two with **20** (inside play) to receive the ball further up and cross. However, **17** moves towards the near post and **21** towards the far post.

In summary, we would say that understanding the paths of soccer performance demands inclusive ideas and concepts that allow to acknowledge how teams' behaviours are organized in relation to the structural constraints of the game. Therefore, it becomes imperative to understand the game scenarios and, above all, their changes.

We accept that the game "responds" to all that we know how to ask, which justifies that the observer should be able to acknowledge the nature and implications of certain tactical behaviours, particularly with respect to their tendency of "polluting" or "oxygenating" the course of matches (Garganta, 2008).

In this context, game observation, the collection of information and its interpretation should be conducted taking into account the possibility of gauging the congruence between the coach's conception and processes developed during competition. Similarly, this will allow to assess the effectiveness of training drills and to understand the result of their impact in competitive settings.

Notes

1 *Phase*—period with well-defined characteristics. Each one of the successive changes displayed by the sequences of play.
2 *Moment*—very brief period of time that takes place between the phases of play.

References

Aboutoihi, S. (2006). *Football: Guide de L'éducateur sportif*. Paris: Editions Actio.
Allard, F. (1993). Cognition, expertise and motor performance. In J. Starks & F. Allard (Eds.), *Cognitive issues in motor expertise*. Amsterdam: Elsevier Science Publishers B.V.
Álvaro, J., Dorado, A., González Badillo, J., Navarro, F., Molina, J., Portoles, J., & Sánchez, F. (1995). Modelo de análisis de los deportes colectivos basado en el rendimiento em competición. *INFOCOES, 1*, 21–40.
Américo, H., Cardoso, F., Machado, G., Andrade, M., Resende, E., & Teoldo, I. (2016). Analysis of the tactical behavior of youth academy soccer players. *Journal of Physical Education, 27*(2710).
Anastasi, A. (1988). *Psychological testing* (6th ed.). New York: Macmillan.
Anderson, J. R. (1987). Skill acquisition: Compilation of weak-method problem solutions. *Psychological Review, 94*, 192–210.
Andrade, M., González-Víllora, S., Casanova, F., & Teoldo, I. (2020). The attention as a key element to improve tactical behavior efficiency of young soccer players. *Revista de Psicologia del Deporte, 29*(2), 47–55.
Andrade, M., Machado, G. F., & Teoldo, I. (2016). Relationship between impulsiveness and tactical performance of U-15 youth soccer players. *Human Movement, 17*(2), 127–131.
Andrés Garcia, E. (2001). Cognição organizacional e ciência da complexidade. In M. Cunha, J. Fonseca, & F. Gonçalves (Eds.), *Empresas, caos e complexidade* (pp. 35–56). Lisboa: Editora RH.
Anguera, M. T., Villaseñor, A. B., Losada López, J. L., & Hernández Mendo, A. (2000). La metodología observacional en el deporte: Conceptos básicos. *Educación Física y Deportes Revista Digital, 5*(24). Recuperado de www.efdeportes.com/efd24b/ obs.htm.
Ardá, A. (1998). *Análisis de los patrones de juego en fútbol 7. Estudio de las acciones ofensivas*. La Corunha: António Ardá. Tese de Doutorado, Departamento de Medicina, Instituto Nacional de Educación Física de Galícia del Universidad de La Corunha, Espanha.
Assis, J., Costa, V., Casanova, F., Cardoso, F., & Teoldo, I. (2020). Visual search strategy and anticipation in tactical behavior of young soccer players. *Science and Medicine in Football*. https://doi.org/10.1080/24733938.2020.182346
Baker, L. (2006). Observation: A complex method. *Library Trends, 55*(1), 171–189.
Balagué, N., & Torrents, C. (2005). Thinking before computing: Changing approaches in sports performance. *International Journal of Computer Science in Sport, 4*(1), 5–13.
Ball, P. (2004). *Critical mass: How one thing leads to another*. New York: Farra, Straus and Giroux.
Bangsbo, J. (1998). *Entrenamiento de la condición fisica en el fútbol*. Barcelona: Editorial Paidotribo.

Bangsbo, J., & Peitersen, B. (2002). *Defensive soccer tactics: How to stop players and teams from scoring*. Champaign, IL: Human Kinetics.

Barreira, D., & Garganta, J. (2007). Transição defesa-ataque em futebol. Análise sequencial de padrões de jogo relativos ao Campeonato Português 2004/05. In F. Tavares, A. Graça, & J. Garganta (Eds.), *Actas do 1º Congresso Internacional de Jogos Desportivos* [em CD-ROM]. Porto: Universidade do Porto, Faculdade de Desporto.

Barreira, D., Garganta, J., & Anguera, M. T. (2013). Avaliação da performance em futebol. In J. Garganta, J. Prudente, & M. T. Anguera (Eds.), *Avaliação da performance em jogos desportivos coletivos* (pp. 133–209). Edição do Centro de Investigação, Formação, Inovação e Intervenção em Desporto (CIFI2D), Faculdade de Desporto da Universidade do Porto. Porto: Greca Artes Gráficas.

Barth, B. (1994). Strategia e tattica nello sport. *Rivista di Cultura Sportiva, 13*(31), 10–20.

Bate, R. (1988). Football chance: Tactics and strategy. In T. Reilly, A. Lees, K. Davis, & W. Murphy (Eds.), *Science and football* (pp. 293–301). London: E & F.N. Spon.

Bauer, G., & Ueberle, H. (1988). *Fútbol. Factores de redimiento, dirección de jugadores y del equipo*. Barcelona: Ediciones Martínez Roca S.A.

Bayer, C. (1994). *O ensino dos desportos colectivos*. Lisboa: Dinalivro.

Beek, P. J., Jacobs, D. M., Daffertshofer, A., & Huys, R. (2003). Expert performance in sport: Views from the joint perspectives of ecological and dynamical systems theory. In J. L. Starkes, & K. A. Ericsson (Eds.), *Expert performance in sports: Advances in research on sport expertise* (pp. 321–344). Stanningley: Human Kinetics.

Benkirane, R. (2002). *A complexidade, vetigens e promessas*. Lisboa: Piaget.

Bertalanffy, L. V. (1968). *General system theory*. New York: George Braziller, Inc.

Biehl, B., Fischer, G. H., Häcker, H., Klebelsberg, D., & Seydel, U. (1975). A comparison of the factor loading matrices of two driver behavior investigations. *Accident Analysis and Prevention, 7*(3), 161–178.

Blomqvist, M., Luhtanen, P., Vänttinen, T., Norvapalo, K., & Hayrinen, M. (2002). Differences in perceptual-motor skills in novice, intermediate and expert soccer players. (Abstract). In M. Koskolou (Ed.), *European College of Sport Science, Proceedings of the 7th annual congress of the European College of Sport Science, Athens, Greece, 24–28 July 2002* (p. 389). Athens, Greece: Pashalidis Medical Publisher.

Blomqvist, M., Vänttinen, T., & Luhtanen, P. (2005). Assessment of secondary school students' decision-making and game-play ability in soccer. *Physical Education & Sport Pedagogy, 10*(2), 107–119.

Bompa, T. (1999). *Periodization: Theory and methodology of training* (4th ed.). Champaign, IL: Human Kinetics.

Booher, H. R. (1978). Effects of visual and auditory impairment in driving performance. *Human Factors: The Journal of the Human Factors and Ergonomics Society, 20*, 307–319.

Borrie, A., Jonsson, G., & Magnusson, M. (2002). Temporal pattern analysis and its applicability in sport: An explanation and exemplar data. *Journal of Sports Sciences, 20*, 845–852.

Bouleau, B. (2002). La modélisation et les sciences de l'ingénieur. In P. Nouvel (Org.), *Enquête sur le concept de modèle* (pp. 101–119). Paris: Presses Universitaires de France.

Boulogne, G. (1972). Organisation de jeu tactique/plan de jeu. *E.P.S., 117*, 52–55.

Buono, A., & Jade, R. (1977). *Le football à Montreal*. Paris: Sport et Plein air.

Capra, F. (1996). *A Teia da Vida*. São Paulo: Editora Cultrix.

Carling, C., Reilly, T., & Williams, A. M. (2009). *Performance assessment for field sports*. New York: Routledge.

Carling, C., Williams, A. M., & Reilly, T. (2005). *Handbook of soccer match analysis: A systematic approach to improving performance*. London: Routledge.

Castelão, D., Garganta, J., Santos, R., & Teoldo, I. (2014). Comparison of tactical behaviour and performance of youth soccer players in 3v3 and 5v5 small-sided games. *International Journal of Performance Analysis in Sport, 14*, 801–813.

Castellano Paulis, J., Perea Rodríguez, A., & Blanco-Villaseñor, A. (2009). Has soccer changed in the last three world cups? In T. Reilly, & F. Korkusuz (Eds.), *Science and football VI: Proceedings on the Sixth World Congress of Science and Football* (pp. 173176). London: Routledge.

Castelo, J. (1994). *Futebol modelo técnico-táctico do jogo: Identificação e caracterização das grandes tendências evolutivas das equipas de rendimento superior*. Lisboa: FMH Edições.

Castelo, J. (1996). *Futebol a organização do jogo: Como entender a organização dinâmica de uma equipa de futebol e a partir desta compreensão como melhorar o rendimento e a direcção dos jogadores e da equipa*. Lisboa: FMH Edições.

Castelo, J. (2002). *O exercício do treino desportivo*. Lisboa: FMH Edições.

Cervera, J., & Malavés, R. (2001). Hacia una concepción unitaria del proceso estratégico en fútbol. *Fútbol Cuardernos Técnicos, 19*, 64–70.

Chase, G. W., & Simon, A. H. (1973). Perception in chess. *Cognitive Psychology, 4*, 55–81.

Chi, M., & Glaser, R. (1992). A capacidade para a resolução de problemas. In R. Sternberg (Ed.), *As capacidades intelectuais humanas. Uma abordagem em processamento de informações* (pp. 250–275). Porto Alegre: Artes Médicas.

Cohen, N. J., & Squire, L. R. (1980). Preserved learning and retention of pattern analyzing skill in amnesia using perceptual learning. *Cortex, 17*, 26–44.

Cohen-Tannoudji, G. (2002). La notion de modèle en physique théorique. In P. Nouvel (Org.), *Enquête sur le concept de modèle* (pp. 29–42). Paris: Presses Universitaires de France.

Colt, H. G., Crawford, S. W., & Galbraith, O. (2001). Virtual reality bronchoscopy simulation. *Chest, 120*, 1333–1339.

Côté, J., & Erickson, K. (2015). Diversification and deliberate play during the sampling years. In Joseph Baker and Damian Farrow (Eds.), *Routledge Handbook of Sport Expertise* (pp. 305–316). New York: Routledge.

Cruyff, J. (2002). *Me gusta el fútbol*. Barcelona: RBA Libros S.A.

Cunha e Silva, P. (1995). *O Lugar do corpo. Elementos para uma cartografia fractal*. Porto: Paulo Cunha e Silva. Tese de Doutorado, Faculdade de Ciências do Desporto e de Educação Física da Universidade do Porto, Porto, Portugal.

D'Antola, A. (1976). *A observação na avaliação escolar*. São Paulo: Loyola.

Drazin, R., & Sandelands, L. (1994). Autogenesis: A perspective on the process of organizing. *Organization Science, 3*(2), 230–249.

Duarte, R., Araújo, D., Correia, V., & Davids, K. (2012). Sports teams as superorganisms. Implications of sociobiological models of behaviour for research. *Sports Medicine, 42*(8), 633–642.

Dufour, W. (1983). Processos de objectivação do comportamento motor. A observação em futebol. *Futebol em Revista*, 4ª série, *1*, 39–46.

Duprat, E. (2007). *Enseigner le football en milieu scolaire (Collèges, Lycées) et au club*. Paris: Editions Actio.

Durand, D. (1992). *La systémique. Que sais-je?* Paris: Presses Universitaires de France.

Eigen, M., & Winkler, R. (1989). *O Jogo. As leis naturais que regulam o acaso*. Lisboa: Ed. Gradiva.

Elferink-Gemser, M. T., Visscher, C., Richart, H., & Lemmink, K. A. (2004). Development of the tactical skills inventory for sports. *Perceptual Motor Skills, 99*(3), 883–895.

Ennis, C., Mueller, L., & Zhu, W. (1991). Description of knowledge structures within a concept based curriculum framework. *Research Quarterly for Exercise and Sport, 62*(3), 309–318.

Epstein, I. (1986). *Cibernética*. São Paulo: Ática.

Eysenck, M., & Keane, M. (1994). *Psicologia Cognitiva. Um manual introdutório*. Porto Alegre: Artes Médicas.

Farrow, D., Chivers, P., Hardingham, C., & Sachse, S. (1998). The effect of video-based perceptual training on the tennis return of serve. *International Journal of Sport Psychology, 29*(3), 231–242.

Fonseca, H., & Garganta, J. (2006). *Futebol de Rua: um Beco com Saída*. Lisboa: Visão e Contextos

Frade, V. (1990). *A interacção, invariante estructural da estructura do rendimento do futebol, como objecto de conhecimento científico uma proposta de explicitação de causalidade*. Porto, Portugal: Projeto de provas de doutoramento, Faculdade de Ciências do Desporto e de Educação Física da Universidade do Porto.

Franks, I. M., Goodman, D., & Miller, G. (1983). Analysis of performance: Qualitative or quantitative. *Science Periodical on Research and Technology in Sport Coaching Association of Canada*, 39–46.

French, K., & Thomas, J. (1987). The relation of knowledge development to children's basketball performance. *Journal of Sport Psychology, 9*, 15–32.

Gallahue, D. L., & Ozmun, J. C. (1998). *Understanding motor development: Infants, children, adolescents, adults* (4th ed.). Boston: McGraw-Hill.

Garcia-Lopez, L. M., Gonzalez-Villora, S., Gutierrez, D., & Serra, J. (2013). Development and validation of the Game Performance Evaluation Tool (GPET) in soccer. *Revista Euroamericana de Ciencias Del Deporte, 2*(1), 89–99.

Gardner, A., & Grafen, A. (2009). Capturing the superorganism: A formal theory of group adaptation. *Journal of Evolutionary Biology, 22*, 659–671.

Garganta, J. (1996). Modelação da dimensão táctica do jogo de futebol. In J. Oliveira, & F. Tavares (Eds.), *Estratégia e táctica nos jogos desportivos colectivos* (pp. 63–94). Porto: Centro de Estudos dos Jogos Desportivos, Faculdade de Ciência do Desporto e Educação Física da Universidade do Porto.

Garganta, J. (1997). *Modelação táctica do jogo de futebol—Estudo da organização da fase ofensiva em equipas de alto rendimento*. Porto: Júlio Garganta. Tese de Doutorado, Faculdade de Ciências do Desporto e de Educação Física da Universidade do Porto, Porto, Portugal.

Garganta, J. (2000). Análisis del juego enelfútbol. El recorridoevolutivode concepciones, métodos e instrumentos. *Revista de Entrenamiento Deportivo, XIV*(2), 5–14.

Garganta, J. (2001). A análise da performance nos jogos desportivos. Revisão acerca da análise do jogo. *Revista Portuguesa de Ciências do Desporto, 1*(1), 57–64.

Garganta, J. (2002). Competências no ensino e treino de jovens futebolistas. *Lecturas: Educación Física y Deportes, 8*(45). Recuperado de www.efdeportes.com/efd45/ ensino.htm.

Garganta, J. (2004). Atrás do palco. Nas oficinas do Futebol. In J. Garganta, J. Oliveira, & M. Murad (Org.), *Futebol de muitas cores e sabores. Reflexões em torno do desporto mais popular do mundo* (pp. 227–234). Porto: Campo das Letras.

Garganta, J. (2005). Dos constrangimentos da acção à liberdade de (inter)acção, para um futebol com pés . . . e cabeça. In D. Araújo (Ed.), *O contexto da decisão a acção táctica do desporto* (Vol. 1, pp. 179–190). Lisboa: Visão e Contextos Lda.

Garganta, J. (2006a). Idéias e competências para "pilotar" o jogo de futebol. In G. Tani, J. Bento, & R. D. S. Petersen (Eds.), *Pedagogia do Desporto* (pp. 313–326). Rio de Janeiro: Guanabara Koogan.

Garganta, J. (2006b). (Re)Fundar os conceitos de estratégia e táctica nos jogos desportivos colectivos, para promover uma eficácia superior. *Revista Brasileira de Educação Física e Esporte, 20*, 201–203.

Garganta, J. (2008). Modelação táctica em jogos desportivos—A desejável cumplicidade entre pesquisa, treino e competição. In F. Tavares, A. Graça, J. Garganta, & I. Mesquita (Eds.), *Olhares e contextos da performance nos jogos desportivos* (pp. 108–121). Porto, Portugal: Universidade do Porto, Faculdade de Desporto.

Garganta, J. (2009). New trends of tactical performance analysis in team sports: Bridging the gap between research, training and competition. *Revista Portuguesa de Ciências do Desporto, 9*(1), 81–89.

Garganta, J. (2012). *Reflexiones sobre la excelencia táctica en el fútbol*. Conferência apresentada ao I Congreso Internacional de Fútbol Ciudad de Valencia. Fevereiro. Auditórium Mar Rojo (Oceanogràfic), Ciudad de las Artes y las Ciencias.

Garganta, J. (2013). A propósito da modelação tática e da relevância da síntese da performance nos jogos desportivos coletivos. In A. Volossovitch & A. P. Ferreira (Eds.), *Fundamentos e aplicações em análise do jogo* (pp. 91–110). Lisboa: Edições FMH.

Garganta, J., & Cunha e Silva, P. (2000). O jogo de futebol: Entre o caos e a regra. *Horizonte, Revista de Educação Física e Desporto, XVI*(91), 5–8.

Garganta, J., & Gréhaigne, J. F. (1999). Abordagem sistémica do jogo de futebol: Moda ou necessidade? *Revista Movimento, 5*(10), 40–50.

Garganta, J., & Oliveira, J. (1996). Estratégia e táctica nos jogos desportivos colectivos. In J. Oliveira, & F. Tavares (Eds.), *Estratégia e táctica nos jogos desportivos colectivos* (pp. 7–23). Porto: Centro de Estudos dos Jogos Desportivos, Faculdade de Ciências do Desporto e de Educação Física da Universidade do Porto.

Garganta, J., & Pinto, J. (1994). O ensino do futebol. In A. Graça & J. Oliveira (Eds.), *O ensino dos jogos desportivos* (Vol. 1, pp. 95–136). Porto: Faculdade de Ciências do Desporto e de Educação Física da Universidade do Porto, Rainho & Neves Lda.

Gibson, J. J. (1979). *The ecological approach to visual perception*. Boston: Houghton Mifflin.

Gigerenzer, G. (2007). *Gut feelings*. New York: Viking Penguin.

Godbout, P. (1990). Observational strategies for the rating of motor skills: Theoretical and practical implications. In M. Lirette, C. Paré, J. Dessureault, & M. Piéron (Eds.), *Physical education and coaching: Present state and outlook for the future* (pp. 209–221). Québec: Presses de l'Université du Québec à Trois-Rivières.

Godik, M., & Popov, A. (1993). *La Preparación del futbolista*. Barcelona: Paidotribo.

Gonçalves, E., Gonzaga, A., Cardoso, F., & Teoldo, I. (2015). Anticipation in soccer: A systematic review. *Human Movement, 16*(2), 95–101.

Gonzaga, A. d. S., Albuquerque, M. R., Malloy-Diniz, L. F., Greco, P. J., & Costa, I. T. d. (2014). Affective decision-making and tactical behavior of under-15 soccer players. *Plosone, 9*(6), e101231 (101231–101236).

Goodwin, B. (1994). *How the leopard changed its spots*. London: Weidenfeld Nicholson.

Gorospe, G. (1999). *Observación y análisis de la acción de juego en el tenis de individuales. Aportaciones del análisis secuencial de las coordenadas polares*. Vitoria. Guillermo Gorospe. Tese de Doutorado, Departamento de Historia y Teoría de la Educación de la Universidad del País Vasco, Universidad del País Vasco, Espanha.

Greco, P. J., & Benda, R. N. (1998). *Iniciação Esportiva Universal Da aprendizagem motora ao treinamento técnico* (Vol. 1). Belo Horizonte: Editora UFMG.

Greco, P. J., Roth, K., & Schörer, J. (2004). Ensino-aprendizagem-treinamento da criatividade tática nos jogos esportivos coletivos. In E. S. Garcia & K. L. Lemos (Eds.), *Temas atuais IX: Educação Física e Esportes* (pp. 52–63). Belo Horizonte: Saúde.

Gréhaigne, J. F. (1989). *"Football de Mouvement". Vers une approche systémique du jeu*. Dijon: Jean-Francis Gréhaigne. Tese de Doutorado, Sciences et Techniques des Activités Physiques et Sportives. Université de Bourgogne, France.

Gréhaigne, J. F. (1991). A new method of goal analysis. *Science and Football, 5*, 10–16.
Gréhaigne, J. F. (1992). *L'Organisation du jeu en football*. Joinville-le-Pont, França: Editions Actio.
Gréhaigne, J. F. (1992). *L' organization du jeu en football*. Paris: Editions Actio.
Gréhaigne, J. F. (2001). *La organización del juego en el fútbol*. Barcelona: INDE Publicaciones.
Gréhaigne, J. F., & Godbout, P. (1998). Formative assessment in team sports in a tactical approach context. *Journal of Physical Education, Recreation and Dance, 69*(1), 46–51.
Gréhaigne, J. F., Godbout, P., & Bouthier, D. (1997). Performance assessment in team sports. *Journal of Teaching in Physical Education, 16*(4), 500–516.
Gréhaigne, J. F., & Guillon, R. (1992). L'utilisation des jeux d'opposition a l'école. *Revue de l'Education Physique, 32*(2), 51–67.
Gréhaigne, J. F., Mahut, B., & Fernandez, A. (2001). Qualitative observation tools to analyse soccer. *International Journal of Performance Analysis in Sport, 1*(1), 52–61.
Guilherme, J. (2004). *Conhecimento específico em futebol. Contributos para a definição de uma matriz dinâmica do processo ensino-aprendizagem/treino do Jogo*. Porto: José Guilherme. Dissertação de Mestrado, Faculdade de Ciências do Desporto e de Educação Física da Universidade do Porto, Porto, Portugal.
Hackfort, D., Kilgallen, C., & Hao, L. (2009). The action theory-based Mental Test and Training System (MTTS). In T.-M. Hung, R. Lidor, & D. Hackfort (Eds.), *International perspectives on sport and exercise psychology: Psychology of sport excellence* (pp. 15–24). Morgantown: Fitness Information Technology.
Hainaut, K., & Benoit, J. (1979). *Enseignement des pratiques physiques spécifiques: Le football moderne tactique-technique-lois du jeu*. Bruxelas: Presses Universitaires de Bruxelles.
Harris, S., & Reilly, T. (1988). Space, teamwork and attacking success in soccer. In T. Reilly, A. Lees, K. Davis, & W. Murphy (Eds.), *Science and football* (pp. 322–328). London: E & F.N. Spon.
Hölldobler B., & Wilson E. (2009). *The superorganism: The beauty, elegance, and strangeness of insect societies*. New York: W. W. Norton & Company.
Holt, N. L., Strean, W. B., & Bengoechea, E. G. (2002). Expanding the teaching games for understanding model: New avenues for future research and practice. *Journal of Teaching in Physical Education, 21*, 162–176.
Hughes, C. (1973). *Football tactics and teamwork*. London: Wakefield: E.P. Publishing Co. Ltd.
Hughes, M., & Franks, I. (1997). *Notational analysis of sport*. London: E & FN Spon.
James, N., Mellalieu, S. D., & Hollely, C. (2002). Analysis of strategies in soccer as a function of European and domestic competition. *International Journal of Performance Analysis in Sport, 2*(1), 83–105.
Júlio, L., & Araújo, D. (2005). Abordagem dinâmica da acção táctica no jogo de futebol. In D. Araújo (Ed.), *O contexto da decisão a acção táctica do desporto* (pp. 159–178). Lisboa: Visão e Contextos Lda.
Kacani, L. (1982). Preparación técnico-táctica del futbolista según su posición en el campo. *El Entrenador Español (Fútbol), 12*, 12–17.
Kannekens, R., Elferink-Gemser, M. T., Post, W. J., & Visscher, C. (2009). Self-assessed tactical skills in elite youth soccer players: A longitudinal study. *Perceptual & Motor Skills, 109*(2), 459–472.
Kelso, S., & Tuller, B. (1984). A dynamical basis for action systems. In M. Gazzaniga (Ed.), *Handbook of cognitive neuroscience* (pp. 321–356). New York: Plenum Press.
Kröger, C., & Roth, K. (2002). *Escola da bola: um ABC para iniciantes nos jogos esportivos*. São Paulo: Phorte.

Lamas, L., & Seabra, F. (2006). Estratégia, tática e técnica nas modalidades esportivas coletivas: Conceitos e aplicações. In D. de Rose Júnior (Ed.), *Modalidades Esportivas Coletivas* (pp. 40–59). Rio de Janeiro: Guanabara Koogan.

Lames, M., & Mcgarry, T. (2007). On the search for reliable performance indicators in game sports. *International Journal of Performance Analysis in Sport, 7*(1), 62–79.

Larkin, P., Mesagno, C., Berry, J., & Spittle, M. (2014). Development of a valid and reliable video-based decision-making test for Australian football umpires. *Journal of Science and Medicine in Sport, 17*, 552–555.

Laughlin, R. B. (2008). *Um universo diferente: Reinventar a física na era da emergência*. Lisboa: Gradiva.

Lee, M.-A., & Ward, P. (2009). Generalization of tactics in tag rugby from practice to games in middle school physical education. *Physical Education & Sport Pedagogy, 14*(2), 189–207.

Lehrer, J. (2009). *Como decidimos*. Alfragide: Lua de papel.

Le Moigne, J.-L. (1990). *La modélisation des systèmes complexes*. Paris: Dunod.

Machado, G., Cardoso, F., & Teoldo, I. (2017). Visual search strategy of soccer players according to different age groups. *Motriz: Revista de Educação Física, 23*(3).

Maciel, J. (2011). *Não deixes matar o bom Futebol e quem o joga. Pelo Futebol adentro não é perda de tempo!* Lisboa: Chiado Editora.

Mahlo, F. (1974). *Acte tactique en jeu*. Paris: Vigot.

Mandelbrot, B. (1991). *Objectos fractais*. Lisboa: Gradiva.

Mangas, C. J. (1999). *Conhecimento declarativo no futebol: Estudo comparativo em praticantes federados e não-federados, do escalão de sub-14*. Porto: Carlos Mangas. Dissertação de Mestrado, Faculdade de Ciências do Desporto e de Educação Física da Universidade do Porto, Porto, Portugal.

Márcio, A., Florêncio, A., Dias, R., Hugo, V., Sá, M., Ribeiro, A., & Santos, R. (1992). Os "Misters" do universo. *A Bola Edição Especial*, 1–15.

Marina, J. A. (1995). *Teoria da inteligência criadora*. Lisboa: Editorial Caminho.

Martins, C., Feitosa, P., & Silva, F. (1999). As principais tendências de planejamento do treino: uma revisão bibliográfica. *Revista Treinamento Desportivo, 4*(2), 71–80.

Martins, F. (2003). *A "Periodização Táctica" segundo Vitor Frade: Mais do que um conceito, uma forma de estar e de reflectir o futebol*. Porto: Filipe Martins. Dissertação de Licenciatura, Faculdade de Ciências do Desporto e de Educação Física da Universidade do Porto, Porto, Portugal.

Matvéiev, L. (1986). *Fundamentos do treino desportivo*. Lisboa: Livros Horizonte.

McGarry, T., Anderson, D. I., Wallace, S. A., Hughes, M. D., & Franks, I. M. (2002). Sport competition as a dynamical self-organization system. *Journal of Sports Sciences, 20*, 771–781.

McGarry, T., & Franks, I. (1995). Modelling competitive squash performance from quantitative analysis. *Human Performance, 8*(2), 113–129.

McPherson, S. (1994). The development of sport expertise: Mapping the tactical domain. *Quest, 46*(2), 223–240.

McPherson, S. L., & Thomas, J. (1989). Relation of knowledge and performance in boys tennis: Age and expertise. *Journal of Experimental Child Psychology, 48*, 190–211.

Memmert, D. (2002). *Diagnostik taktischer leistungskomponenten: Spieltestsituationen und konzeptorientierte expertenratings*. Heidelberg: Daniel Memmert. Tese de Doutorado, Universidade de Heidelberg, Alemanha.

Memmert, D., & Harvey, S. (2008). The Game Performance Assessment Instrument (GPAI): Some concerns and solutions for further development. *Journal of Teaching in Physical Education, 27*(2), 220–240.

Mendes, L. (1979). *As tácticas do futebol.* Rio de Janeiro: Ediouro Publicações S/A.
Mérand, R. (1976). *L'éducateur face à la haute performance.* Paris: Sport et Plain Air.
Mesquita, I. (1998). *A instrução e a estruturação das tarefas no treino de voleibol. Estudo experimental no escalão de iniciados feminino.* Porto, Portugal: Isabel Mesquita. Tese de Doutorado, Faculdade de Ciências do Desporto e de Educação Física da Universidade do Porto.
Mesquita, I. (2006). Ensinar bem para aprender melhor o jogo de voleibol. In G. Tani, J. Bento, & R. Petersen (Eds.), *Pedagogia do Desporto* (pp. 327–343). Rio de Janeiro, Brasil: Guanabara Koogan.
Mesquita, I., Farias, C., Oliveira, G., & Pereira, F. (2009). A intervenção pedagógica sobre o conteúdo do treinador de futebol. *Revista Brasileira de Educação Física e Esporte, 23*(1), 25–38.
Moles, A. (1995). *As ciências do impreciso.* Porto: Afrontamento.
Mombaerts, E. (1991). *Football, de l'analyse du jeu à la formation du joueur.* Joinville-lePont, França: Edition Actio.
Morin, E. (1973). *Le paradigme perdu: la nature humaine.* Paris: Seuil.
Morin, E. (1991). *Introdução ao pensamento complexo.* Lisboa: Publicações Instituto Piaget.
Muller, E., Garganta, J., Santos, R., & Teoldo, I. (2016). Comportamento e desempenho táticos: estudo comparativo entre jogadores de futebol e futsal. *Revista Brasileira de Ciência & Movimento, 24*(2), 100–109.
Muller, E., Teoldo, I., & Garganta, J. (2018). Análise tática no futsal: estudo comparativo do desempenho de jogadores de quatro categorias de formação. *Revista Brasileira de Ciência do Esporte, 40*(3), 248–256
Nitsch, J. R. (1985). The action-theoretical perspective. *International Review for Sociology of Sport, 20*(4), 263–282.
Olivares, H. T. (1978). *Realidad y fantasia del fútbol total.* Madrid: Augusto E. Pila Teleña.
Oliveira, J. (1993). *Os meios de treino.* Porto, Portugal: Relatório das provas de aptidão pedagógica na Faculdade de Ciências do Desporto e de Educação Física da Universidade do Porto.
Olsen, E., & Larsen, O. (1997). Use of match analysis by coaches. In T. Reilly, J. Bangsbo, & M. Hughes (Eds.), *Science and football III* (pp. 209–220). London: E & FN Spon.
Oslin, J. L., Mitchell, S. A., & Griffin, L. L. (1998). The Game Performance Assessment Instrument (GPAI): Development and preliminary validation. *Journal of Teaching in Physical Education, 17*(2), 231–243.
Parreira, C. A. (2005). *Evolução tática e estratégias de jogo.* Brasília: Escola Brasileira de Futebol.
Pereni, A., & Di Cesare, M. (1998). *Zone play: A technical and tactical handbook.* Spring City: Reedswain.
Perl, J. (2004). A neural network approach to pattern learning in sport. *International Journal of Computer Science in Sport, 3*(1), 67–70.
Phelan, S. (2001). Do caos à complexidade no planeamento estratégico: Implicações para a teoria e para a prática. In M. Cunha, J. Fonseca, & F. Gonçalves (Eds.), *Empresas, caos e complexidade* (pp. 9–20). Lisboa: Editora RH.
Piaget, J. (1964). Development and learning. *Journal of Research in Science Teaching, 2*(3), 176–186.
Piaget, J. (1983). *Psicologia da Inteligência.* Rio de Janeiro: Zahar
Piaget, J. (1993). *A representação do espaço na criança.* Porto Alegre: Artes Médicas.
Pinto, J. (1996). A táctica no futebol: abordagem conceptual e implicações na formação. In J. Oliveira & F. Tavares (Eds.), *Estrátegia e táctica nos jogos desportivos colectivos* (pp. 51–62). Porto: Centro de Estudos dos Jogos Desportivos, Faculdade de Ciências do Desporto e de Educação Física da Universidade do Porto.

Pinto, J., & Garganta, J. (1989). Futebol português: Importância do modelo de jogo no seu desenvolvimento. *Horizonte, Revista de Educação Física e Desporto, 33*(6), 94–98.

Pinto, J., & Garganta, J. (1996). Contributo da modelação da competição e do treino para a evolução do nível do jogo no futebol. In J. Oliveira & F. Tavares (Eds.), *Estratégia e táctica no jogos desportivos colectivos* (pp. 83–94). Porto: Centro de Estudos dos Jogos Desportivos, Faculdade de Ciências do Desporto e de Educação Física da Universidade do Porto.

Placek, J. H., & Griffin, L. L. (2001). The understanding and development of learners' domain-specific knowledge: Concluding comments. *Journal of Teaching in Physical Education, 20*(4), 402–406.

Queiroz, C. (1986). *Estrutura e organização dos exercícios de treino em futebol*. Lisboa: Federação Portuguesa de Futebol.

Queiroz, C. M. (1983). Para uma teoria de ensino/treino do futebol. *Ludens, 8*(1), 25–44.

Rezende, A., & Valdés, H. (2003). Métodos de estudo das habilidades tácticas (1). Abordagem comparativa entre jogadores habilidosos e iniciantes expert & novice. *Educación Física y Deportes*. Revista Digital, *9*(65). Recuperado de www.efdeportes.com/efd65/tatica.htm.

Richard, J.-F., Godbout, P., & Griffin, L. L. (2002). Assessing game performance: An introduction to the Team Sport Assessment Procedure (TSAP). *Physical and Health Education Journal, 68*(1), 12–18.

Roca, A. (2011). *Perceptual-cognitive expertise and its acquisition in soccer*. Liverpool: André Roca. Tese de Doutorado, Research Institute for Sport and Exercise Sciences, Liverpool John Moores University, Liverpool, England.

Roca, A., Ford, P., McRobert, A., & Williams, A. M. (2011). Identifying the processes underpinning anticipation and decision-making in a dynamic time-constrained task. *Cognitive processing, 12*(3), 301–310.

Roca, A., Ford, P., McRobert, A., & Williams, A. M. (2013). Perceptual-cognitive skills and their interaction as a function of task constraints in soccer. *Journal of Sport & Exercise Psychology, 1*(35), 144–155.

Rohde, H., & Espersen, T. (1988). Work intensity during soccer training and matchplay. In T. Reilly, A. Lees, K. Davis, & W. Murphy (Eds.), *Science and football* (pp. 68–75). London: E & F.N. Spon.

Sebastián, J. F. (1996). *Futebol. Entrenamiento físico basado en la tactica y la estrategia. Los sistemas de juego y su evolucion*. Madrid: Gymnos.

Silva, A. (2004). *Padrões de jogo no processo ofensivo em futebol de alto rendimento: Análise dos jogos da segunda fase do Campeonato do Mundo Coréia-Japão 2002*. Madri: António Silva. Dissertação de Mestrado, Universidad Autónoma de Madrid, Madri, Espanha.

Silva, A., & Rias, C. (1998). 5° Fascículo Inglaterra e Holanda. Extremos tocam-se. In R. Santos (Ed.), *O mundo do Futebol* (pp. 130–161). Lisboa: A Bola.

Silva, B., Garganta, J., Santos, R., & Teoldo, I. (2014). Comparing tactical behaviour of soccer players in 3 vs. 3 and 6 vs. 6 small-sided games. *Journal of Human Kinetics, 41*, 191–202.

Silva, M. (2007). *O desenvolvimento do jogar, segundo a periodização táctica*. Pontevedra: MC Sports.

Smith, D. (2003). A framework for understanding the training process leading to elite performance. *Sports Medicine, 33*(15), 103–126.

Solomenko, V. (1982). Juego sin balon. *El Entrenador, 14*, 72–75.

Stacey, R. (1995). *A Fronteira do caos*. Venda Nova: Bertrand Editora.

Sun Tzu. (1996). *A arte da guerra*. Rio de Janeiro: Record.

Tani, G. (2002). Aprendizagem motora e esporte de rendimento: Um caso de divórcio sem casamento. In V. J. Barbanti, A. C. Amadio, J. Bento, & A. T. Marques (Eds.), *Esporte e atividade física. Interação entre rendimento e saúde* (pp. 145–162). São Paulo: Editora Manole.

Tavares, F., Greco, P. J., & Garganta, J. (2006). Perceber, conhecer, decidir e agir nos jogos desportivos coletivos. In G. Tani, J. Bento, & R. Petersen (Eds.), *Pedagogia do Desporto* (pp. 284–298). Rio de Janeiro: Guanabara Koogan.

Taylor, H. L., Talleur, D. A., Emanuel, T. W., Rantanen, E. M., Bradshaw, G. L., & Phillips, S. I. (2002). *Incremental training effectiveness of personal computers used for instrument training: Basic instruments.* Moffett Field, CA: NASA Ames Research Center.

Teissie, J. (1969). *Le football* (2nd ed.). Paris: Vigot Fréres.

Tenenbaum, G., & Lidor, R. (2005). Research on decision-making and the use of cognitive strategies in sport settings. In D. Hackfort, J. Duda, & R. Lidor (Eds.), *Handbook of research in applied sport and exercise psychology: International perspectives* (pp. 75–91). Morgantown, WV: UNKNO.

Tenga, A., Kanstad, D., Ronglan, L. T., & Bahr, R. (2009). Developing a new method for team match performance analysis in professional soccer and testing its reliability. *International Journal of Performance Analysis of Sport*, *9*, 8–25.

Teodorescu, L. (1975). *Probleme de teorie si metodica* în *jocurile sportive*. Bucuresti: Ed. Sport-Turism.

Teodorescu, L. (1984). *Problemas de teoria e metodologia nos jogos desportivos* (J. Curado, Trad.). Lisboa: Livros Horizontes Lda.

Teoldo, I. (2010). *Comportamento tático no futebol: Contributo para a avaliação do desempenho de jogadores em situações de jogo reduzido.* Porto, Portugal: Israel Teoldo. Tese de Doutorado, Faculdade de Desporto da Universidade do Porto.

Teoldo, I., Garganta, J., Greco, P. J., & Mesquita, I. (2009). Avaliação do desempenho tático no futebol: Concepção e desenvolvimento da grelha de observação do teste "GR3–3GR". *Revista Mineira de Educação Física*, *17*(2), 36–64.

Teoldo, I., Garganta, J., Greco, P., & Mesquita, I. (2010). Análise e avaliação do comportamento tático no futebol. *Revista da Educação Física/UEM*, *21*(3), 443–455.

Teoldo, I., Garganta, J., Greco, P., & Mesquita, I. (2011). Proposta de avaliação do comportamento tático no futebol baseada nos princípios táticos fundamentais de jogo. *Revista Motriz*, *17*(3), 511–524.

Teoldo, I., Garganta, J., Greco, P., Mesquita, I., & Maia, J. (2011). Sistema de avaliação táctica no futebol (FUT-SAT): desenvolvimento e validação preliminar. *Revista Motricidade*, *7*(1), 69–84.

Teoldo, I., & Silvino, M. P. (in press). Analysis of tactical behavior in full- and small-sided games: Comparing professional and youth academy athletes to enhance player development in soccer *Journal of Sport Science*.

Teoldo, I., Silvino, M. P., & Sarmento, H. (in press). Comparing the tactical behavior of young soccer players in full- and small-sided games *International Journal of Performance Analysis in Sport*.

Tschiene, P. (2001). Lo stato attuale della teoria dell'allenamento. Analise dello stato attuale della teoria dell'allenamento e della sua influenza sulla pratica nello sport di alto livello. *Rivista di Cultura Sportiva, Anno XX*, *52*, 2–6.

Utaker, A. (2002). Analogies, métaphores et concepts. In P. Nouvel (Org.), *Enquête sur le concept de modèle* (pp. 203–221). Paris: Presses Universitaires de France.

Vaeyens, R., Lenoir, M., Williams, A. M., Matthys, S., & Philippaerts, R. M. (2010). The mechanisms underpinning decision-making in youth soccer players: An analysis of verbal reports. In B. Drust, T. Reilly, & M. Williams (Eds.), *International research in science and soccer: Proceedings of the First World Conference on Science and Soccer* (pp. 21–28). London: Routledge.

Valdano, J. (2002). *El miedo escénico y otras hierbas*. Madrid: Aguilar.

Vilar, L., Araújo, D., Davids, K., & Button, C. (2012). The role of ecological dynamics in analysing performance in team sports. *Sports Medicine*, *42*(1), 1–10.

Ward, P., & Williams, A. M. (2003). Perceptual and cognitive skill development in soccer: The multidimensional nature of expert performance. *Journal of Sport & Exercise Psychology*, *25*(1), 93–111.

Ward, P., Williams, A. M., & Hancock, P. A. (2006). Simulation for performance and training. In K. A. Ericsson, N. Charness, P. Feltovich, & R. R. Hoffman (Eds.), *The Cambridge handbook of expertise and expert performance* (pp. 243–262). Cambridge: Cambridge University Press.

Werner, S. (1995). *El duelo entre dos: libro de ejercicios de uno contra uno*. Barcelona: Paidotribo.

Williams, A. M. (2000). Perceptual skill in soccer: Implications for talent identification and development. *Journal of Sports Sciences*, *18*, 737–750.

Williams, A. M., & Burwitz, L. (1993). Advance cue utilisation in soccer. In T. Reilly, J. Clarys, & A. Stibbe (Eds.), *Science and football II: Proceedings of the Second World Congress of Science and Football* (pp. 239–244). London: E & F.N. Spon.

Williams, A. M., Davids, K., & Williams, J. G. (1999). *Visual percepcion & action in sport*. London: E & F.N. Spon.

Williams, A. M., & Hodges, N. J. (2005). Practice, instruction and skill acquisition in soccer: Challenging tradition. *Journal of Sports Sciences*, *23*(6), 637–650.

Worthington, E. (1974). *Learning & teaching soccer skills*. London: Lepus Books Hal Leighton Printing Company.

Wrzos, J. (1984). *La tactique de l'attaque*. Bräkel: Broodecoorens.

Yan, Z., Jingjing, G., Danmin, M., Xia, Z. H. U., & Yebing, Y. (2011). Subjective evaluation of mental fatigue and characteristics of attention during a driving simulation. *Social Behavior & Personality: An International Journal*, *39*(1), 15–20.

Zerhouni, M. (1980). *Principes de base du football contemporain*. Fleury: Orges.

Index

Note: Page numbers in *italics* indicate a figure and page numbers in **bold** indicate a table on the corresponding page.

Academy for Sports Excellence 187
active observation 196
Ajax 14, 15
assessment *see* tactical assessment
Astronomy comparison 27–28
attractors 75

ball, illustration of trajectories *28*
Brazil: children development process 68; "WM" and "WW" systems in 13, *13*
Brazilian National Team: systems "1-4-2-4" 11, *12*, 13; "1-4-3-3" 11, *12*

centre of play 26, *26*; defensive phase 46; offensive phase 31, *32*; principle of balance 53; principle of concentration 57; principle of defensive coverage 50; principle of defensive unity 59–60; principle of delay **47**; principle of depth mobility 37; principle of offensive coverage 34; principle of offensive unity 43; principle of penetration 32; principle of width and length 39
Centre of Research and Studies in Soccer 139
chance 73n1
chaos theory 74–75; fractal organization 96–97
Chapman, Herbert: coach 8–9; "WM System" *9*
Classical System, game representation 8, *8*
coach 8–9; assessment *179*; ideas of 5; synergy between players and 133–134

competition, reciprocity between training and *191*
conception of play 80, *82*
conceptual lens, modelling process 75
culture of play 92; training and 190

decision-making, elements of tactics *19*
declarative knowledge 188n2; training 93, 94
defence/attack transition: (GK+5) *vs* (5+GK) drill + 2 floaters 128–129; (GK+8) *vs* (8+GK) drill 131–132; (GK+9) *vs* (9+GK) drill 130–131; 11X11 drill 132–133; 1X1 situations 124; 4X4 drill 127–128; 4X4 drill + four floaters 126–127; 6 versus (3+3) drill 125–126; 6X6 drill + 2 floaters 129–130; drills 123–133; soccer training 99–100
defensive organization: (GK+10) *vs* (10+GK) drill 121–123; (GK+7) *vs* (7+GK) drill 119; (GK+7) *vs* (8+GK) drill 118–119; (GK+8) *vs* (8+GK) drill 120–121; 1X1 drill + 2 floaters 116; 4X4 drill + 2 floaters 116–117; 6X6 drill 117–118; defensive transition 203–204; drills 115–123; interdependence 84
defensive phase, core tactical principles 29, 46–62; management of space *46*; principle of balance 53–54, **54–56**, *56*; principle of concentration 57, **57–58**, *58*; principle of defensive coverage 49–51, **52–53**, *53*; principle of defensive

unity 59–60, **60–62**, *63*; principle of delay 47, **47–48**, *49*; *see also* tactical principles of game
defensive set-plays 204
defensive third 205; functional characterization 205; sectorial characteristics *205*
Department of Tactical Assessment 139
docking, notion of 84
drills: coach's intervention in 106–107, *107*; defence/attack and attack/defence transition 123–133; defensive organization 115–123; diagonal positioning in 1-4-3-3 structure 102, *103*; fractal organization of 108; (Gk+4) *vs* (2+Gk) + 2 floaters 102, *103*, 104, *105*, 106, *106*; (Gk+6) *vs* (6+Gk) drill with man-to-man marking *101*; (Gk+6) *vs* (6+Gk) drill with zone defence organization *102*; lines in depth in 1-4-3-3 structure *104*; lines in width in 1-4-3-3 structure 104, *105*; offensive organization 108–115; operational training level 100–108; specificity of Model of Play and 106–108; Specific Model of Play 107–108; *see also* defensive organization; offensive organization
Dutch National team 14, 15

Eastern Europe, soccer training 90–91
emergence, soccer 84–85
Eton College 6
European Leagues 181
Eye Tracking System 138, 188

field tests: Game Performance Assessment Instrument (GPAI) 146–147; Game Performance Evaluation Tool (GPET) 150; KORA tests battery 147–149; System of Tactical Assessment in Soccer (FUT-SAT) 150–166; Team Sports Performance Assessment Procedure (TSAP) 143–146, *145–146*
Football Association: first known rules 6; foundation of 6–7; offside 6, 7
Football Exchange program 139
fractal: notion of 96; organization of training process 97
Frade, Vitor, tactical periodization 92

futsal, as element for player development 68–72
FUT-SAT 141; *see also* System of Tactical Assessment in Soccer (FUT-SAT)

game: adaptation and evolution into 8; analysis for better training and playing 192–193; arrangements of players on field *7*; Classical System of 8, *8*; dimensions of 3; inseparability of concepts *82*; mapping of 83; observation for understanding 208; principles in soccer 83–85; Pyramid 8, *8*; tactical principles of 24–62; tactics emerging from 6–16; *see also* soccer
game context, term 189n4
game intelligence 78
Game Performance Assessment Instrument (GPAI) 140, 141, 146–147
Game Performance Evaluation Tool (GPET) 140–141, 150
Game Test Situation 140
German National Soccer Team 187
Gigerenzer, Gerd, on decision-making 78
goalkeeper; functional characterization 204; sectorial characteristics *205*

Integrated Training, Latin America 91
intermediate third: functional characterization 205; sectorial characteristics *205*
internal logic, soccer game 20–22
International Football Association Board 27, 65
intuition, term 78
Italian National Team, Pozzo as coach 9

knowledge: declarative, in training 93, 94; of players 5; procedural, in training 94; role in problem solving 94; video of declarative test for defensive phase *183*
KORA (Konzept Orientertes Rating) 140, 141; offering and orienting (O.O) 147, 148, *148*; recognizing spaces (R.S) test 147, 148, *149*; tests battery 147–149
Kovacs, Stephan 14, 15

laboratory tests: cognitive assessment 186–188; Mobile Eye Tracking System

188; Tactical Skills Inventory for Sports (TACSIS) 186; TacticUP® 169, 169–181; video-based tests 181–185; Vienna Test System (VTS) *187*, 186–187
Latin America, Integrated Training 91
Liverpool John Moores University 139
logic, soccer game 20–22

magic square, "WM system" 9
management of space: core principles in defensive phase *46*; core principles of offensive phase *32*; principle of balance *56*; principle of concentration *58*; principle of defensive coverage *53*; principle of defensive unity *63*; principle of delay *49*; principle of depth mobility *39*; principle of offensive coverage *36*; principle of offensive unity *45*; principle of penetration *34*; principle of width and length *42*
Meisl, Hugo: coach 9; coach of Austrian National Team 10–11; "System" of *11*
Michels, Rinus 14, 15
Mobile Eye Tracking System 188
model/modelling: concept of 75; soccer using 76; process 75; tactical 76
Model of Play: competition and training *83*; concept of 80–81; creation of 96

Northern Europe, soccer training 91

observational methodology 197
offensive organization: 2X2 drill + 4 floaters 109; 3X3 drill + 2 floaters 108–109; drills for 108–115; (GK+4) *vs* (4+GK) drill + 6, 110; (GK+6) *vs* (6+GK) drill + 2 floaters 111–112; (GK+7) *vs* (7+GK) drill + 2 floaters 114; (GK+8) *vs* (8+GK) drill 110–111; (GK+10) *vs* (8+GK) drill 114–115; (GK+10) *vs* (10+GK) drill 112–113; offensive transition 203
offensive phase, core tactical principles 29, 31–45; management of space for *32*; principle of depth mobility 37, **38**, *39*; principle of offensive coverage 34–35, **35–36**, *36*; principle of offensive unity 42–43, **43–45**, *45*; principle of penetration 32–34, **33**, *34*; principle of width and length 39–40, **40–42**, *42*; *see also* tactical principles of game
offensive routines *206, 207*
offensive set-plays 204
offensive third 207; functional characterization 207; sectorial characteristics *205*
offside rule 6, 7; reduction of effective play-space 59

paradigms 3
passing zone, concept of 73n3
passive observation 196
performance, understanding, in sports games 198
performance analysis, elementary and complex perspectives in **196**
periodization: competition 136; training 89–91, 136; word 92
Peripheral Perception test 186
phases of play, soccer game 20–22, *21*
Physics 27
play, styles of 15, 16
player development, futsal as element for 68–72
players: arrangements on field *7*; counter-attack of 208; designation of 78–79; offensive routines *206, 207*; positional arrangement and movement *206*; positional attack 207; specific knowledge of 5; synergy between coach and 133–134
playing culture, implementation of 77
playing management, action principles and rules 74
playing systems 16; importance of training configuration 95–97
play-space, soccer 84–85
Pozzo, Vittorio: coach 9–10; WW system 10, *10*
predictability, coach's ideas and players' specific knowledge 5
principle of balance: characteristics of **54–56**; defensive phase 53–54; FUT-SAT assessment **161–162**; management of space *56*
principle of concentration: characteristics of **57–58**; defensive phase 57; FUT-SAT

assessment **162–163**; management of space *58*
principle of defensive coverage: athletes' performance and response time for *176*; characteristics of **52–53**; defensive phase 49–51; FUT-SAT assessment **160–161**; management of space *53*; representation of idea of risk to goal *50*
principle of defensive unity: characteristics of **60–62**; defensive phase 59–60; FUT-SAT assessment **163–164**; management of space *63*
principle of delay: characteristics of **47–48**; defensive unity 47; FUT-SAT assessment **159–160**; management of space *49*
principle of depth mobility: characteristics of **38**; FUT-SAT assessment **155–156**; management of space *39*; offensive phase 37
principle of offensive coverage: athletes' performance and response time for *176*; characteristics of **35–36**; FUT-SAT assessment **154–155**; management of space *36*; offensive phase 34–35
principle of offensive unity: characteristics of **43–45**; FUT-SAT assessment **158–159**; management of space *45*; offensive phase 42–43
principle of penetration: characteristics of **33**; FUT-SAT assessment **154**; management of space *34*; offensive phase 32–33
principle of width and length: characteristics of **40–42**; FUT-SAT assessment **156–157**; management of space *42*; offensive phase 39–40
problem solving, role of knowledge 94
procedural knowledge 188n3; training 94
Pyramid, game representation 8, *8*

Qatar 187
qualitative approach, soccer game *195*
quantitative approach, soccer game *195*

Sacchi, Arrigo 15
scale invariance 96
scales 134n1

scheme: concept 22; system of play and 22–24; tactical *23*
Sebes, Gustav 14; Hungarian team 11; "System" of *12*
sequential analysis 197
soccer: analysis for better training and playing 192–193; basic positional arrangement and movement tendencies *206*; categories of problems in 79; concept of "Model of Play" 80–81; defensive organization-defensive transition 203–204; defensive set-plays 204; dimensions of 3; elementary and complex perspectives in performance analysis **196**; elements of team 82–83; emergence of 84–85; evolution of game 16; evolution of processes of analysis and interpretation *195*; as game of opinions 191; interdependence of 84; internal logic and phases of play 20–22, *21*; language of 76–77; learning to see to better understand 190–191; macrocategories framing tactical observation of *202*; mapping ideas to play 77–78; means and methods in observation, analysis and interpretation of *194*; non-linearity of 84; observation and recording of tactical events in matches 199–208; offensive organization-offensive transition 203; offensive routines *206, 207*; offensive set-plays 204; as phenomenon from various polarities *201*; principles in 83–85; procedures in observation, analysis and interpretation of 193–199; roadmap for functional characterization for tactical role 204–205; scheme and system of play 22–24; sectorial characteristics of team *205*; study of game story line 201–202; tactical action of 85; tactical concepts and principles *200*; tactical principles of *30*; tactics and strategy 18–20; tendencies in training 90–91; training 90–95; Training Theory 89–90; understanding and mapping out game of 74–77; using models 76; *see also* tactical assessment
soccer technical staff 199

Soccer View® graphical information on software 167, *168*
sociobiology 198
space *see* management of space
spatial references, core tactical principles *26*, 26–27
specificity, definition of 4
Specific Model of Play 99–100
sport sciences, observational methodology 197
sports training: principle of specificity 191; purpose of 191
strategic-tactical knowledge 19
strategy: origin of word 18; tactics and 18–20
superorganism, term 198
system of play, concept 22, 23
System of Tactical Assessment in Soccer (FUT-SAT) 141; balance principle **161–162**; categories, sub-categories, variables and definitions **152–153**; characterization of field test 165–166, **165–166**; concentration principle **162–163**; core tactical principles through **154–164**; defensive coverage principle **160–161**; defensive unity principle **163–164**; delay principle **159–160**; depth mobility principle **155–156**; graphical information on software Soccer View® 167, *168*; observation instrument 152, **152–153**; offensive coverage principle **154–155**; offensive unity principle **158–159**; penetration principle **154**; physical structure of field test *167*; protocol 166–169; purpose and structure 150–151, *151*; structural organization of variables *151*; width and length principle **156–157**

tactical assessment 135; characteristics and instruments 135–137; range and limitations of instruments 137–143; Team Sports Performance Assessment Procedure (TSAP) 143–146, *145–146*; *see also* field tests
tactical modelling: definition of 76; mapping ideas to play soccer 77–78; players and coach interventions 192–193

Tactical Performance Index (TPI) 151
tactical periodization, Vitor Frade and 92
"tactical-physical" form 15, 16
tactical principles of game 24–62; characterization of 25–29; core principles 26, *30*; general principles 25, *30*; operational principles 25, *30*; spatial references in conception of core *26*, 26–27; specific principles 29; teaching-training process and 29–31, 62–67; *see also* defensive phase, core tactical principles; offensive phase, core tactical principles
Tactical Skills Inventory for Sports (TACSIS) 186
tactical systems, playing 79
tactical training: conceptual level of 97–100; defensive organization 99, 115–123; drills as operational level 100–108; fundamentals for consideration 93–95; importance of configuration for playing 95–97; offensive organization 108–115; soccer 90–95; *see also* drills
tactics: as complex dimension 3–5; concept of 95; definitions of 3; elements comprising *19*; paths by 6; strategy and 18–20; understanding of 4–5; Vitor Frade and 92
TacticUP® 141, *179*; analysis of athletes' performance 172; assessment of two players *178*; benefits of 180–181; for coaches 180; coach's opinion about player 177; collective assessments 174–177; comparative analysis of athletes' performance 174; comparative analysis of athletes' performance and decision-making 174, 176; comparing assessment by coach and *179*; defensive coverage principle *176*; graphical comparison of athletes' response time 172; graphic information scheme *171*; individual assessments 172; interpreting results 170–172; for management staff 180; offensive coverage principle *176*; for performance analysts 181; periodic assessments 177; for players 181; representative image of moment

for sequence of play *170*; result of individual response time *173*; results for defensive midfielders *175*; sequence of play 169; for soccer schools 180–181

teaching-learning process: layout of players in geometric configurations *65*; Me+Ball+Space+Teammates+Opponents+Conditioners stage 62, 65; Me+Ball+Space+Teammates+Opponents stage 62, 64–65; Me+Ball+Space+Teammates stage 62, 64; Me+Ball+Space stage 62–64; player development and 71–72; proposal for spatial organization and adaptations for game **66**

teaching-training process: stages of 62; tactical principles and 29–31, 62–67

Team Sports Performance Assessment Procedure (TSAP) 140, 141; assessment of player's action zones *145*; field test 143–146; nomogram for assessment performance *144*; nomogram with two performance scores *146*

"technical-tactical" form 15, 16

Teodorescu, León 76

Theory of Relativity 27

"Total Football" 14

training: conceptual level 97–100; configuration for playing 95–97; declarative knowledge in 93, 94; drills as operational level 100–108; Eastern Europe 90–91; General Training Theory 89–90; interpretation of players 98; Latin American tendency 91; Northern Europe 91; objective of structured process 89; overview of game to improve 192–193; problem solving methods 94; procedural knowledge 94; reciprocity between competition and *191*; soccer 90–95; synergy between coach and players 133–134; *see also* tactical training

Training Theory, soccer 89–90

Universidad de Castilla-La Mancha 150
Universidade Federal de Viçosa 139
University of Sidney 184
University of Utah 184

video-based tests 181–185; life-size video of declarative knowledge test for defensive phase *183*; picture of participant's answer by protocol of decision-making test *184*; picture of participant's answer by protocol of situational probability test *185*; representative picture of moment the player in possession of ball *182*; representative picture of options of solution for play *182*

Vienna Test System (VTS) *187*, 186–187

"WM System," Chapman's *9*
Wunderteam, Meisl as coach of 10–11
"WW System," Pozzo's 10, *10*

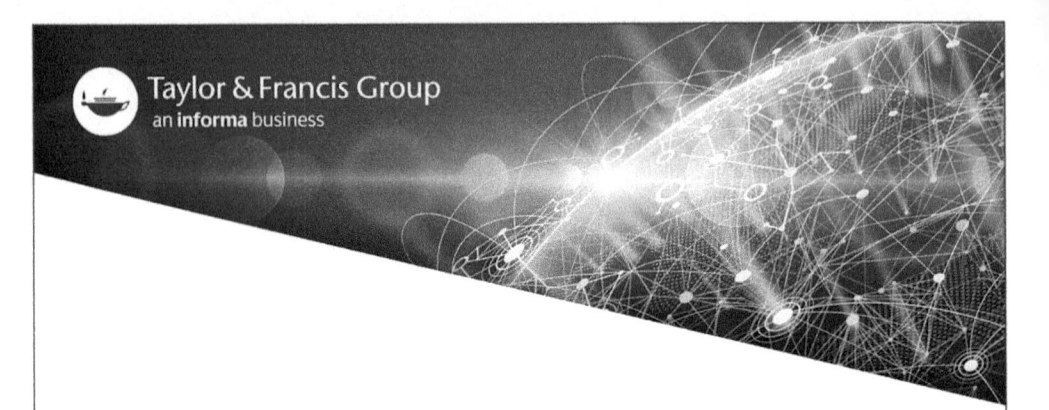